THE COLLECTED WORKS OF
G. K. CHESTERTON

X

PART I

THE COLLECTED WORKS OF
G. K. CHESTERTON

X

COLLECTED POETRY
PART I

Compiled and with an Introduction by
Aidan Mackey

IGNATIUS PRESS   SAN FRANCISCO

© 1994 Ignatius Press, San Francisco
All rights reserved
ISBN 0-89870-390-5 (HB)
ISBN 0-89870-391-3 (SB)
Library of Congress catalogue number 85-81511
Printed in the United States of America

CONTENTS

GENERAL EDITORS' INTRODUCTION

Gilbert Keith Chesterton was one of the most prolific writers of the twentieth century. He delighted the English speaking world with his political and theological essays, novels, biographies, short stories, plays and travel works. Chesterton also distinguished himself as a poet. He penned thousands of poems that described his reactions to events and people. On Sigmund Freud he wrote:

> The ignorant pronounce it Frood,
>   To cavil or applaud.
> The Well-informed pronounce it Froyd,
>   But I pronounce it Fraud.

He also gave us great epics that portray Christendom's battles against the barbarian hordes. "The Ballad of the White Horse" celebrates King Alfred the Great's 871 A.D. victory over the Danes while "Lepanto" describes the West's triumph over the Turks in 1571.

In the "Ballad of the White Horse", Chesterton warns of the new barbarians — the secular humanists:

> "They shall not come with warships,
>   They shall not waste with brands,
> But books be all their caring,
>   And ink be on their hands. . . .
>
> "They shall come mild as monkish clerks,
>   With many a scroll and pen; . . .
>
> "By this sign you shall know them,
>   The breaking of the sword,
> And man no more a free knight
>   That loves or hates his lord.
>
> "Yea, this shall be the sign of them,
>   The sign of the dying fire;
> And Man made like a half-wit
>   That knows not of his sire. . . .
>
> "By all men bond to Nothing,
>   Being slaves without a lord,
> By one blind idiot world obeyed,
>   Too blind to be abhorred;

> "By God and man dishonoured,
>   By death and life made vain,
> Know ye the old barbarian
>   The barbarian come again—".

Critic Charles Williams, in his 1930 work *Poetry at Present*, best described G. K. C.'s efforts as a poet:

> Mr. Chesterton's verse, even when it is not concerned with historic battles—Ethandune, Lepanto, the Marne—has generally the sound of a battle within it. There are drawn swords from the first page to the last: material, intellectual and spiritual; the swords of Arthur and Roland, of Ben Tillett and Paul Deroulède, of the Mother of God and Michael the Archangel. Everything is spoken of in terms of war, either actual or potential. For even when there is no enemy the state of being described is a state where man is strung to a high pitch of expectation and his delight is already militant. The babe unborn in one poem looks forward to "leave to weep and fight", and his old men die either in conflict or in the joy or fear of conflict. Man must be either a hero or a coward.

This volume contains the first part of the great man's collected poems. We are pleased and honored that Mr. Aidan Mackey of Bedford, England has served as the editor. Mr. Mackey is one of the world's leading Chestertonians. He directs the Chesterton Study Centre and has served as Chairman of the Chesterton Society. He has devoted over half a century to promoting the memory and works of G. K. Chesterton.

After the 1988 death of Chesterton's literary executrix, Dorothy Collins, Mr. Mackey was granted access to the voluminous Chesterton papers in her attic. While reviewing these documents, Mr. Mackey discovered hundreds of poems. These "lost" works are published, for the first time, in these volumes.

GEORGE J. MARLIN
RICHARD P. RABATIN
JOHN L. SWAN
General Editors

PATRICIA AZAR
JOE MYSAK
REV. RANDALL PAINE, O.R.C.
Associate Editors

BARBARA D. MARLIN
Assistant

INTRODUCTION

By Aidan Mackey

In his verse, as in most of his endeavors, G. K. Chesterton is difficult to assess because his individuality is so marked that he cannot usefully be compared to any of his peers. He belonged to no school; he never attempted to lead any movement in poetry; and although in his early years, his rhythms are imitative of Swinburne's, he quickly developed a style unmistakably his own.

He cannot be pigeon-holed, because he worked with equal facility in so many fields, and, even among his admirers — perhaps especially among his admirers — there is no consensus of opinion as to the one in which he was most successful. If I were constrained to pin a single label on him, then it would have to be that of propagandist. And this will, I believe, make him the more readily understandable.

His written work as a whole is, I believe, most readily understood if he is seen as a propagandist. Almost from the beginning he had a coherent philosophy of life and people from which he never deviated, and he dedicated his life and work to propagating it. All forms of communication — the novel, the debating platform, literary criticism, social and political comment, plays, letters to the press, detective stories, religious writing and controversy, art studies, essays and verse — were vehicles by which he reached out, over the heads of specialists and critics, to the ordinary people he so unaffectedly loved.

His whole life was one consistent and fierce, though almost unfailingly good-tempered, attack on the planners, sociologists and bureaucrats who sought (and still seek) to supervise and regulate the lives and pleasures of people — most especially of poor people. He was very much more in tune with the joys and sorrows and grievances of ordinary people than were most of the intellectuals of his day, who tended, then as now, to think in terms of abstract social problems rather than of common folk and their lives. He was the poet of the ordinary, denying that anything was or could be uninteresting; his verse celebrates lamp-posts and daisies and railway stations. Above all he gave unceasing thanks for "The Great Minimum", that gift of mere existence, to which any added joy is almost superfluous, and certainly to be regarded as an unlooked-for and undeserved bonus.

Chesterton saw himself as a journalist, and in this he was accurate in the sense that he wrote for his day; he had no desire at all for permanent fame, and none of his writing was done for posterity; all was penned for immediacy of impact upon the people and problems of his day. Even his finest and most profound books, such as *The Everlasting Man*, are scattered throughout with names of people who mean nothing to us today, for it would never have occurred to him that many of the people with whom he argued would pass into oblivion whilst his own work and thought endured.

Inevitably, this means that some of his verse, written for a topic or event of the day, has little meaning for us today without explanatory notes which would in some cases smother the barb he had fired. It would, for instance, require a brief essay to render "A Song of Swords" (p. 414) easily accessible to us now. More importantly, it means that he wrote most of his verse in haste and did not polish and revise nearly as much as would a more single-minded writer. The truly dedicated poet does not ride, but is ridden by, his muse; but for Chesterton poetry was there to serve and not to be served. There were too many other things in life of far higher importance to him than poetry—especially his own poetry.

Chesterton, then, is not to be numbered among the great poets of our inheritance, and most certainly he himself would have derided any such suggestion. The following pages, however, will show how very often he wrote great and near-great poetry, and most literate people have, whether or not they are aware of the fact, a good many lines and stanzas of his verse securely installed as part of the furniture of their minds.

Even his lightest poems, such as those in his novel, *The Flying Inn*, carried his rollicking yet devastating shafts launched at the cant and humbug of the planners, politicians and self-appointed reformers of his day. The thrust and accuracy of his barbs is remarkable, and English satiric attack has few better examples than "AntiChrist, or The Reunion of Christendom: An Ode".

It was, however, virtually always at the idea and not at the person that he aimed his weapon. Even in the two exceptions to that rule which come to mind, "Sonnet with the Compliments of the Season" and "Elegy in a Country Churchyard", the target is allowed anonymity.

Chesterton took very seriously the ideas and causes for which he fought throughout his life, but it never occurred to him that his own writing, whether in prose or verse, was of lasting importance. It was several times pointed out to him that in his splended epic, "The Ballad of the White Horse", he had the left wings of the opposing armies at the battle of Ethandune facing each other but, as his wife Frances wrote to one correspondent, G. K. C. did not believe that anyone would care or think it of any importance.

When we consider the breath-taking quantity of his literary output (an article for *Illustrated London News* every week from 1905 until his death in 1936, with hardly a week missed except during his illness in 1914; a weekly article in *The Daily News* for eleven years; essays, poems, reviews, letters, etc., in almost a hundred different journals; his writing for the papers, *The Eye-Witness* and *The New Witness*, edited by his brother Cecil, followed by his own editorship of *G. K.'s Weekly*; the travelling and lecture tours; all these in addition to the torrent of books), some unevenness in his work cannot be wondered at.

The faults are there to be seen but, beyond any reasonable doubt, so are the glories. Even the speed at which he wrote had the advantage of giving his verse a freshness and vigour that heightens its appeal to us. An originality of approach to the age-old theme of love would seem to be an impossibility, yet Chesterton achieves it, and achieves it triumphantly, time after time.

These considerations cannot but make life difficult for the critic whose integrity and judgement will not allow him to be dismissive, as are so many lesser commentators. The *doyen* of literary critics, Desmond McCarthy wrote in *The Sunday Times* (September 17, 1933):

> This is the second time I have read the collected poems of Chesterton through, and whatever doubts I have about this poetry I am in no doubt about this: Mr Chesterton is not a minor poet. Nor is he a great one—that is equally certain. A

minor poet (it is an exceedingly vague term) may, as is well known, produce
one or two imperishable poems; but his vision does not embrace so much. . . .
Both Chesterton and Kipling stand in that sense apart as faulty, fervid poets
whose approach to poetry is nevertheless the grand one through which great-
ness is achieved. . . . In my boyhood there was a critical flag flying in all the
reviews, inscribed "The Renaissance of Wonder". Wonder seems to Chesterton
the permanently appropriate attitude towards life; wonder, with faith behind
it. . . . Humility and the courage which springs from humility, not that which
springs from pride, are his favourite virtues. These make him sing as a poet—or,
when he doesn't sing—shout. He has the great poet's capacity to feel most what
he values most. But unlike the great poet, his art is second to his purpose. . . . I
never tire of a chivalrous radiance that shines in his best work, shines with a glitter
of tears that are tears of joy; or of the solemnity of that climax his rhetoric some-
times reaches, when it has fought its way through paradoxes, jokes and conceits
to a final simplicity of expression.

But it was that fine, though now neglected, critic John Collinge
Squire who most clearly saw Chesterton's true position, describing
him as the poet of "of the market-place", and commenting:

We have here, in the intermittent work of an unflagging publicist and man-of-
letters, a body of good, and diversely good, work which would suffice to make
reputations for a dozen small dedicated poets, and a body of less good verse which
remains interesting because only one man and one craftsman could have written it.

He saw that Chesterton's reputation had suffered because of this
diversity as well as his massive output:

People like clear definitions and a label. If a writer produces a little good verse, and
nothing else, he is evidently a poet, and will be sympathetically considered as
such. . . . Chesterton's poetry, as it were, has been hidden by the dust he has
raised. . . . A great deal of Mr Chesterton's verse has serious, though usually not
ruinous, faults. He is a very exuberant man. The coupling of complete, and full-
blooded, expression with fastidious care is unusual. Carefulness normally leads to
cramping and timidity, and gusto to carelessness. Mr Chesterton has always
scorned to conceal even his most 'vulgar' tastes, and he has let his genius take him
where it would. . . . The mixture does no harm: it is all to the credit of his
honesty in a frightened, neighbour-watching age; it is a great thing that on one
page there is to be found a poem beginning, "A word came forth in Galilee, a
word like to a star", and on the next, with one which opens, "Jones had a dog; it
had a chain". . . . His defects are the defects of his qualities; his ear for splendid

sound, his intellectual agility, his natural un-self-conscious copiousness. Lesser
men often have fewer obvious faults.

My own feeling is that we gain more than we lose from the fact that
G. K. C. seldom took time to hone and polish his verse. If to be a great
poet one must have produced a body of near-flawless work, then he has
certainly disqualified himself. For the great, dedicated poets there is very
frequently a point at which inspiration must take second place to the
sheer grind of wrestling with technique, and the task of making some
uncooperative line scan, and this may hold up composition for a long
time. Chesterton seldom exercised that patience.

It is often said that he never revised his work. This is not true, but
it was far from being his normal practice. He was a poet of overflow-
ing vitality, of high purpose and, it must be said, sometimes of high
carelessness. An idea would sometimes recur to his mind and re-
emerge in an altered form or length, but this is not the same as the
meticulous polishing of a particular piece. One example of his re-
working of a theme (quite possibly having forgotten that he had
earlier committed it to paper) can be seen in "The Troubadour of
God", which I have seen in several versions. The one that seems the
earliest is a fragment, of which the only complete stanza does not appear
in that form in other versions. The fullest version did not see publica-
tion until after his death when it appeared in *G. K.'s Weekly*, February
3, 1938. What variants I can find will be included in the second volume
of this edition.

If, as I contend, there is greatness in having produced very many
poems of real depth and quality and, perhaps even more important,
to have minted countless lines and stanzas that have lodged them-
selves firmly in the hearts of many thousands of people who may
hardly know the name of the poet, then Chesterton cannot be de-
nied a significant place in our hall of poetic fame. As Oliver Ed-
wards, writing in the *London Times*, on May 15, 1958, put it:

> He was, it seems to me, more consistently a poet than any other kind of
> writer. . . . There is in his poems less persiflage and more passion than in any of
> his other work. He plumbed more sombre depths, he rose to greater heights.

Perhaps it would be possible to satisfy the demands of both justice and accuracy only if we acknowledge G. K. C. to be (a concept which would greatly amuse him) not one, but half-a-dozen poets: the ballad-monger, the satirist, the troubadour, the comic, the psalmist and the warrior-poet.

Chesterton, I believe, must be seen as a whole or we lose much of his integrity and importance. He cannot be compartmentalized or cut down; there are those who say, "I love his essays (or his fiction, or his verse or his literary criticism) but I don't want to bother about his religious beliefs (or his social philosophy, or his controversies)", but such readers must miss a great deal, for he was a thinker made in one piece and all his thought and writing offers a unified and coherent view of life.

As I have noted, some of his poems exist in more than one version, but in many cases the variation is slight and without significance, so I have not thought it worthwhile to distract the attention of the reader with it. With others, I have noted that a variant version does exist, quoting changes, and in one or two cases, such as "The Song of the Cradle", the versions differ so greatly that I have treated them as being separate poems and have given both versions.

One of the criticisms that may be made of this collection is that it includes inferior poems that some readers would prefer to remain forgotten; some the point of which has been blunted by the passage of time, and many others that Chesterton himself did not include in his *Collected Poems*.

If, however, I had decided to select and winnow, some major difficulties would have arisen. Firstly, that there are few poems in which there is nothing of value or interest that we would regret losing; secondly, that he himself was, like John Keats and others of our greatest poets, prepared to preserve work that he came to regard as faulty and immature. In a brief note in *The Wild Knight and Other Poems*, 1900, he commented that the poems "have been selected and arranged rather with a view to unity of spirit than to unity of time or value; many of them being juvenile." Then in 1933 when Methuen issued a new edition of the *Collected Poems*, he wrote a Prefatory Note to the section *Poems* (1915):

This collection was made a long time ago and includes items written a very long time before that: things that are indeed merely juvenile. But I have decided that it is very difficult to disentangle the threads in a patchwork which may already be thought threadbare; and I have let these schoolboy verses remain side by side with some that I wrote at least in maturer years and on more momentous occasions.

As a further answer to those who would say that poems that were not collected by the poet himself should not be included in this permanent record, it should be sufficient to list a few of those which, for one reason or another, he failed to collect. In a few cases, such as the three poems (including the splendid "Gloria in Profundis" that appeared in the Faber & Gwyer series of 'Ariel Poems', and those in the little book of religious verse *The Queen of Seven Swords*, the reason for the omission may possibly lie in the realm of copyright. A few others, such as "To Saint Michael in Time of Peace" and "To the Jesuits in Spain", were written after the compilation of the *Collected Poems*. But very many others, I am certain, were merely overlooked, for it was only in the last ten years of his life that Dorothy Collins was at hand to bring some degree of order and system to filing and storage. It would be quite ludicrous to imagine Gilbert himself diligently sifting through files of dozens of periodicals and newspapers in search of his own verse.

It would, in fact, be very difficult to determine just what he intended (if, indeed, he gave any thought at all to the matter) and which alterations and omissions were deliberate and which were fortuitous. For instance, for the enlarged edition of the *Collected Poems* which Methuen published in 1933 he moved his sonnet "The Convert", which had appeared on page 84 of the original (1927) edition, to make it the final poem in the volume.

This, clearly, was deliberate. Equally clearly, it was done not because he held that poem in special esteem, but because of the importance to him of its subject. On the other hand, the early poem "A Word", which had been first collected in *Poems* (1915), was also included in the first edition of *Collected Poems*. It was then dropped from the 1933 and subsequent British printings, yet retained in all American printings.

We can, I believe, draw no conclusion from all this except that the confusing situation, and other oddities and omissions, arose simply through lack of systematic editing and the fact that no one had the overall task of keeping track of all of his verse. This, of course, applies also to much of his other writings; very many of the essays and articles as yet uncollected are quite as good and relevant as are those that were gathered into books. This I have long known because of the wealth of unpublished material I have had the opportunity to study, and it is now amply demonstrated in the collections of his essays from the *Illustrated London News*, which form so considerable and valuable a part of these Collected Works.

My own view is that sufficient time has now elapsed since the poet's death for it to be legitimate to say that in so far as it is possible, the whole of his verse should be made available.

Our further need now is for a new, much smaller, volume of selected poems that would allow readers and critics to extend to him the courtesy due to every writer and particularly to every poet — to be judged by his finest work.

Other poems again, and this represents a large body, were written for the entertainment of friends and family, with no intention whatsoever of publication. As well as a number of important serious poems, these include some of his very best comic verse, which will delight the growing number of his readers, not only for their quality but also because they are so personal, again and again revealing the huge warmth and geniality of his character.

Of these, very few readers would wish to be deprived. For me, the years of tracking down (a task that will never be completely achieved) these fugitive pieces have been one of the most exacting, but most exciting and rewarding aspects of compiling this offering. As an example, I saw, about a year ago, a reference to a biography of A. G. Gardiner. Knowing that Gardiner had been editor of the *Daily News* at the time when G. K. C. was writing his Saturday articles for it, I ordered the book to find what Gardiner might have said about him. I found in it the delightful verses "Some Revelations of Journalism", which Chesterton had written for Gardiner's little daughter, Stella.[1]

---

[1] Stephen E. Koss, *Fleet Street Rebel: A. G. Gardiner and the 'Daily News'* (Archon Books, 1973).

Very recently, well after the contents of this first volume had gone to the publisher, I was sent two minor but completely fresh poems, inscribed by G. K. C. in books given to friends, and I have no doubt at all that the publication of this edition will flush out more from their hiding-places. It will, therefore, be a very long time before we dare to assert that we have a complete and definitive edition.

There are other problems in editing Chesterton. He almost never dated his work, and much of it, even very early compositions, now exists only in typescript. Some poems may be given an approximate date by their appearance in periodicals, but this can never be conclusive; those that are in holograph form furnish a rough guide because of the development of his hand-writing, and a few are linked to specific, identifiable events.

The great majority, however, thwart any attempt to arrange them chronologically so, after a good deal of heart-searching, I have adopted a thematic approach and have arranged the poems under nine subject-headings. I accept that this method, too, has its shortcomings, and the reader will see that many poems are susceptible of being placed in one of two or even more groups, so that there is a strong but unavoidable element of the subjective in the decision. I can only plead that the Prefatory Note I quoted earlier shows that this method does conform to Chesterton's own approach.

Another problem I encountered is that he sometimes wrote verses using very soft pencils or chalks, and age has rendered some of these unreadable. Then there are pages that have been lost, pages torn out to make a spill with which to light one of his small cigars, passages indecipherable because of stains from tea, wine or ink. I also found a few cases in which his hand-writing was so hurried or tired that little can be made out, and his habit of using journalisitic abbreviations adds greatly to the difficulty. In some instances I have inserted, within brackets, a word or phrase that seems likely to have been what Chesterton had in mind, but in cases where the authentic text is insufficient to the offering of a coherent and significant passage, it must be reckoned as being a poem lost.

The enormous amount of material that was, for over half a century, stored at Top Meadow Cottage (the home of Dorothy Collins on the grounds of Top Meadow) and is now in the British Library gives the clearest possible picture of the exuberant and care-free attitude Chesterton held toward his material when once it had served its immediate purpose. The wonder is not that some part of it has been lost, but rather that so much of it has survived—preserved, of course, by others.

ACKNOWLEDGMENTS

My work on Chesterton's verse goes back over so many years and has covered so much ground, that I am certain to fail to express my debt to some of the people who have helped me in tracking down, verifying, locating sources, and so forth. I ask their pardon and will hope to rectify any omissions in the second volume.

The late Dorothy Edith Collins had been as a daughter to Gilbert and Frances Chesterton and as his literary executor had carried on the tradition of hospitality of that household. She and, since her passing, her associate at Top Meadow Cottage, Judith Lea, have not only given me free access to the enormous amount of material in their custody but have shown kindness in many ways during my frequent visits. My debts to them, personal as well as literary, are numerous.

Special mention must be made of The Marion E. Wade Center at Wheaton College, Illinois, where the magnificent holdings of Chesterton and other Christian thinkers have always been at my disposal. In 1988 the Center awarded me the Clyde S. Kilby Research Grant for my work on Chesterton's poetry, and I am deeply grateful for this and much other encouragement.

George Marlin, general editor of the Collected Works of which this volume is a part, and a constant supporter of the G. K. Chesterton Study Centre, and Carolyn Lemon, of Ignatius Press, whose task it has been to guide this through the stages of editing and production have put me greatly in their debt.

Professor Denis Conlon, until recently of the University of Antwerp, and Mr. Geir Hasnes, of Trondheim, Norway, who is completing a full new descriptive bibliography of Chesterton that will eventually form part of the Collected Works, have both given unstinted help and advice.

The Chesterton Review, edited by Ian Boyd, C.S.B., and published from St. Thomas More College, Saskatoon, Canada, prints much elusive and uncollected material by G. K. C., and several of these poems made their first appearance in its pages.

The archivist of St. Paul's School has more than once given me the benefit of his expertise, particularly with the poem to which I gave the title, "A Return to St. Paul's School".

The Wahlert Memorial Library of Loras College, Dubuque, Iowa, very kindly sent me a copy of their Chesterton Exhibition Catalogue containing the poem "Lines for Mr. Thomas Hutchinson".

The Rt. Hon. Kenneth Baker, M.P., while Home Secretary, found time to send me copies of the poems inscribed by G. K. C. in *Robert Browning* and in *The Ball and the Cross*.

Messrs R.F.G. Hollet & Son, of Sedburgh, Mr. Roy Pitches, of Dunstable, and my friend Peter Budek of Bedford, all booksellers, and Mrs. Eileen Mable, of the Charles Williams Society, have given valuable help. It was in *Fleet Street Radical*, Stephen E. Foss' biography of A. G. Gardiner (Archon Press, 1973) that I found the delightful poem to which I refer in my introduction.

My wife, Dorene Mary, and our seven daughters — Claire in particular, who did much of the cataloguing — have suffered much over many years while I pursued ballades and quatrains to the neglect of all else. And my thanks are due to Alan and Jane Drury and other friends who have given me both encouragement and practical help.

Finally, in advance and in hope, I warmly thank all those who, following the publication of this volume, will write to me about other verses that I may have missed. I am quite sure that there are many in private hands, inscribed in presentation copies or in visitors' books, that have yet to come to light. I may be reached through Ignatius Press, or at The G. K. Chesterton Study Centre, 15 Shaftesbury Avenue, Bedford, MK40 3SA, England.

I

JUVENILE AND EARLY POEMS

Daisy Song

The Sower's face is secret
    The Sower's stride is long
Accross the painless places
    The homeless voids among
(Join we hands over sunset lands
    Sing we the daisy song)

    Behind the great grey Sower
    Towhom all voids belong
    The sun-seeds float and eddy
    The fire-grains drift and throng
(Join we hands over sunset lands
    Sing we the daisy song)

THE AGE OF REASON

An endless line of tubs, all in an endless row
And a little child at play who rolls them to and fro.
But each contains a man — rattled about like a stone
A man of a Philosophic Age, when each man lives alone.

(ca. 1896 – 98)

ALGERNON SYDNEY[1]

Aye, beloved, as thou sayest, 'tis not fear nor failing will,
'Tis not for the block and headsman waiting me on yonder hill,
That my firm step is not joyous, nor my fearless forehead gay,
As I once had thought it should be, as I go to death today.
Can my ringing ears be deafened to the shameful cry and sound,
Can my weary eyes be blinded to the scenes that rage around?
How should English heart be merry, how should English step be proud,
While the culverins of Holland speak our country's shame aloud?
While a rout of weakling jesters revel in the Tudor's hall,
While the claims of hounds and harlots sway the council of Whitehall,
While the pride that blazed at Cressy crawls at France's throne for gain.
She who drove the vast Armada bows her craven crest to Spain.
All the nobler strifes have vanished, all the nobler lives have died,
Ancient Cavalier and Roundhead sleep forgotten side by side.

[1] Algernon Sidney (or Sydney), 1622 – 83, was a politician and soldier. The second son of Earl of Leicester, he was wounded at Marston Moor and rescued with difficulty. Later he was deeply involved in politics and intrigues. He was charged with High Treason for "conspiring and compassing the death of the king" (Charles II), and after a perjured and unfair trial was beheaded. The reference to the "culverins of Holland" is to the Dutch war, during which, in 1667, the Dutch sailed up the Thames and destroyed the British ships in the Medway.

England foremost in the revel, England slowest to the fray,
How should English heart be merry, how should English step be gay?
And is this indeed the ending, this the crown of all our toil,
When we waged that truceless battle with oppression's dragon-coil?
When a duped and chafing tyrant thundered at the Common's door,
When we bound their kings and nobles, vanquished upon Marston
  Moor,
When the crafty Northern were-wolf to his native wilds was driven,
When we smote the lying Agag in the face of earth and heaven.
All the ancient forms we shattered, all the gallant blood we shed
For the cause that now is fallen, for the hope that now is dead.
When we shaped our stern Millenium of the gospel and the sword,
Where each soul should walk unsullied in the worship of the Lord;
Thus toward that far ideal life and freedom did we lend,
And we toiled, and fought, and sorrowed—and this chaos is the end!
We were foolish, and it may be, following a wandering gleam;
Is the dream's awakening sweeter that we know it was a dream?
Yet the dream was high and noble, may not yet the ages show
Some far-off divine fulfilment of the young hope long ago?
Though our scattered few be mournful, though these drunken mobs
  be gay;
Better seek and fail as we did, than to seek and find as they:
Better die in rocky pathways, struggling for the peaks on high,
Than lie rotting in the valley where the slaves and cowards lie.
Onward through the awful spaces, on through doubt and death,
  and hell,
Will we seek the lost ideal in whose cause we fought and fell.
Yonder looms the block and headsman, yonder swell the rabble's cries,
And I go from hence to seek it through the starred eternities.

                                 (The Debater, Nov. 1891)

ALONE

Blessings there are of cradle and of clan,
    Blessings that fall of priests' and princes' hands;
    But never blessing full of lives and lands,
Broad as the blessing of a lonely man.

Though that old king fell from his primal throne,
    And ate among the cattle, yet this pride
    Had found him in the deepest grass, and cried
An 'Ecce Homo' with the trumpets blown.

And no mad tyrant, with almighty ban,
    Who in strong madness dreams himself divine,
    But hears through fumes of flattery and of wine
The thunder of this blessing name him man.

Let all earth rot past saints' and seraphs' plea,
    Yet shall a Voice cry through its last lost war,
    'This is the world, this red wreck of a star,
That a man blessed beneath an alder-tree.'

                                        (late 1890s)

A BEATEN PATH

Whitening upward,
    Clambering still,
Under the brown hedge,
    Over the hill;
Shimmering, slipping,
    Pattering on,
Goeth the path,
    Where the feet have gone.

What were their footsteps,
  Eager or slow?
What were their faces?
  Where did they go?
Why by the sea-cliffs?
  Why by the glen?
Over the green brow
  Whitherward then?

City or homestead,
  Battle or bride,
What do we seek
  On the other side?
Over the meadows
  Yellow and white
Am I an elf-prince
  Cap feathered bright?

Skies stoop fiery
  A swirl of wings,
Purple and golden
  The fen flag swings
Isled in the yellow
  Seas of the west
She who is beautiful
  Lieth in rest.

Over the waste fields,
  Sea-grey and dun,
Track I the stars
  More sweet than a sun?
More than the poppies,
  Reddens the glooms,
Fire as of haloes,
  Flush as of plumes,
Unsealed on the slopes
  Is the world's white day,
And the face of a baby
  Looks out in the hay.

Over the heathlands,
  Dreary and red,
Prodigal, seek I,
  The house of the bread?
The wall and the pathway,
  The orchard below,
Are shapes of a childhood
  Lost long ago
The last rook floats
  From the golden dome
All things are peaceful
  I have come home.

Hem of the wheatfields
  Dome of the hill
Passed by the white path
  Clambering still
With pride or wonder
  With hope or doubt
As Life's white thread
  We follow it out.
Till to end all journeys
  The wide world o'er
    The footpath stops
      At an open door.
                    (mid 1890s)

BEFORE A STATUE OF CROMWELL[1]

Once there was a time in England, for a random space alone
When the tyrannies of Europe bowed themselves at England's throne,
When the servant of the nation thought no shame to serve the Lord
When the sufferings of the stranger could be righted with the sword.

[1] At the time of the persecution of the Jews in Russia.

'Twas a time of desperate menace, mid the crash of civil strife
'Twas a time of lawless kinghood, hanging on a single life
'Twas a flash of desperate genius, swallowed by an endless sea
When the ancient flag of England was the star of all the free.

O thou grim old captain, watching from the land beyond the grave
Like a wounded king and warrior, all the strivings of the brave.
We are girt with codes and cautions, nets of policy and plan
Bonds that bar the path of vengeance to the holy wrath of man
Cannot, though our blood be flaming, as we grope the nets among
Fling the battle-gage in thunder at the startled feet of wrong
But must speak with formal reverence, urge with pleading look and
    word
Truth that such should rather meet with urged with battle flame
    and sword.
Thou who fenced the poor of Piedmont, thou who set the Hebrew free
Take our forms and codes and treaties,
        Give us but an hour with thee.
Peace!
There is no fear of slaughter, list not for the clash of steel
Well the braggart powers of Russia know the age with which
    they deal.
'Tis an age of peace and commerce, bloodless land and stainless sea,
Cries of 'peace' where there is no peace: where no peace should
    ever be!

Are our thoughts with old Crusaders, with knight-errantry our sighs
Here at least the laughing Devil works his will beneath our eyes
Little need we seek for causes neath the charnel and the sod
While a brave and tortured people cry the shame of men to God!
You that work the will of Russia, howling Christ against the few
He will take some crowd of heathen ere He opens the gates to you.

Christ has borne from you more insult than from Israel he has borne
Ye have placed the scourge of murder where they placed the reed of
    scorn

Where they flung the robe of Caesar, mocking him with Rome's
renown,
Ye have crowned your God as Pharoah and his curse be with his crown.
On, go on in safe dominions, 'tis in times of peace we dwell
Commerce with a bridge of silver joins the gates of Heaven and Hell
Let your servants work their fancies, speak not of [   ]¹ were best
Need a woman's shriek at midnight break the calm of Europe's rest
Snatch the nearest tool to torture, be it cannon, be it creed,
Let the frown of dead religion be the mask of living greed,
Fear not that mankind will touch thee for the torment of a Jew,
Kings and states sit silent round you, does not God sit silent too.

Was there theft? A slave has done it. Is there wrong? The system blame
God forbid the lips of Europe should pronounce a royal name
Cain's old craft has been in practice: but our eyes [remain cast down].²
We must not look too closely at the brow that wears a crown.

For your realm is calm and ordered which the white Czar ruleth o'er.
Comes no shout of clamorous voters, flies no flaring tricolour,
Only comes the cry of Rachel, wild and piercing o'er the dead
Only on your bubbling gutters runs the glow of rebel red!

O that somewhere in the future, yonder trampled rule to save
We may send the war cry burning on the lips of all the brave
In all generous hearts where deeper than all race and creed and clan
Lies the throbbing vein of anger at the common shame of man.
Do we seek for cause of battle, chivalry and old emprise
Yonder in the streets of Russia, 'neath the stars of God it lies.

(ca. 1890–92)

---

¹ I have seen several typed and part of one holograph copy. This blank occurs in all.
² The ending of this line was indecipherable, and an early typescript left a blank here.

THE BELL

Stars flame
Winds flood
Under the old tower's
Grey old hood
Blue dome
And stars strong
Mist's changes
Wind's song.
My song is good.
            (ca. 1895–98)

A BLESSING

I live in an age of varied powers and knowledge,
Of steam, science, democracy, journalism, art;
But when my love rises like a sea,
I have to go back to an obscure tribe and a slain man
To formulate a blessing.
                    (notebooks, ca. 1894–96)

A BLESSING

Sunlight in a child's hair.
It is like the kiss of Christ upon all children.
I blessed the child: and hoped the blessing
                          would go with him
    And never leave him;
And turn first into a toy, and then into a game
    And then into a friend,
And as he grew up, into friends
    And then into a woman.
                    (notebooks, ca. 1894–97)

THE CALVARY

In the dark of this cloud-laden even
   Still upraised, son of man, still alone
Yea, 'mid empires still shifting and breaking
   This place is thine own.

All thrones are left fallen and naked
   All treasures corrupt and all gains
O Prince of four nails and a gibbet
   Thy Kingdom remains.

On an age full of noises and systems
   Where comfortless craze follows craze
Where the passions are classified forces
   Where man is a phrase.

On an age where the talkers are loudest
   From thy silence, thy torment, thy power
O splendour of wrath and of pity
   Look down for an hour.

Go hence: To your isles of the blessèd
   Go hence, with the songs that you sing:
For this is the kingdom of pity
   And Christ is the king.

                 (ca. 1892)

THE CARPENTER

The Meditations of Marcus Aurelius.
Yes: he was soliloquising, not making something.
Do not the words of Jesus ring
Like nails knocked into a board
    In his father's workshop?
            ("The Notebook", 1894–97)[1]

COMPARISONS

If I set the sun beside the moon,
And if I set the land beside the sea,
And if I set the town[2] beside the country,
And if I set the man beside the woman,
I suppose some fool would talk about one
    being better.
            (notebooks, 1894–98)

THE CRUCIFIED

On a naked slope of a poor province
A Roman soldier stood staring at a gibbet,
Then he said, "Surely this was a righteous man,"
And a new chapter of history opened,
Having that for its motto.
            ("The Notebook", ca. 1895)

---

[1] On "The Notebook", see Maisie Ward, *Gilbert Keith Chesterton* (New York: Sheed and Ward, 1943), pp. xiv–xv and 58–68. She writes that "The Notebook" is, among Chesterton's exercise books, the "only one of real biographical importance, a book deliberately used for the development of a philosophy of life, dated in two places", p. xiv.

[2] One version in print has "tower".

DAISY-SONG

The sower's face is secret,
  The sower's stride is long
  Across the pathless places
  The homeless voids among.
(Join we hands over sunset lands,
  Sing we the daisy-song.)

Behind the great grey sower
  To whom all voids belong
  The sun-seeds float and eddy
  The fire-grains drift and throng.
(Join we hands over sunset lands,
  Sing we the daisy-song.)
                    (1890s)

DANTON

On the grim and crowded tumbrils high he reared his giant frame,
While the doubtful crowd seemed awe-struck at the murmuring of his
    name
"Sight most strange," he muttered, "strangest e'en these blood-stained
    streets have seen;
I, the fiercest of the Tribunes, passing to the guillotine.
Not in all those maddened millions, tossing wild with flame and steel,
Who with deadly blaze and thunder shook the towers of the Bastille—
Not in all that furious rabble flaunting with the oak-leaf sign,
Burnt a heart as hot as Danton's, clenched a hand as rich as mine!
Bear you the Tricolour yonder? Fling its colours over me,
Chief or captive, let me perish neath the flag of Liberty.
Liberty for whom I laboured, Liberty for whom I sinned,
Let me see her banner o'er me, flapping in the mighty wind:
As it flapped of old above us, where the serried pikes did glance,
When our thunder cry was swelling the awakened voice of France!

When we all were young and hopeful in the old time long ago,
When we scathed their haughty nobles under wild old Mirabeau!
Dost thou see us, old commander, somewhere in the still abyss?
Dost thou see the mighty union of thy children come to this?
Ay, throng thick thou yelling rabble, read with screams the shameless
    sky,
As ye thronged to see your tyrants, throng to see your champion die.
Well may dark St. Juste regard me with an ugly look, askance;
I am going, he is staying, well for me and ill for France.
Well may Monsieur David yonder mark me with artistic eye,
Let him tell his pale Maximilien,[1] Danton did not fear to die.
Let him tell his cold Dictator that his time shall also come—
See his blood on yonder hatchet, hear his knell on yonder drum;
And my murdered blood shall choke him as he gasps the coward's lie
And there mobs cajoled recall me as they watch the tyrant die;
And we now have reached the scaffold, and we all are near the end;
Good Camille, you will be faithful to your old Cordelier friend.
Nay, I first, my friends, the greatest must receive the foremost lot,
And my name will be remembered—it were better far forgot!
Friends, farewell, and be ye witness Danton dies without a fear.
Dear Camille, may God be with you—Monsieur Samson, I am here."

                                (*The Debater*, ca. 1892)

---

[1] Maximilien Robespierre.

EASTER SUNDAY

The Christ is risen the preachers say
  "Cry, for today is Easter Day".

Yea; if the dead might rise; then he
  Might rise for one thing verily.

He has not heard the mouths that moved
  The faint and fallen that he loved

The wheels that rack, the lips that rave
  Stern is God's guard about the grave.

Peace—for the priests in gold array—
  Peace—for today is Easter day.

The bannered pomp: the pontiffs wise
  (Great God—methinks he might arise)

Might break for once from death's eclipse
  To smite these liars on the lips.
                    (1895)

EDUCATION

I would say to all parents
Do you take things equally
How do you know that you are not
In the place of Joseph and Mary.
          (notebooks, 1894–97)

EGO

The sea is a dragon coiled and crowned
Strange hues wreathing the whole earth round.

The sea is a Tomb with crypt and roof
Where the bones of the brave are walled in proof.

The well shall mirror thy face to thee
There is naught but foam on the face of the sea.

This is the word the wise man says
Thread the ways of the grey sea-maze.

Be torn and ground by the sea-fangs fell
Only look not into the well.

Scarlet and gold the poppies there
Through brown dusk as a fire-hedge flare.

Through fire and fragrance I thrust apace
I looked in the well and saw my face.

I saw my face and the face was fair—
Better the deep sea choked me there.

Methought I stood in the shining street
Filled with the rush of many feet.

Face after face the faces pass,
God's hand shatter the cursed glass.

Methought I stood where the spirits pass
Glassed in the seas of fire and glass.

Richly plumed as an autumn wood
Great and gorgeous the angels stood.

Beneath dark feet did the fireglass gleam
Their faces were my face in a dream.

For he that seeth his face in the well
Sees it in heaven and earth and hell.

Methought I saw in the skies alone
One that sat on a great white throne.

His robes were braided of rose and gold
With buried daybreaks and sunsets old.

But across his visage a great cloud sat
For no man liveth that looks thereat.

The cloud was rimmed with an edge of fire
Because it hideth the world's desire.

Face after face the faces came
Only the faces were all the same.

Face after face the faces shine
Only that every face was mine.

Gold and ruby and blue and green
Every garb had a varied sheen.

Then the cloud 'gan break in the kindling air
And my soul surged up in a frantic prayer.

"Strike me dead, of thy mercy's sake
Dead and damned ere the great cloud break.

Plunder a man of bride and friends
Of all that his own soul comprehends.

But take not out of his wretched lot
The thing that he comprehendeth not.

I saw a child on a windy fell
Yea, as I passed I loved him well.

His yellow head in the deep grassed hills
With the yellow heads of the daffodils.

His face was bright, with the fields behind,
His hair was full of the sun and wind.

Yea, for a baby's gold heads sake
Strike me dead ere the grey cloud break.

For he that seeth his face in the well
Sees it in heaven and earth and hell

Save my brow, where the earth's light fell
From the star of a huge sin new in hell.

Let me not look and see mine own
Face and form on the great white throne."

Veins as of gold the grey cloud rive
Who shall look upon God alive?

The grey cloud sundered and slid away
God's face shown is the judgement day.

And high in a clearness crowned and isled
The face of God was the face of the child.

(mid 1890s)[1]

EVENING

Here dies another day
During which I have had eyes, ears, hands
And the great world round me;
And with tomorrow begins another.
Why am I allowed two?

(early notebooks, 1894–97)

---

[1] An earlier version was of five stanzas only, with little difference from the first five given here.

Ego.—.

The sea is a dragon coiled and crowned
Strange trees wreathing the whole Earth round

The sea is a tomb with wall and roof
Where the bones of the brave are stored in proof

But where the sea and the sea-fields meet
The Well by the Sea is still and sweet

This is the word the wise man says
Thread the walls of the grey sea maze

Be torn and ground by the sea-fangs fell
Only look not into the Well.

———— · ————

FAIRY-TALE

Captain Sword and Dr Gunn
Sail the sea beneath the Sun.
All fantastical they stand
Quaint as fishes on the land
Captain Sword with sparkling luck
Like a sword-fish flashed and struck
Dr Gunn, with peal on peal,
Exploded like a conger-eel.

                    (1884–86)

A FRAGMENT

And the Woods, with gnarled and cruel
    Hoary humour of the earth
Cry as at a barren Woman
    Evil jests of death and birth

At the lean lamp-iron standing
    Hideous as a hanging tree
Lonely amid nature's palace
    Of her blazoned chivalry

But the sentinel of cities
    Keeping watch o'er human things
Answered like a weaponed burgher
    To those fair old laughing Kings.

When was the green blood of lilies
    Shed upon a cross of shame
I have seen your King, and crowned him
    In a beggar lewd and lame.

And when Man with his flame banner
   Break your old tyrannic pales—
And where built a single spider
   Laugh and weep a million tales.

This shall be your best of boasting
   That some poet, poor of spine
When full fatted with our wisdom
   Full and sated with our wine

Shall slink and make a treaty
   With the tree-roots and the showers—
Weep against the grey-town mother
   Fawn upon the scornful flowers

Lay his head among the roses
   Where a quiet cuckoo sounds
And no sword made sharp for traitors
   Hack him into meat for hounds.
                (mid 1890s)

FRAGMENT

Once more the man stood, saying "A cottage-door
     Wherethrough I gazed
When I turned back—though I be vile and poor
     Yet my eyes blazed

For I have weighed the mountains in a balance
     And the skies in a scale
I come to sell the stars—old lamps for new
     Old stars for sale."

Then the first voice tell all the thunder through
     A tone less rough
"Thou has begun to love one of my works
     Almost enough."
                (mid 1890s)

GIRLS AND BOYS

Look at them blowing at these flowers!
This game is good enough for girls,
But you and I are trousered men,
And mean to end as belted earls.
And when we've shot with bows and bolts,
And shot our arrows, used our swords,
I have no doubt that we shall both
Be members of the House of Lords:
For these hereditary joys
Are given to the boldest boys.

(mid 1890s)

THE GOD OF THE LIVING

Not of the dead: of the face on face,
Crowned and damned in a twilight place,
Where the dumb lips gape and the weird lamp gleams,
And the glories dissolve into dust and dreams
Not of the dead, of the void of sighs
Where yesternight, with her children, lies,
Amid stars and mists: of the lone cry tossed
To the far low tread of an age long lost,
The sleepy realms of a sunken star,
God is the God of the things that are.

Though the fair myths moan and the faint creeds sigh,
Yet the hoarse crafts roar and the days rush by,
In a deafening circle, wheel in wheel,
In a fog of smoke and a shriek of steel,
God sits aloft in the noisy air,
The master of workers everywhere,
The dreamer's lips have a golden word
But the voice of life is the voice of the Lord,
Steam or raincloud, spark or star,
God is the God of the things that are.

(school period, 1890–92)

A GRACE

You say grace before meals.
All right.
But I say grace before the play and the opera,
And grace before the concert and pantomime,
And grace before I open a book,
And grace before sketching, painting,
Swimming, fencing, boxing, walking, playing,
    dancing;
And grace before I dip the pen in the ink.

(early notebook, mid 1890s)

GRASS AND CHILDREN

Grass and children
There seems no end to them.
But if there were but one blade of grass
Men would see that it is fairer than lilies,
And if we saw the first child
We should worship it as the God come on earth.

("The Notebook", 1890s)

THE GREAT LORD ARCHIBALD

Sing of the Great Lord Archibald
Sing of his glorious name
Sing of his covenenting faith
And his evelasting fame.

One day he summoned all his men
To meet on Cruerchin's brow
Three thousand covenenting chiefs
Who no master would allow

Three thousand Knights
With clamores drawn
And targets tough and strong
Knights who for the right
Would ever fight
And never bear the wrong.

And he creid (his hand uplifted)
"Soldiers of Scotland hear my vow
Ere the morning shall have risen
I will lay the trators low
Or as ye march from the battle
Marching back in battle file
Ye shall there among the corpses
Find the body of Argyll.

Soldiers, Soldiers onward onward
Onward soldiers follow me
Come, remember ye the crimes
Of the fiend of fell Dundee
Onward let us draw our clamores
Let us draw them on our foes
Now then I am threatened with
The fate of false Montrose.

Drive the trembling Papists backwards
Drive away the Tory's hoard
Let them tell thier hous of villians
They have felt the Campbell's sword."

And the next morn he arose
And he girded on his sword
They asked him many questions
But he answered not a word.
And he summoned all his men
And he led them to the field.

And We creid unto our master
That we'd die and never yield.
That same morn we drove right backwards
All the servants of the Pope
And Our Lord Archibald we saved
From a halter and a rope
Far and fast fled all the trators
Far and fast fled all the Graemes
Fled that cursed tribe who lately
Stained their honour and thier names.

(ca. 1884–85)[1]

THE HERO

"Heaven preserve the Lord's anointed
God defend our Sacred King."
As dark-browed Stuart passes
Hark the loyal clamours ring.

---

[1] Earliest surviving poem, ca. 1884–85. It is an adaptation of one of Aytoun's "Lays of the Scottish Cavaliers", but completely reverses Aytoun's sentiments. The young Chesterton's spelling has been retained.

Ha, but look you, where he passes,
What are those dark gallows trees?
What are those grim chain-hung corpses
Swinging clanking in the breeze.

'Tis the bones of Vane and Hampden
Torn from burial's sacred bound
Champions of the ancient freedom
Of the crowd who yell around.
What are those mouldering corpses
Flung into that bit of mire
'Tis the bones of two dead women
For the actions of their sire.
Shame to England! Shame to Manhood!
That such vile revenge should be.
Is this Christian Church's mercy
Is this knightly chivalry?

Listen to the hoots and shouting
Of the drunken panders base
Round the gibbeted bones of heroes
Whom alive they dared not face.
Listen, mingled with their yelling
What is that far-distant roar
Speaking to us through the distance
From the Thames' farther shore
'Tis the cannon of the Dutchman
To their shouting makes reply.
Let it thunder! 'Tis an answer
Worthy of so base a cry.

He the man the mighty soldier
He the ruler whose remains
Hang there as a feast for ravens
Clanking in the gallows chains.

He had chased all Holland's navy
Back into the Zuyder Zee
As he smote the Papish tyrant
On the Spaniard's native sea.

(boyhood poem, 1886)

THE HIGH MASTER AND THE ABBOT OF FULHAM

All ye who list a ballad sad
All ye who list a ballad new
— O hearken, hearken, ladies gay
— And melancholy ladies too.

— O hearken, hearken ladies gay
O pray you hearken unto me
And ye shall hear of the stoutest Prince
That dwelt in all the West Countie.

O hearken, hearken ladies gay
I rede ye hearken unto me
And ye shall hear of the proudest priest
Of all the priests in Christentie.

King Walker in the board-room sat
I trow he drank the good red wine
And to him came the holy Hilyard
God send that lot it be not mine.

"Now Christ thee saine, thou holy Hilyard
Now Christ thee saine and see
May I be Watkyn if I can
What thou would'st have with me"

"Now Christ thou saine, thou Mighty Walker
Now Christ thou sain, and also see,
It is a good half-holiday:
I come to ask of thee.

I know the jolly rifle-corps
Thy merry men, Lord King:
And I ask their guard for the Queen's daughter
To her own home to bring:

Then Walker from the table rose
And a great oath sware he
"And what to me is the Queen's daughter
And who the devil may she be."

                    (unfinished or lost, ca. 1894–95)

THE HOLY OF HOLIES

Elder Father, though thine eyes
    Shine with hoary mysteries
Canst thou tell what in the heart
    Of a cowslip blossom lies?

Smaller than all lives that be
    Secret as the deepest sea
Stands a little house of seeds
    Like an Elfin's granary.

Speller of the Stones and weeds,
    Skilled in Nature's Crafts and Creed,
Tell me what is in the heart
    Of the smallest of the seeds.

God Almighty and with Him
    Cherubim and Seraphim
        Filling all Eternity.
            Adonai Elohim.
                    (mid 1890s)[1]

---

[1] This is as in *Collected Poems* and was written ca. 1894. An earlier version is called "The Germ"; in it the first line starts, "Meadow Father", and the first two lines of verse two read:

> Secret as the inmost sea,
> Tiny to infinity.

There are no other differences.

The Holy of Holies

'Elder Father, though thine eyes.
Shine with hoary mystery,
Canst thou tell what in the heart
Of a cowslip blossom lies?

'Smaller than all lives that be
Secret as the deepest sea
Stands a little house of seeds
Like an Elfin's granary —.

'Speller of the Stones and weeds
Skilled in Nature's Crafts & Creed.
Tell me what is in the heart
Of the smallest of the seeds.

God Almighty & with Him
Cherubim and Seraphim —
Filling all Eternity
—Adonai Elohim—   —

HUMANITY

O'er the night-black city gazing, broken by the blaze and spark,
Where the light of human presence seemed more ghastly than the dark,
I beheld the far-off lamp-light mark the tavern and the den,
Till my soul grew sick and weary of the dreary life of men,
"Vain are canons and ideals, vain are creeds and duties all
To the last our blood is tinctured with the madness of the fall,
Onward moves the march of progress, but 'neath all its pride and fame
Flash the same the ruffian's weapons, flash the harlot's eyes the same;
Sin consumes our brethren's spirits, death consumes our brethren's clay,
Blood of our blood boils with passion, bone of our bone wastes away;
And we move among each other, breathing in our human breath
All our ghastly inner knowledge of the law of sin and death,
In our souls the stormy presence of the things without a name,
On our brows the dark confession of the common thought of shame.
On from fathers unto children pass the evils black and fell,
Through the veins of mortal millions course the burning springs of hell.
So I live, my ruin dating to some far ancestral dawn—
Live, and with my human being damn the helpless child unborn.
Oh, to break the cursed fetters, oh, to leave them and be free,
Risen, guiltless, flower-like, star-like, in a land of purity,
Where I then should feel no longer, moving in a silent place,
Throbbing in my human essence all the vileness of my race,
Loose the old brute-bond of nature, let my spirit, girt with wings,
Hover, nameless, formless, sinless, amid everlasting things."
Through the place, upon my speaking, came a rush of angels' wings,
Bore me through the starry spaces to a place of purer things;
Regions of a golden sunset, 'neath the evening star that lay,
Dark-eyed spirits softly walking in the evening courts of day;
Troops of strange, bright aureoled maidens thronged through mystic
  glen and grot,
Souls on golden wings went by me, and I looked and knew them not.
In the bowers of purple woodlands spirit-children were at play,
And they scanned me as I passed them and in wonder turned away,

And my soul cried out within me with a bitterer distress,
That one face I loved might meet me in my heavenly loneliness.
Then across my sorrowing spirit came the thought of vanished earth,
Of the fields that knew my childhood, of the love that gave me birth.
"I would give all mystic lilies for a spray of woodland brier,
I would give all saintly glories for a gleam of cottage fire;
I would give all taintless spirits born beyond my earthly ken
For the hand grasp and the welcome of the meanest child of men.
Give me back the earthly contact, homely ill and homely good,
Link me with a race of sinners in the painted bond of blood;
Let me feel a common nature, whence I never can be free,
In whose realm one broad pulsation beats to all eternity.
Let me feel the hands of brothers in the darkness grasping mine,
As we stumble on together from the low to the divine.
Give me back my mortal nature, mortal death and mortal birth,
Keep your mystic, spotless spirits, take me back again to earth."
Through the place upon my speaking came a rush of angels' wings,
Bore me downward through the space to the place of mortal things;
And I saw once more the city, glimmering with its blaze and spark,
Every light a brother's watchfire, kindled in the silent dark;
And throughout the crowded homesteads, while the hours of sleep
  endure,
Slept the happy and the starving, slept the sinful and the pure;
And o'er all the darkened city, over hall and hut, and den,
Lay a mute and mighty presence of the brotherhood of men.

                                   (*The Debater*, March 1892)

HUMANITY

A poet, pallid and perverse,
With witless love and watery curse
Rose up to Heaven with hosts sublime
Of the insatiable time.
He rent the angels' cohorts through
And broke Heaven's blazonry of blue,

And even more he cried, "What ban
Can Jesus give, who was a man?"
The last red guard was fighting still
Against the jeering Prince of Nil,
And as he rushed across the bay
The insulted lord of star and spray
Lifted his head, "Thou sayest true—
I was a man: but what are you?"

(ca. 1891–92)

IDOLATRY

Shall we turn from the mysterious dark with the pagan prayer and spell,
As wholly a hideous dream from the gloom of the gateway of Hell?
Shall we say of the wild-eyed savage who crouches with gibber
　and moan,
Where the dead stone god sits glaring, that the worship is dead as the
　stone?
Not so; for the worshipper lives, and with him the worship grew,
And the fear of his heart is deep and the prayer of his lips is true;
The worshipper lives and prays, and with him the worship began,
Though the fetish that towers be a fetish, the man that kneels is a man;
And a spark of the world-wide worship, dim kindled within him now,
Has guided the hands that fashioned and prompted the knees that bow.
Whence came that strange, mystical impulse, with the strength of true
　sacrifice strong,
Before symbols of earth and of heaven, before canons of right and of
　wrong?
Out of the deep, mysterious—we know not whence it began—
Out of the deep, all-present, from the depths of the Nature of Man.
Yon dark barbarian, crouching with the wild and abject mien,
Is, more than the sage or the prophet, the priest of the things unseen;
That groveller's wail in the darkness that rings to the silent sky
Is more than lore or gospel the proof of a life on high.

Not alone to yon graven horror the man was kneeling then;
There is more than a fancy hidden in the soul of the children of men.
Not alone to yon ghastly idol the savage prays to-day.
He prays to the presence within him that has prompted his heart to pray.

(*The Debater*, Feb. 1892)

IF I COULD SING

If I could sing as you can sing
Then would I prize a burning marl,
One simple and resplendent thing,
Too utterly to pule or parle.
If I could sing as you can sing
    I would not snarl.

If I had sinned as you have sinned,
Ere saints could scoff at wings that singe
This much of manhood would I find,
  To thank God for the shames that tinge
If I had sinned as you have sinned,
    I would not cringe.

(Written on a fly-leaf
torn from a book, ca. 1895)

IMPERMANENCE

Earth is a prey of the hours
Life is dividing of days
Sorrow and happiness fly
Vanish dishonour and praise
Yet, toil we on toward something that lieth before our way,

Yearnings are shattered and healed
Battles are lost and are won
All the old visions are dead
All the old faces are gone
Only remains on the Earth the voice that is crying "on!"

Vanish the echoes of feet
That once in my chamber have trod
Die in the darkness without
With the silence of death they are shod
All but the roll and the march of the measureless purpose of God.

Hearts that were near unto mine
Lie far, with a waste between
Coldness is in the eyes
Where tenderness once has been
All but the Heart that is true and the face that I never have seen.

Friends may be round me still
Yet in full many a one
Something there is till
Our happiest days are gone
Only remain on the Earth the voice that is crying "on"

Vanish the love of the past
Vanish the friends of to-day
But moveth a presence within me
That is stronger and truer than men
God of my Soul! My God! Thou wilt not vanish away.

(mid 1890s)

IN THE EVENING

It is the little brown hour of twilight.
I pause between two dark houses,
    For there is a song in my heart.
If I could sing at this moment what I wish to sing,
The nations would crown me,
    If I were dumb ever afterwards.
For I am sure it would be the greatest song in the world,
And the song every one has been trying to sing
      Just now!
    But it will not come out.

(1894)

INSCRIPTION IN "POEMS & BALLADS"

A poet with a painted face
And fair gold curls and cruel grace
Broke through the heavens' opal rim
Pelted with flowers the cherubim
On the seven gateways smote and cried
And broke towards the Crucified
Then its Voice womanish and wild
Cried out "Lo, Man! Clay's common child
Thou that wert God, what art thou now?"

The insulted reared his bloodstained brow
And said "Even so: thou sayest true
I was a man. But what are you?"
(ca: 1898–1900)

INTERLUDE

Here where the golden apples grow
Came Christ more strong than Hercules
Walking the sea with wounded feet
And found the lost Hesperides.

And here might all the times have met
The pagan dance, the monkish dream,
The Golden Age, the Second Coming,
The infinite Saturnian theme.

The hero passes to other labours
The nymphs are dead, and dry the trees;
All living creatures passed; and left
The Dragon the Hesperides.

(late 1890s)

INTERLUDE

There sunken in deep woods they sang their song
And while they sang, the Kings of many lands
Strove to add land to land and field to field,
And earth was all a dust of driving bands;
And the Dutch broom and the British pennant strove
And the mad Swede sprawled out to smite the Pole
And the Czars and Sultans watched their aged rites
And never guessed a song could save a soul.

(ca. 1896)

THE INVISIBLE

God knows I would not blame you, dear,
   I do not know what thing am I
How hard a burden on your back,
   How stale an eyesore to your eye.

I never knew myself at all,
   I trod the tangled woods, but ne'er
Came to the mystic well or saw
   What monster might be mirrored there.

I saw all faces save my own—
   How should I see it now, who rise,
Stand between Heaven and Earth and Hell
   And only see the brave blue eyes.
               (mid 1890s)

"IT IS NOT WELL FOR MAN TO BE ALONE"

She was my sister through the hours that fly
   Till then . . .

Nothing I said: only in every vein
   My father Adam moved in ancient might
And on my body, bone and blood and brain
   Came the dark strength of that primeval might

When sex was cried aloud to weed and worm
   In seven thunders from the hidden throne
The night when germ cried darkly unto germ
   "It is not well for man to be alone."
              (ca. 1896–99)[1]

---

[1] Fragment written For Frances.

THE KINGDOM OF HEAVEN

Said the Lord God, "Build a house,
    Build it in the gorge of death,
Found it in the throats of hell,
    Where the lost sea muttereth,
Fires and whirlwinds, build it well."

Laboured sternly flame and wind,
    But a little, and they cry,
"Lord, we doubt of this Thy will,
    We are blind and murmur why,"
And the winds are murmuring still.

Said the Lord God, "Build a house,
    Cleave its treasure from the earth,
With the jarring powers of hell
    Strive with formless might and mirth,
Tribes and war-men build it well."

Then the raw red sons of men
    Brake the soil, and lopped the wood,
But a little and they shrill,
    "Lord, we cannot view Thy good,"
And the wild men clamour still.

Said the Lord God, "Build a house,
    Smoke and iron, spark and steam,
Speak and vote and buy and sell;
    Let a new world throb and stream,
Seers and makers, build it well."

Strove the cunning men and strong,
    But a little and they cry,
"Lord, mayhap we are but clay,
    And we cannot know the why,"
And the wise men doubt to-day.

Yet though worn and deaf and blind,
  Force and savage, king and seer
Labour still, they know not why;
  At the dim foundation here,
Knead and plough and think and ply.

Till at last, mayhap, hereon,
  Fused of passion and accord,
Love its crown and peace its stay
  Rise the city of the Lord
That we darkly build to-day.

(1892)[1]

KRUGER

The little sardines of the tin
Lie calmly side by side within
So when our Victory is o'er
Briton shall lie at peace with Boer
We shall provide the tin, I guess
And Kruger will the oiliness.

(ca. 1900)

LEGEND OF THE PESSIMIST

The Lord God sat over space for a seat
Seven suns were under His feet.

The Lord God's riddle the Lord God said
"The daisy crown has a ring of red."

---

[1] This early poem appeared first in *The Debater*, but was not collected until *Poems 1915*. Despite John Sullivan's note in his bibliography that it was dropped from *Collected Poems*, 1927, it was included, but was dropped from later British printings.

Past chaos, giants adrift and dim
  The soul of the pessimist answered him.

"Stars are nakedness, worlds are woe
  This is the thing my tongue shall show."

Strong moons flickered and heavens bowed
  As the Lord God laughed in His place aloud.

"How wilt thou do this, mighty one?"
  "Give me five gifts and it is done."

"Ring me round in a living flame
  —a little gift to begin the game."

"Arch my brow like the sky's own dome
  Merrily on our work doth come."

"Set in it eyes as flames that see
  How shall I else make nought of thee?"

"Shape my lips like a trumpet curled
  Fashioned to flout thee and thy world."

"World of thunderclap, kiss of strife
  Wake within me the star of life."

"Titans travailling, world-wide wings
  This is the marvel of wonderous things."

Sunshine thickens and grasses thrive
  Only and under a man alive.

His eyes are suns to blaze and beat
  Down on the daisy at his feet.

Only a word his lips have said
  "The daisy crown has a ring of red."

Read God's riddle he that knows
  Down in the fields where the daisy grows.
                    (ca. 1890–92)

A LIMERICK

There was an old person of Lapland
Who objected to see on a map land
   If that were only all sea
   Then mankind would be free
This idealist person of Lapland.
(ca. 1884 – 85)[1]

LONDON

A thousand housetops under the dome
And every house is one man's home,
With love and quarrel and truth and sin.
I should find if I walked therein
Under the eaves of every house
Secrets, laughter and sullen brows,
And bitter battles and comrades kind
And the love of a woman I should find
[Every anger] and hope there comes,
In any home of a thousand homes.

And strangest yet, find them in the press
Who say that the world is emptiness.
(mid 1890s)[2]

[1] Very early. On a sheet of exercise book paper, preceded by a limerick by his brother Cecil, and followed by one by E. C. Bentley, whom G. K. first met at Bewsher's (the prep school for St Paul's) in 1883.

[2] Unfinished. The two words in brackets are struck through in the original holograph, but no substitution was made.

LOVE

Do I say no-one has loved as I love?
I believe thousands have loved as I love
And if thousands have loved a thousand times more than I love
        Why so much the better.

                                    (early to mid 1890s)

LOVE OF GOD

Hide thou thy face in clouds and mysteries
Wield as thou wilt thy power that makes and mars
But hear, that in thy roaring wheel of stars
One atom dares to love thee ere it dies.

                                    (early 1890s)

MADONNA MIA

About Her whom I have not yet met
        I wonder what she is doing
        Now, at this sunset hour,
Working perhaps, or playing, worrying or laughing,
Is she making tea, or singing a song, or writing,
        or praying, or reading?
Is she thoughtful, as I am thoughtful?
        Is she looking now out of the window
        As I am looking out of the window?

                                    (mid 1890s)

A MAID'S WAY

Seven sons of the dust that are
Worthy of daisy, stone and star
Made in vigil and suffering
Worthy to hear the blackbird sing,
Roofed in the woods above;
But a maid's heart is as God's heart
And who shall speak thereof.

Seven Knights their brows that rear
Cleansed and christened of sacred fear
Seven warriors strong and sad
Seven Christs in armour clad,
His kin and kith:
But a maid's way is as God's way
And who shall strive therewith.

(mid 1890s)

THE MITRE

They made for the priest a mitre of many feathers
Of all birds in the sky;
The blue-birds burning like noon, and the great green parrots;
And blazing by
The humming-birds small like the humming bees, but brilliant
With a hundred gems;
And the great dark crimson cardinals one slow fire
To their feathered
And the holy helmet, the helmet of flaming feathers
Lifted his head
Like the rainbow crown out of heaven, the hope of martyrs,
That lifts the dead.
"But in all our days no feather fell from an angel",
The old priest said.

(ca. 1890)

MOTHER OF ALL

O strange old shadow among us, O sweet-
    voiced mystery,
Now in the hour of question I lift my voice
    unto thee.
Stricken, unstable the creeds and old things
    fall and are not.
The temples shake and groan and whisper we
    know not what.
The shapes and the forms of worship wherein
    the divine was seen
Are scattered and cast away on the fields of
    the things that have been.
A terrible stir of change and waking
    through all the land,
Till we know not what things to believe or
    what knowledge be near at hand.
Therefore I turn to thee, the nameless
    infinite,
Mother of all the creeds that dawn and
    dwell and are gone,
Voice in the heart of man, imperative,
    changeless, blind,
The call to the building of faith through
    the ages of all mankind. . . .
        ("The Notebook", mid 1890s)

THE NATIVITY BY BOTTICELLI

Do you blame me that I sit hours before this picture?
But if I walked all over the world in the time
I should hardly see anything worth seeing that is not in this picture.
        (notebooks, mid 1890s)

A NURSERY RHYME

We all are little infants
   As far as I can see.
Romping and sprawling all about
   One painted Nursery.

We all of us have small ideas
   Of what is wrong and right
And sometimes we dispute our views
   —and sometimes even fight.

Some tie gold paper round our heads
   And play at being kings
And others sit against the wall
   And think of serious things.

We are not always very good
   We strut and shriek a lot.
We have our games they all must have
   And toys that they must not.

But still we are not very bad,
   We own a generous spark.
     (Incomplete; early, ca. 1892?)

PARABLES

A raven flapped o'er the rich man's roof,
O'er golden turrets and white walls proof.
And the rich man looked on the blackening sign
From his drowsy lamp and his fiery wine:
And he thought of the red blood, fierce with sin,
That gleamed in the cup and the wine therein.
He thought of the mad tears gathered up,
To fill the glory that filled the cup.

He thought of the dim wine's secret red,
And the men that struggle and scream for bread,
And he gazed and murmured the bird to see,
"God feeds the raven, but men feed me."
Reigns and revels are gone and past,
Shall not the good time come at last?

A wild flower flamed at the rich man's feet,
For the fitful showers and the shines to greet
It had climbed its course from the riven down,
Till it ringed its brow with a glory-crown.
And the rich man gazed on the wild-eyed flower,
In his weight of robes, like a golden tower;
And he thought of the gaunt hands, fierce with sweat,
That netted the garb in a lustrous net.
He thought of the worn eyes, blind with pain,
That watched the web as it waxed amain;
He thought of the weaver's labouring breath,
And the nets that drag to a nameless death,
And he lifted his voice, the flower to see,
"God clothes the lilies, but men clothe me."
Reigns and revels are gone and past,
Shall not the good time come at last?
                              (*The Debater*, ca. 1891)

PARABLES

There was a man who dwelt in the east centuries ago,
And now I cannot look at a sheep or a sparrow,
A lily or a cornfield, a raven or a sunset,
A vineyard or a mountain, without thinking of him;
If this be not to be divine, what is it?
                    ("The Notebook", ca. 1894–97)

PAST AND PRESENT

Far in the dim past, the dark house of childhood
She moves like a sunbeam, a glimmer of day.
Old voices are with me, old eyes look upon me
Far in the dark house where children could play.

Far in the dead time, the day, past recalling
Barred, buried deep in the crypts of the brain
Save, when the gates are unbarred in the silence,
Stir like a spectre the old bones again.

New friends are with me, the brave ones, the true ones
New work is by me, the work of today.
Only at times comes the vague burning sorrow
Rings the sweet laugh of an old voice at play.

Dead, little playmate: not dead, yet departed.
Dead in a woman who dwells far away.
Dead in the dream house, the dust house, the death house,
Far in the dark house where children could play.

God who repaireth the fall of the sparrow
Crowneth the lost rose once more with her crest,
He alone bindeth the heart that is broken,
On now to action. In death shall be rest.

(mid 1890s)

PERMANENCE

Do you call the ideal the impossible?
But the impossible is the Eternal
Many changes await human thought
And Herbert Spencer shall vanish
And Isiah shall remain.

(early 1890s)

PRAISE

What Time the sun to dark is trod,
The moon to blood thereunder,
What Time the secret face of God
Moveth its lips of thunder.

I will stand up and speak a Word
Yea, one great Word, I ween
"To me gold leaves were golden, Lord"
"To me green leaves were green".
(ca. 1895–97)

THE PRESENT TIME

Mother of Riddles, dark desperate vivid
Crowned with a longing that burns as a star
Not on my lips be the cry of the thankless
Weak, discontented, thy mission to mar.

High in thine hand is the lamp of the ages,
Linked at thy side are the past and unborn,
Thou art the now and God's shame be upon us
Black: if we fail thee or leave thee forlorn.

Cowards may flout thee, sad mother of labours,
Tremblers shrink back to the peace of the dead
Yet shall each age have its rear and its vanguard
Some that have lingered and some that have led.

Gone is the hour of earth's forces primeval
Bent o'er the cradle where man's race began
Now riseth, Science with stars and with Thunders
Binding the earth with the marvel of man.

Doubters may wail or a law that is rusted
  Faith in the spectres that fade and that flee
May thy great master, worn toilers and homeward
  Grant to us faith in ourselves and in thee.

Faith in our destiny; faith in our children
  Not in a book, or a church or a caste
Faith, that despite all the growling of greybeards,
  God does not sulk in the tombs of the past.

Shall we grow weak with the dream of a childhood
  Realms of a memory: flowers of a grave.
While through the tangle of ages for ever
  God sets a sword in the hands of the brave.

                              (early, ca. 1892)

THE SCORN OF GOD

Who is the lover of the world? : him choose
Who sitteth still upon a stone to stare.
Till the brown birds have nested in his hair
And moss and lichen grown upon his shoes.

Like skies and mountains, he abides the same,
In his strange folly, lest a fly be spilled
Only his eyes with slow fire orbed and filled
Spell from a face of night, a heart of flame.

The finches carp at him : a tree too low
The lichens use him for a stone or clod—
Yet still he sitteth—yea, as still as God.
Whom, if He moved and slew us, we should know.

Dark walls with stones like eyes: hunched and bowed,
Daunt not the champion of the flaming heart
Aloft I stand on fiery crags apart
And cry to all the fallen worlds aloud.

In stormy Kiss, darkening the stars, he came
God over chaos, in colossal strife.
In the first twilight traced the globe of life
And with his lips of earthquake, spake thy name.

In hope of thee toiled nature's cycles seven
With every leaf a finger showing thee
And every walking beast a prophecy
And every flying bird a sign in heaven.

Go, snarl and snivel over clay and clod
Curse life and fatten, thou art safe, and own
In sun and rain and fruit in season grown
The shining silence of the scorn of God.

SEA AND STAR

The wave broke in, and the star came up
O'er the flower in the fields by the sea
And the purple vault of the evening sky
Domed pale above the three.

The long wave rose, an elfin wall,
And bent, a flickering crown,
And from its fields the lonely flower
Cried out, the sands adown.

"I oped to many a golden morn
I close to many an eve
Yon, gleam, a pearly ridge, and break
A stain of froth to leave."

Then from the far star's burning tongue
Its loosened thunders came
"You bloom and break, a petal-ring
I dwell a deathless flame."

The wave upon the yellow floors
Cast down its dazzling crown
And gurgling all its grey old throats
The hungry sea drew down.

And days went by: the frost-fangs bit
The hoarse blasts came and went
And broken in the furrows bare
The fiery flower lay rent.

Aeons went by: and in the night
An old light's race was run
Blasted and bitter dark, the star
Sank in its blinding sun.

But when the soul out of the wave
At God's feet broke, in rest,
There rose a new star in his crown
A new flower on his breast.

(early 1890–92)

SIMON DE MONTFORT

Moonrise gleams above the mountain, sunset glimmers through the
  wood,
Dreary float King Henry's banners, silent o'er the field of blood;
Pause the spears of fiery Edward, fierce before the heap of dead,
Where my foemen's shields are cloven, and my wearied sword is red.
At the dawn my sons were round me, and before yon armèd show,
Gave our souls to the eternal, and our bodies to the foe;
One by one they fell around me, with my banner over all,
Falling sword in hand like heroes, falling even as I shall fall.
I have ruled a mighty people I have held a captive King,
I have tasted pride and glory, all that love and power can bring;
Now in my old age and sorrow I must take the field again,
And my cherished work is shattered, and my dearest lives are slain.

Forward, all ye thankless yeomen, onward, all ye Norman spears,
Give me in my breast the guerdon of a score of toiling years!
Onward every crested tyrant, onward every armèd slave,
And I ask for nothing of you, nothing but a soldier's grave.
Yet amid the gloom of failure, the advancing shade of death
Flutters in my soul a whisper, like a meadow breeze's breath.
See the fruits of all thy labour far beyond this gloomy plain —
Never man that died for justice gave his life and blood in vain.
And a dark mist wraps the foemen, and in golden light on high
Dawn strange visions seldom given save to men about to die;
From the wild North, whence my love came, comes a people fierce and
    brave,
That shall drive yon haughty Edward wearied to a tyrant's grave.
Through the storms of feudal battle, through the gloom of despot's
    reign,
'Spite of king, and priest, and baron, Freedom's fire breaks out again;
Freedom's banner flames and flutters, Freedom's war cries rise and ring,
Angry mobs and stern battalions menacing a perjured King;
And a soldier ruling England, as I ruled it in my day,
Rough and stormy voice of Freedom spoke in faction and in fray;
And a second tyrant striving to uphold a priestly power,
Flying baffled o'er the ocean in a dark and stormy hour;
And a purer kinghood ruling lawfully the times to be,
And a nobler future dawning for the country of the free,
Far beyond yon sceptred puppet, far beyond his bolder son,
Dawns the promise of fulfilment for the work that I have done;
Onward! every bandit weapon, onward! every hireling spear,
For my dream is fading yonder and my hours are numbered here.

(The Debater, Sept. 1891)

THE SNAIL

I saw a vision of the morning age
   A farm with mammoths in the stable fed
A man stroking strange hounds: and o'er his head
   A pterodactyl singing in a cage.

Gigantic elks dragged ploughs on uplands high
    All the world's wild youth wrought around him rose
Huge and half-witted things, to chaos close
    He loved them: and I knew that it was I.

Bearing this snail I stand on crags above
    And cry aloud to all the worlds that fell—
Daring the darkness of the brain of hell
    To breed one horror that I cannot love.

(mid 1890s)

SOME PROPHECIES

Woe unto them that keep a God like a silk hat,
    that believe not in God, but in a God.
Woe unto them that are pompous for they will
    sooner or later be ridiculous.
Woe unto them that are tired of everything, for everything
    will certainly be tired of them.
Woe unto them that cast out everything, for out of
    everything they will be cast out.
Woe unto them that cast out anything, for out of
    that thing they will be cast out.
Woe unto the flippant, for they shall receive flippancy.
Woe unto them that are scornful for they shall receive scorn.
Woe unto him that considereth his hair foolishly,
    for his hair will be made the type of him.
Woe unto him that is smart, for men will hold him
    smart always, even when he is serious.

("The Notebook", 1894–95)

A SPELLING LESSON

A giant with an ox's head
  Straddled across a morning land
Vast deserts and an empty sky
  Had room for such a thing to stand.

With legs apart: a derelict
  The Deluge wetted to the knee
"My name is Aleph" thus he said
  "And every A is drawn from me."

"But all my brother-signs are dead
  And we are nothing one by one
Therefore I stand here meaningless
  A crippled monster in the sun.

For weeks I crossed the deserts drear
  Till a great shape the distance broke
Like two arches sharp and high
  A living ruin stood and spoke

"My name is M. the first and best
  And all M's written are my brood
But I am last of all my race
  For me life hath not any good.

It melted days behind my march
  Till found in those circles grey
A giant pointing with three arms
  Blown, like a sea-blown tree, one way

"E. is my name" the remnant cried
  "Yet can I not for wisdom wive
Look round these plains, you will not see
  Another letter left alive."

In the last borders of the world
  I saw ruined sunset under
Three columns that like three dead trees
  Fell half together, half asunder.

And from that low and sloping wreck
    A cry came "Cruel are the skies
Cruel the sand: my name was N.
    And with me the world's wisdom dies."
                                    (ca. 1897–98)

SUDDENLY IN THE MIDST

Suddenly in the midst of friends,
Of brothers known to me more and more,
And their secrets, histories, tastes, hero-worships,
Schemes, love-affairs, known to me
    Suddenly I felt lonely.
Felt like a child in a field with no more games to play
Because I have not a lady
        to whom to send my thought at that hour
        that she might crown my peace.
                                    (ca. 1895)

SUFFERING

Though pain be stark and bitter
And days in darkness creep
Not to that depth I sink me
That asks the world to weep.
                (late 1880s)[1]

---

[1] A boyhood poem—he suffered much from both earache and toothache.

SUNSET AND DAWN

The child looked through the lattice old,
  And watched the reddening west;
Thought he, "I'll chase that gloaming fire,
  E'er it can sink to rest."

He ran over the evening fields,
  He climbed the wooded steep,
He paddled through the rushes dim
  Where the hidden brook is deep.

Nor stayed to watch, in wooded gloom,
  The glow-worm's mystic spark;
Nor snatch the poppies floating red,
  Nor blue-bells wild and dark.

He followed still the dying glow,
  O'er meadow, wood and hill;
And faint and sad, and far from home,
  Pursued the sunset still.

The stormy clouds, the fierce red rifts,
  The gleams of fitful gold,
With drifting mist and dying light
  In changing grandeur rolled.

At last, in utter weariness,
  With struggle long and vain;
With gasp and sigh, and closing eyes,
  He sank upon the plain.

" 'Tis all in vain, the light will die,"
  The hopeless seeker wept;
And with a long and sad farewell,
  Rolled on the heath and slept.

And the red, red glow died away in the west,
  And night sank blue and dark;
And high above his still, pale face,
  The starlight lit its spark.

At last he woke, with sudden cry,
   His eyes towards the East,
Saw flooding all the Heavens with gold
   The red day's fiery crest.

Once more he marked, with flashing eye,
   Fringing the hills' dark blue,
The broad and burning belt of red
   That did not die, but grew.

Thus following some old, dying light
   That now has had it's day,
We strongly, desperate, for a while,
   Then baffled turn away.

Turn from the old and single Form
   We had pursued in vain,
Yet in the region least we think,
   May meet the light again.
                (*The Debater*, Mar. 1891)

THE TEA POT

Raised high on tripod, flashing bright, the Holy Silver Urn
Within whose inmost cavern dark, the secret waters burn
Before the temple's gateway the subject tea-cups bow
And pass it steaming with thy gift, thy brown autumnal glow.
Within thy silver fortress, the tea-leaf treasure piled
O'er which the fiery fountain pours its waters undefiled
Till the witch-water steals away the essence they enfold
And dashes from the yawning spout a torrent-arch of gold.
Then fill an honest cup my lads and quaff the draught amain
And lay the earthen goblet down, and fill it yet again
Nor heed the curses on the cup that rise from Folly's school
The sneering of the drunkard and the warning of the fool.

Leave to the Stuart's cavalier the revel's blood-red wine
To hiccup out a tyrant's health and swear his Right Divine
Mine, Cromwell's[1] cup to stir within, the spirit cool and sure
To face another Star Chamber, a second Marston Moor.
Leave to the genius-scorner, the sot's soul-slaying urns
That stained the fame of Addison, and wrecked the life of Burns
For Etty's[2] hand his private Pot, that for no waiter waits
For Cowper's lips his "Cup that cheers but not inebriates."

Goal of Infantine Hope, Unknown, mystic felicity
Sangrael of childish quest much sought, aethereal "Real Tea"
Thy faintest tint of yellow on the milk and water pale
Like Midas' stain on Pactolus, gives joy that cannot fail.
                                        (ca. 1890 or earlier)

THE TEMPLE OF EARTH

Skies grey or green,
    The brown old dome
Of earth, our home,
    The same is seen.

O'er forest-gate
    O'er mountain-wall,
The dome o'er all
    Glooms dark and great.

But through skies swart
    In hours of old
White bars or gold
    Broke bright athwart.

Some storm-rift shone,
    Bade see and greet,
Tremendous feet
    That stood thereon.
                (1891–94)

---

[1] Oliver Cromwell's teapot was among the first to be used in Britain.

[2] William Etty, the painter (1787–1849), always carried his own teapot, and in hotels, etc., made his own tea.

The Temple of Earth

Skies grey or green,
The brown old dome
Of earth our home,
The same is seen

O'er forest-gate
Or mountain-wall,
The dome o'er all
Glooms dark & great

But through skies swart
In hours of old
White bars or gold
—Broke bright athwart

Some storm-tuft shone,
Back see & greet.
Tremendous feet
That stood thereon.

A TESTAMENT

This is my Testament of all my gear
My limbs to larch; my eyes to marigolds,
My locks to grass: and thou, bird of the wolds
Build in my brain for nest and never fear

But if on blasted peaks the wheeling Kite
Darkens a ghastly sunset as I die
I will stretch arms from that lone crag and cry
"Thank God the Vultures have a feast tonight".
(ca. 1896–98)

'THANK GOD'

I ask not, though my fiery tears be sore,
That skies should pity or that men should mourn,
Nay, rather teach me with what sunny scorn
The great earth laughs and labours evermore.

Thank God the stars are set beyond my power
If I must travail in a night of wrath
Thank God my tears will never vex a moth
Nor any curse of mine cut down a flower.

Men say the sun was darkened: yet I had
Thought it beat brightly, even on Calvary
And he, that hung upon the torturing tree
Heard all the crickets singing and was glad.
(mid 1890s)

THANK-YOU

I thank thee, O Lord, for the stones in the street
I thank thee for the hay-carts yonder and for the houses
    built and half-built
That fly past me as I stride.
But most of all for the great wind in my nostrils
As if thine own nostrils were close.

                  (notebooks, 1894–97)

THEORY

As one who looks from rocky dales,
   Still shadowed from the reddening morn,
Beholds above the gloaming slopes
   The pale crests fiery in the dawn;

And lit on their uplifted brows
   The glimmer of the far-off snow,
Like some pale star whose nearer light
   The toiling worlds shall never know.

But when the broad sun's rising glow,
   Flush with its fires the glittering ice,
And torrents from the foaming clefts
   Leap flying o'er the precipice;

And broadening like a mighty sea,
   Shall sweep on human field and home,
And shadowy depth and shadowy crest
   Are shattered into clouds of foam—

Learn all who spurn ideal dreams
   Of righted wrong and bettered woe;
The truth that seemed a star above,
   May roar a flood of death below.

               (*The Debater*, Jan. 1892)

THERE IS A HEART

There is a heart within a distant town
Who loves me more than treasure or renown
Think you it strange and wear it as a crown.

Is not the marvel here; that since the kiss
And dizzy glories of that blinding bliss
One grief has ever touched me after this.

(notebooks, mid 1890s)

THREE THINGS

There are three things that make me think;
    things beyond all poetry:
A yellow space or rift in evening sky:
A chimney or pinnacle high in the air;
And a path over a hill.

(notebooks, mid 1890s)

TO HIS LOVE

I cannot make less red the rose's fold,
Less white the wave,
Less blue the sea, less bright the garner's gold,
Less dark the grave,
Nor make thy soul less beautiful and bold,
Queen of the brave.

(notebooks, mid 1890s)

TWILIGHT

—And the evening and the morning were the first day.
                                    — Genesis

With treading of Night as a vintage
    Half-reddened, half-ruin
With a rending of Night as a quarry
    Half cleared and half-won
We gather, the workers, the makers
    The brave who can feel
God fashioned the sun for a furnace
    The world for a wheel.

This old earth where all labour and longing
    Grow heavy with guilt
Is it not as a morning half-broken
    A city half-built
This old earth where our faiths grow unequal
    Our faces afraid
Is it not a creation half-finished
    An Eden half-made?

With binding of Night as a harvest,
    For granaries dim
With feeling of Night as a forest
    Trunk, tangle and limb
We answer the makers who learn,
    —Amid thicket and brier,
God reared to us forest for fuel
    And fuel for fire.

As the glebe crieth out to the plowman
    For team and for share,
As the harvest cries out to the reapers
    To smite and not spare,
With cries from the void of the shapeless
    Of shapes that shall be.
With a mightier cry than perfection
    The world cries to me.

With searching of night as an orchard
    Its fruitage to claim
With dredging of night as an ocean
    For things without name
We answer, the makers who know
    In the bramble and wood
God laid to us upland for fallow
    — And fallow for food.

What praise to the gates of the forest
    The domes of the hill
What hymns for the cloudland — what honour
    For mead and for rill
The shaping of ship out of pine-trunk
    Of pot out of clay
The changing of all into other
    — Of dawn into day.

With spelling of Night as a book
    Hieroglyphic with Moons
With touching of Night as a lyre
    To a shadow of tunes
We answer, the makers, who learn
    From below, from above,
God gave to us matter for living
    — And living for love.

With the rising of mind and of stratum
    In smoke and in steel
With the triumph of labour that passes
    With engine and wheel
With the changing of fair out of fallen
    — Of new out of old
Lo: Man, a beginning, an outline
    — A grey before gold.

                  (mid 1890s)

ULTIMATE

The vision of a haloed host
    That weep around an empty throne;
And, aureoles dark and angels dead,
    Man with his own life stands alone.

'I am,' he says his bankrupt creed;
    'I am,' and is again a clod:
The sparrow starts, the grasses stir,
    For he has said the name of God.

              (1890s)

THE UNION

Scowl on ye dead that hug the dead, and cleave the air with cries.
While the slow hand of England clears the blood-mist from her eyes.
Ye shall not drug her back to sleep with songs that (slur) and brag,
Ye little bards that flaunt abroad the Union's tattered flag.
Ye shall not stay her holy hands with laughter or with wail
Go: cry aloud the Union's name: ye do not know its tale.

In the dark night of slaughtered kings when chaos roared in flood,
When all men's day was turned to dark; men's waters [turned to] blood.
When men were blind, and fury-led; that night in fear and [fright]
With nameless sounds and stifled cries and clash and groan of [fight]
With the hard fear that binds and slays, the hates that cringe and [yield],
The forts were filled, the fetters forged, the happy peace was sealed.
Go: sing your songs; no answer comes from ruin, rock or hill;
The Union held its secrets fast: it holds the secrets still.

              (early 1890s)[1]

---

[1] This early poem, ca. 1892–94, is probably an anti-Jingoist outburst, referring to the Union of England, Ireland, Wales and Scotland. The page of exercise-book paper upon which the verse is scrawled, has been torn in places along the right-hand edge. The words enclosed in brackets may not, therefore, be correct.

A VISION OF EDENS

"I do not believe the Bible story can be true.
I believe there were five Adams."
                    — Conversations of Leonard Magnus.

1. Is the stern old story shattered,
    Questioned, doubted, or denied,
    Of the world wherein our father
    Fell from innocence to pride?

    Is that wondrous antique tracing
    Of the giant primal bliss,
    Is it lost, outgrown, abandoned,
    Rated, scouted—and for this?

    Strange the tale was, rude of image:
    Full of symbols: eastern, old,
    Yet one thought did burn into us
    From that glimmering age of gold.

    From the loins of one great father
    Came each nation, race and horde,
    From one raw red clay, awakened
    By the nostrils of the Lord.

    Masqued by birth or creed or Kinghood,
    Still the living fact remained,
    Brother at the throat of brother,
    Brother crowned and brother chained.

    You, who trace elsewhere the issue
    Of the primal man and wife;
    You who see through mists of ages
    Five great fountain heads of life—

    Do not yield your story lightly;
    No, nor blame it, or forsake.
    Only read a tale, a vision
    That came to me, when you spake.

2. In the mytic eastern forest
   Where pomegranates' blood-red lips
   Here and there in the green twilight
   Gaped like moons in fierce eclipse;

   In his gorgeous domed Eden,
   In the lustrous southern wood,
   Thoughtful, eager, swarthy, subtle,
   There the Semite father stood.

   Twitched the brown hands, long and cunning,
   Hands that, labouring night and day,
   Piled the weird colossal temples
   That the ages cannot slay.

   Gleamed in eyes like antique jewels
   Things then hid from human ken,
   Sudden voices, starry visions,
   Prayers and laws of mighty men.

   "Are not all things mine to rule them,
   Fruits and foliage, moon and star,
   Am I not the latest, holiest,
   Wisest of the things that are?"

   Loud his cry was through the forest;
   It was echoed by a cry
   From his slighter, gentler help-mate
   Gathering reeds her bower anigh.

   And between them lay a creature,
   Gyre on gyre, a burning thing,
   Evil-eyed and subtle-coloured,
   As of rainbows, ring on ring.

   Whirred the pigeons from the cedar,
   Crashed the coveys from the brake,
   Lonely, lurid, fear-inspiring,
   Thus it raised its voice and spake:

"Are not all things thine to govern,
Art not thou the lord of dust,
Stronger than the laws that made thee,
Subtler than the Powers that trust?

"Grasp the reins of power and passion,
Be as gods are where you stand,
Master pleasure, vengeance, knowledge,
Lo, the fruit is to your hand."

Smitten, swayed with fierce temptation,
Thrice he bowed and groped, afraid,
Then his hand, abrupt, presumptuous,
— On the great pomegranate laid,

Came an utter darkness, noisy
With the crashing of great woods,
Earth's foundation choked and cloven
With the roaring of old floods.

Screamed the chaos, screamed and dwindled
And the twain, the fallen stand,
Hand-in-hand upon the deserts
Of a pathless morning land.

3.   In the yellow mists of morning,
     In the furthest east, below,
     Peaks of pale, fantastic mountains
     Flanked with rice-fields, capped with snow;

     In the quaint-rilled meads of sunrise,
     In the twinkling orange wood,
     Moon-faced, pensive, blandly smiling,
     Calm the first of Mongols stood.

     Clattering with his wooden sandal,
     Wielding aesthetic rake,
     Tracing sunset-tinting vases
     Made to look at — and to break.

Making comic gods to worship,
painting them profanely blue;
Lying on his back and smiling,
Having nothing else to do.

"Are not all things mine to play with,
Sun, chrysanthemum and sea;
Am I not the latest, sharpest,
First of all things that shall be?"

Loud he chirped, but in his pathway
Slow there rose a glittering thing,
Dragon-fanged and fiery-crested,
Wreathed fantastic for a spring;

Swept the grey storks from the rushes,
Sprawled the spiders from the brake,
Blazing, coiling, limbless, endless,
Thus it raised its voice and spake:

"Are not all things thine to govern,
Art not thou the lord of dust,
Stronger than the laws that made thee,
Subtler than the powers that trust?

"Grasp the reins of power and passion,
Be as gods are where you stand,
Master pleasure, vengeance, knowledge,
Lo, the fruit is to your hand."

Dazed, bewitched and fascinated
Stood the Mongol, rose at last,
Saw the orange gleam above him,
Sprang aloft and held it fast.

Dragon-clouds came o'er the sun-disc,
Rose the sea in spires of spray,
Fruit trees danced and wild flowers scampered,
All the Eden raved away.

Snapt convolvulus and lily,
Vanished heights and surf and grain,
And the fallen stood together
On a never-ending plain.

4. In the ghostly virgin forests
Of the windly, grassy west,
Where the squirrel fills the garner,
Where the blue jay builds the nest;

In the never-ending darkness,
In the dense, unbroken wood,
Serpent-bodied, copper-visaged,
Grim the earliest red man stood.

Bending on his bow of ash-tree,
Watching where, on uplands brown,
Lay the great deer of the woodland
That a single shaft brought down.

"Are not these all mine to marshal,
Tree and squirrel, down and deer,
Am I not the latest, lightest,
Swiftest of the creatures here?"

Lightly to his squaw he turned him,
But there blackened on his sight
One huge coil of living darkness,
Like a giant birth of night.

Flashed the rabbits from the burrows,
Whirled the wild fowl from the lake;
Dusky, shapeless, orbed in circles,
Thus it raised its voice and spake:

"Are not all things thine to govern,
Art not thou the lord of dust,
Stronger than the laws that made thee,
Subtler than the powers that trust?

"Grasp the reins of power and passion,
Be as gods are where you stand,
Master pleasure, vengeance, knowledge,
Lo, the fruit is to your hand!"

Stared aloft the wild red giant,
High his painted arms he flung,
Where, amid the tasselled tree-boughs,
Knots of glistening berries swung.

Broke beyond a deafening thunder,
Reeled and bent the rending woods,
And with sound and foam and darkness
Came the desolating floods.

O'er their coming, domed the tempest,
Lightning flare and thunder's yell,
Under them the woods and wigwams
Tumbled hopeless and pell-mell.

Sank the forests, sank the torrents,
And the twain stood hand in hand
In the grey, unbroken circle
Of a bare and level land.

5. Mid the trunks and roots gigantic
Of the primal forests grey,
Where the damp mist hid the torrent
And the white wolf dogged the prey,

In the voiceless, leafy vistas,
In the vasty Northern wood,
Strong of limb and frank of feature,
Proud the Aryan father stood.

In his eyes the star of conquest,
In his hand the axe of stone;
Might within him, worlds before him,
All he looked on was his own.

"Are not all things mine to rule them,
Road and river, herd and hound,
Am I not the latest, fairest,
Bravest of the things around?"

In the thickets crashed a something,
Heavy, long, it cleared a place,
And the grey jaws of a monster
Yawned before his lifted face.

Slunk the grey swine from the apples,
Dived the herons from the brake;
Gaping, glaring, forest-rending,
Thus it raised its voice and spake:

"Are not all things thine to govern,
Art thou not the lord of dust,
Stronger than the laws that made thee,
Subtler than the powers that trust?

"Seize the reins of power and passion,
Be as gods are where you stand,
Master pleasure, vengeance, knowledge,
Lo, the fruit is to your hand!"

Pale with passion grew the Aryan,
Madly to the tree he strode;
'Neath his arms the great bows splintered,
In his hand the apple glowed.

Woke the four great winds of heaven,
Rushed together with one sound,
Sank the circle of the forests,
Reeled and swayed the riven ground.

Horrors, noises, deafness, darkness,
Clutched and drowned them like a tide;
And upon a trackless level
Stood the fallen, side by side.

6. In the inmost fieriest circle
    Of the secret southern lands
    Where the emerald-roofed oasis
    With its bamboo columns stands,

    Ringed with tall, fantastic palm trees,
    Like a single-filing wood.
    Black and gaunt as Behometh,
    There the primal Negro stood.

    Bowed his massy, glistening shoulders,
    Bared his mighty, grinning teeth,
    Screwed his blind and heavy eyelids
    Scarce a glister shot beneath.

    "Are not all things mine to please me,
    Feather, stone (banana too),
    Am I not the latest, largest,
    Strongest of the things in view?"

    Grinned the dreamer, and before him
    Reared a creeping goblin-growth,
    Heavy-handed, many-jointed,
    Dragged its ugly length in sloth.

    Flared the red flamingoes upwards,
    Sailed the ibis in their wake;
    Sullen, floating, squat, flat-headed,
    Thus it raised its voice and spake:

    "Are not all things thine to govern,
    Art thou not the lord of dust,
    Stronger than the laws that made thee,
    Subtler than the powers that trust?

    "Grasp the reins of power and passion,
    Be as gods are where you stand,
    Master pleasure, vengeance, knowledge,
    Lo, the fruit is to your hand!"

Slow, the giant, round whose temples
Danced the palm leaves like a wreath,
Squirmed, and took the big banana
With one clash of his great teeth.

At his face there sprang a darkness,
Dizzy, stunning like a blow,
And he never told what followed,
Seeing that he did not know.

Till at last the twain woke slowly,
Rubbed their knees and stared and smiled,
For they sat alone together
On a dumb and dismal wild.

7.   One great plain and five great chieftains
Drawing nearer each to each,
Rearing fast, like broods of giants,
Sons to foster and to teach.

As a wolf-pack on the mountains
Suddenly its fellows scents,
So the five vast tribal musters
Sighted one another's tents.

Then the five chiefs pealed a summons
For each other's place and birth,
And the five roared back together:
"I am father of the earth!"

Then the outskirts swayed and jostled,
Questioned, quarrelled and defied,
Till one wild man, blind with passion,
Smote another, that he died.

And the red blood on the prairie
For a moment gleamed and curled,
Then in five great torrents o'er it
Met the first fight of the world.

And the screaming human oceans,
Black, white, yellow, red and brown,
Over continents and ages
Surged and struggled up and down.

First the white-skinned men came trampling,
Bold of heart and strong of hand,
Then the yellow race came swarming
From its yellow eastern land.

First the myriads out of Afric
Swept the fiery sons of Shem,
Then the star-led Semites, turning,
Took and did the same to them.

To and from the racial battle
Trampled o'er the primal earth,
Drove and crashed and smote and shouted
For the secret of their birth.

Now the Mongol scourged the Aryan
For a stranger, for a pest,
Now the Aryan stoned the Mongol
In his cities in the West.

Now the Semite spurned the Aryan
"Hold aloof: we are the Lord's."
Now the Aryan held the Semite,
Beaten, branded, bound with cords.

Now the red man flayed the white man,
Scorched and scalped with knife and flame;
Now the white man shot the red man
Like a brainless head of game.

Now the white man held the black man
Toiling in a shameless law;
Now the black man took the white man,
Took him peppered: took him raw.

To and from the blinded struggled,
Shocked and staggered, reeled and swirled,
For the case was undecided,
Which was father of the world.

And the family enquiry
To this day is going on;
Once with rended trees and boulders,
Now with battery and gun.

Yet the vision was not ended,
For methought upon a land
'Neath a crested wall of mountains
Met the five kings, hand to hand.

And when morning reddened darkly
On the high and shelving heath,
Lay the five great rulers moaning,
Stricken nigh unto the death.

And above them, on the upland,
Did a tall, weird being show,
Limbs in red clay cast gigantic,
Hair and beard like blinding snow.

And his voice like the low thunder
Of an old forgotten flood:
"What is this that tears my substance,
What is this that sheds my blood?"

In the ten wild eyes upgazing,
Sprang a memory and a pain:
"Father Adam, Father Adam,
Hast thou shown thyself again?"

"We were blind and had forgotten,
See our banners are unfurled;
Father Adam, Father Adam,
Thou wert father of the world!"

Yet the vision was not ended,
Ere it fled, a gleam, a word,
Nations round the knees of Adam,
Hand in hand before the Lord.

Varied, tolerant, united,
Satisfying diverse needs;
Where the Mongol stained his vases,
And the Indian strung his beads.

Where the harmless Ethiopian
Ate and hunted, laughed and fought,
Where the rod of Europe governed
And the harp of Israel taught.

(ca. 1889–90)[1]

VOICES

The axe falls on the wood in thuds, "God, God."
The cry of the rook, "God," answers it,
The crack of the fire on the hearth, the voice of the brook, say the
    same name;
All things, dog, cat, fiddle, baby,
Wind, breaker, sea, thunderclap
Repeat in a thousand languages—
    God.

("The Notebook", mid 1890s)

[1] This juvenile poem, clearly less accomplished than that contributed to *The Debater*, probably dates from about 1889–90. It has not previously been collected, but was first printed in the *Catholic Herald* on December 5, 1952.

A WALK

Have you ever walked along a road
  Of such a mind
That you doubted you might meet
  God at any turn of the path?
A lady plays the piano
  And I light two candles.
Sun, moon, and stars
Are not so beautiful as those candles.
Do you think they are not just as
  Good as any stars in the firmament
    Because they go out sooner?
        (mid 1890s)

WILLIAM OF ORANGE

So the chattering knaves have vanished, by a mercy all are flown,
And in the slowly deepening twilight I am silent and alone,
Silent I am thought by nature, 'tis a legacy I bear,
From my grim old grandsire yonder, and a virtue great, but rare;
And for solitude, the desert, if its drear red plain I sought,
Could not be more lonely to me, than this bustling English court,
All my soul beyond the ocean to my ancient home is flown,
And the palace of a stranger holds me weary and alone.
Ancient friends have died around me, and alone I hold the fight,
Served by mean and fawning traitors, hateful to my thought and sight,
Lies a shadow over Bentinck, and our minds we may not join.
Schomberg sleeps with blood that mingles darkly with the rushing
  Boyne;
And a newer race is round me, cold and strange to look upon,
In the calm of grasping Churchill, and the smile of proud St. John;
Men who drink the State's donation in the toasts of exiled names,
Men who wear the stars of William, while they break the seals of
  James.

Though I doubt not many a homestead, through this happy northern
    land,
Oft could show in Whig and Tory, noble heart and toiling hand.
But this people cannot love me, base or faithful, low or high,
To the worst I am a master, to the best but an ally.
Once only, when danger threatened, and I faced it sword in hand,
With beneath the Irish river, and in front the Irish band—
And the English, never silent, to the praises of the brave,
Hailed me as a king and comrade, sent to govern, and to save.
It were better I had fallen on that stern, but glorious day,
Where the Rapparee, and red-coat, mingled in the roaring fray.
Better that the grazing bullet had been driven through my breast,
And beneath the Boyne's dark waters laid my weary limbs to rest;
But I lived to see their kindness in my old age dim and cease,
And that flash of glory fading in the drearier work of peace.
Toiling without thanks or honour, while the men I save stand by.
In a work that must be finished ere I earn my right to die;
Still the old fight roars around us, trumpets blow, and chargers
    prance,
And a hundred tribes are writhing 'neath the tyrant heel of France.
And we yet must teach the lesson Louis' spangled crowds among,
Though old William's heart is heavy, yet his brain and hand are strong;
Yet shall Luxembourg and Condé see our armies going forth,
And the blazoned throne of Louis shake beneath the banded north,
But the victor must be lonely, dark and silent as the tomb,
Save one memory in my spirit smiling gently on my gloom;
Yonder stands she, smiling ever, 'mid the Stuart's painted frowns,
Like a woodland garland lying 'mid a wealth of jewelled crowns,
Smile then on, and let me fancy 'tis once more thy presence fair,
Which I see and watch, forgetting 'tis thy painted semblance there;
Let them stay without, the schemers, plan or quarrel, or agree,
And for this one hour of evening, let me be alone with thee.

                                        (*The Debater*, May 1891)

A WORD

A word came forth in Galilee, a word like to a star;
It climbed and rang and blessed and burnt wherever brave
    hearts are;
A word of sudden secret hope, of trial and increase
Of wrath and pity fused in fire, and passion kissing peace.
A star that o'er the citied world beckoned, a sword of flame;
A star with myriad thunders tongued: a mighty word there
    came.

The wedge's dart passed into it, the groan of timber wains,
The ringing of the river nails, the shrieking of the planes;
The hammering on the roofs at morn, the busy workshop roar;
The hiss of shavings drifted deep along the windy floor;
The heat browned toiler's crooning song, the hum of human
    worth
Mingled of all the noise of crafts, the ringing word went forth.

The splash of nets passed into it, the grind of sand and shell,
The boat-hook's clash, the boat-oars' jar, the cries to buy and
    sell,
The flapping of the landed shoals, the canvas crackling free,
And through all varied notes and cries, the roaring of the
    sea,
The noise of little lives and brave, of needy lives and high;
In gathering all the throes of earth, the living word went by.

Earth's giants bowed down to it, in Empire's huge eclipse,
When darkness sat above the thrones, seven thunders on her
    lips,
The woes of cities entered it, the clang of idols' falls,
The scream of filthy Caesars stabbed high in their brazen halls,
The dim hoarse floods of naked men, the world-realms' snapping
    girth,
The trumpets of Apocalypse, the darkness of the earth:
The wrath that brake the eternal lamp and hid the eternal hill,

A world's destruction loading, the word went onward still—
The blaze of creeds passed into it, the hiss of horrid fires,
The headlong spear, the scarlet cross, the hair-shirt and the
briars,
The cloistered brethren's thunderous chaunt, the errant champion's
song,
The shifting of the crowns and thrones, the tangle of the
strong.

The shattering fall of crest and crown and shield and cross and
cope,
The tearing of the gauds of time, the blight of prince and
pope,
The reign of ragged millions leagued to wrench a loaded
debt,
Loud with the many-throated roar, the word went forward
yet.
The song of wheels passed into it, the roaring and the smoke,
The riddle of the want and wage, the fogs that burn and
choke.

The breaking of the girths of gold, the needs that creep and
swell,
The strengthening hope, the dazing light, the deafening
evangel,
Through kingdoms dead and empires damned, through
changes without cease,
With earthquake, chaos, born and fed, rose,—and the word
was "Peace."

(early 1900s)

THE WORLD'S MISER

A Miser with an eager face
Sees that each roseleaf is in place.

He keeps beneath strong bolts and bars
The piercing beauty of the stars.

The colours of the dying day
He hoards as treasures — well He may!

And saves with care (lest they be lost)
The dainty diagrams of frost.

He counts the hairs of every head,
And grieves to see a sparrow dead.

Among the yellow primroses
He holds his summer palaces.

And sets the grass about them all
To guard them as His spearmen small.

He fixes on each wayside stone
A mark to show it as His own,

And knows when raindrops fall through air
Whether each single one be there.

That gathered into ponds and brooks
They may become His picture-books,

To show in every spot and place,
The living glory of His face.

        (early 1890s)

WORSHIP

"All thy works praise thee, O Lord."

A silence on the wooded slopes, a silence on the sea,
And would that heaven so were praised by such a peace in me.
I am a man, my heritage a curse of fire and sword,
While o'er my head the purple hills in silence praise the Lord.
From the old earth doth worship rise a hymn of ordered deeds,
But we have rent it into sects and coined it into creed.
His myriad phrases lift their hymns in ordered calm divine,
While we must struggle for a name and slaughter for a sign.
God's solemn rocks and sunny fells their hymns are still the same;
But we have strewn them with the dead we slaughtered in His name,
And while the sweet old nature song goes up from wood and hill,
The worshippers of mortal race are madly wrangling still.
And this is he; the lord of earth, the image of the Lord,
Whose worship blasteth as a curse and smiteth as a sword,
I grasp the rods and dare to claim an Eden-right divine,
To rule the living world that lifts a purer prayer than mine.
Yet lord he is, on every hand, his power is with his claim,
He rends the secret of the rocks and grasps the thunder-flame.
The cloudy confines of the earth as portals he unbars,
And tracks o'er all the silent heaven the purpose of the stars,
As a young child, mid birds and beasts with chiding and caress,
Subdues and sways their patient strength with mock imperiousness,
So mid the Titan powers of earth the child of Heaven lay,
Of wilder mood and frailer form, but loftier race than they,
While earth's mute forces blindly bent before the mystic throne,
Are conscious of a presence vague, adored but all unknown,
Man lifts a reckless gaze and strives o'er all the glimmering night,
To trace the vast unmeasured form, too awful for his sight.
Though nature's spirits lift their hymns without a doubt's alloy,
From field and hill, from flower and fruit, a psalm of ordered joy,
When far behind and far below their echoes fade and die,
Goes lonely up beyond the stars the bitter human cry.

There is a place of inner life where nature cannot come,
Where all her visions are a blank and all her voices dumb.
A deep of silent consciousness no bridge of thought can span,
Where in the lonely places meet the souls of God and man.
Aye, this is he, the lord of earth, though lone his doom and dire,
A wild-eyed, dual mystery, a strife of dust and fire,
A flame is set upon his brow, a sword within his hand,
And on his own wild way he goes, a waster of the land.
He stirred, a far-off germ of life, at old Creation's root,
Climbed ever, with a dawning will, the cycles of the brute.
Groped blindly through unconsciousness, sought out an unknown
    goal,
And found the vision of himself, the temple of his soul,
Within that shrine a secret lies where nature has no share,
Within that shrine for ever burns the mystic lamp of prayer,
In dreaming myth and frantic creed, in flame and battle-wrath,
In stormy flash and mystery, that secret goeth forth.

A glory round the wooded hills, a splendour of the sea,
And something of that sunset rest hath laid its hand on me.
Here, too, is peace, within, without, a praying world I scan
The fiery peace of eventide, the passion faith of man.

                                   (*The Debater*, July 1892)

XMAS DAY

Good news: but if you ask me what it is, I know not;
It is a track of feet in the snow,
It is a lantern showing a path,
It is a door set open.

                        ("The Notebook", 1894–97)

II

RELIGIOUS POEMS

Praise

What Time the sun To dark is Trod,
The moon to blood thereunder,
What Time the secret face of God
Moveth its lips of Thunder.

I will stand up and speak a Word
Yea, one great Word, I ween
"To me gold leaves were golden, Lord"
"To me green leaves were green".

G. K. Chesterton.

ADVENIAT REGNUM TUUM

Not that the widespread wings of wrong brood o'er a moaning earth,
Not from the clinging curse of gold, the random lot of birth;
Not from the misery of the weak, the madness of the strong,
Goes upward from our lips the cry, "How long, oh Lord, how long?"
Not only from the huts of toil, the dens of sin and shame,
From lordly halls and peaceful homes the cry goes up the same;
Deep in the heart of every man, where'er his life be spent,
There is a noble weariness, a holy discontent.
Where'er to mortal eyes has come, in silence dark and lone,
Some glimmer of the far-off light the world has never known,
Some ghostly echoes from a dream of earth's triumphal song,
Then as the vision fades we cry, "How long, oh Lord, how long?"
Long ages, from the dawn of time, men's toiling march has wound
Towards the world they ever sought, the world they never found;
Still far before their toiling path the glimmering promise lay,
Still hovered round the struggling race, a dream by night and day.
Mid darkening care and clinging sin they sought their unknown home,
Yet ne'er the perfect glory came—Lord, will it ever come?
The weeding of earth's garden broad from all its growths of wrong,
When all man's soul shall be a prayer, and all his life a song.
Aye, though through many a starless night we guard the flaming oil,
Though we have watched a weary watch, and toiled a weary toil,
Though in the midnight wilderness, we wander still forlorn,
Yet bear we in our hearts the proof that God shall send the dawn.
Deep in the tablets of our hearts He writes that yearning still,
The longing that His hand hath wrought shall not His hand fulfil?
Though death shall close upon us all before that hour we see,
The goal of ages yet is there—the good time yet to be:
Therefore, tonight, from varied lips, in every house and home,
Goes up to God the common prayer, "Father, Thy Kingdom Come."

(The Debater, 1891)

THE ARENA

Causa Nostrae Laetitae
(Dedicated to the University of Notre Dame, Indiana)

There uprose a golden giant
On the gilded house of Nero
Even his far-flung flaming shadow and his image swollen large
    Looking down on the dry whirlpool
    Of the round Arena Spinning
As a chariot-wheel goes spinning; and the chariots at the charge.

        And the molten monstrous visage
        Saw the pageants, saw the torments,
    Down the golden dust undazzled saw the gladiators go,
        Heard the cry in the closed desert,
        Te salutant morituri,
    As the slaves of doom went stumbling, shuddering,
        to the shades below.

            "Lord of Life, of lyres and laughter,
            Those about to die salute thee,
        At thy godlike fancy feeding men with bread and
            beasts with men,
            But for us the Fates point deathward
            In a thousand thumbs thrust downward,
        And the Dog of Hell is roaring through
            the lions in their den."

    I have seen, where a strange country
    Opened its secret plains about me,
One great golden dome stand lonely with its golden image, one
    Seen afar, in strange fulfilment,
    Through the sunlit Indian summer
That Apocalyptic portent that has clothed her with the Sun.

    She too looks on the Arena,
    Sees the gladiators in grapple,
She whose names are Seven Sorrows and the Cause
    of All Our Joy,

Sees the pit that stank with slaughter
Scoured to make the courts of morning
For the cheers of jesting kindred and the scampering
of a boy.

> "Queen of Death and deadly weeping
> Those about to live salute thee,
> Youth untroubled; youth untortured; hateless war
> and harmless mirth
> And the New Lord's larger largesse
> Holier bread and happier circus,
> Since the Queen of Sevenfold Sorrow has
> brought joy upon the earth."

Burns above the broad arena
Where the whirling centuries circle,
Burns the Sun-clothed on the summit, golden-sheeted, golden shod,
Like a sun-burst on the mountains,
Like the flames upon the forest
Of the sunbeams of the sword-blades of the Gladiators of God.

> And I saw them shock the whirlwind
> Of the World of dust and dazzle:
> And thrice they stamped, a thunderclap; and thrice
> the sand-wheel swirled;
> And thrice they cried like thunder
> On Our Lady of the Victories,
> The Mother of the Master of the Masterers of the World.

> "Queen of Death and Life undying
> Those about to live salute thee;
> Not the crawlers with the cattle; looking
> deathward with the swine,
> But the shout upon the mountains
> Of the men that live for ever
> Who are free of all things living but a Child;
> and He was thine."   (1930)[1]

[1] In 1930 Chesterton lectured at the University of Notre Dame, Indiana. Two of the things that impressed him were the football games and the golden-domed church of the Blessed Virgin on the campus.

ART COLOURS

On must we go: we search dead leaves,
  We chase the sunset's saddest flames,
The nameless hues that o'er and o'er
  In lawless weddings lost their names.

God of the daybreak! Better be
  Black savages; and grin to gird
Our limbs in gaudy rags of red,
  The laughing-stock of brute and bird.

And feel again the fierce old feast,
  Blue for seven heavens that had sufficed,
A gold like shining hoards, a red
  Like roses from the blood of Christ.

(late 1890s)

THE ARTIST

When all the flowers were full and fair
When skies were quiet overhead
I took my pen and smiled a smile
  Whereat the flying birds dropped dead.

For on my page to heaven blazed
The shameless and tremendous words
My life's one prayer that I wrote down
  Amid the blossoms and the birds.

"O Devil ruling Heaven and Earth
I could have made a better hell
Than this, where here and there a tale
  By brutal accident goes well."

"Shorten our torments in blind rage
Be angry with us if we die
Leaving thy dotard wits to fill
  The darkness of Eternity.

I smiled for pride and power of song
Like a blind god I closed my eyes
Then saw, I know not why, new words
   Written across those sunken skies.

"The blackbird's song: the grasses' scent:
And your strange smile have risen far
To join the choir that praises God
   For the first fancy of a star."
                           (late 1890s)

AVE MARIA

Hail Mary, thou blessed among women, generations shall rise
                                        up to greet,
After ages of wrangles and dogma, I come with a prayer to
                                        thy feet.
Where Gabriel's red plumes were a wind in the lanes of thy
                                        lilies at eve,
We love, who have done with the churches, we worship, who
                                        may not believe.
Shall I reck that the chiefs we revolt with, stern elders
                                with scoff and with frown,
Have scourged from thine altar the kneelers, and reft from
                                thy forehead the crown?
For God's light for the world has burnt through it, the thought
                                whereof thou wert the sign,
As a sign, for all faiths are as symbols, as human, and man
                                        is divine.
We know that men prayed to their image and crowned their own
                                passions as powers,
We know that their gods were their shadows, nor are 'shamed of
                                this queen that was ours:
We know as the people the priest is, as the men are the
                                        goddess shall be,
And all harlots were worshipped in Cyprus, all maidens and
                                mothers in thee.

Who shall murmur of dreams or be sour when the tale of thy
               triumph is told,
When thy star rose a sun and a meteor o'er empires and cities
               of old?
When against the dim altars of passion, the garlands of
               queens god-embraced,
Come the peace of a poor Jewish maid in the lily-like pride
               of the chaste,
Came weak, without swords of the flesh, without splendours of
               lyres or of pen,
As a naked appeal to things pure in the hearts of the children
               of men;
And e'en as she walked as one dreaming, sweet, pale as the
               evening star,
The spell of the wanton was snapped, and the revel of gods
               rolled afar,
And she brightened the glens that were gloomy, and softened
               the tribes that were wild,
Till the world grew a worshipping choir round the shapes of a
               mother and child.

O woman, O maiden and mother, now also we need thee to greet:
Now in ages of change and of question, I come with a prayer
               to thy feet,
In the earthquake and cleaving of strata, the lives of low
               passions we see,
And the horrors we bound in dark places rejoice, having hope
               to be free;
Wild voices from hills half-forgotten laugh scorn at all
               bonds that restrain:
O queen of all tender and holy, come down and confound them again!
They dream that another shall oust thee, a lower rise strong
               o'er the higher,
And tread on the stars of thy night and the rose that was
               born of thy brier;
She is wreathed with red rose that is thornless, with warmth
               never stinging as fire,

She is pleasure, and this is the end of the world and the
world's desire.

O dead worlds of valour and faith, O brave hearts that strove
hard to be pure,
O wonderful longing of man, the old taint of his being to cure,
Old voices in strange exaltation, with lightning and star
taking part,
When like song of the wind in his ears were the statutes,
rejoicing the heart:
When he yearned with a terrible joy to the laws that avenge
and restrain:
Sleep, children of faith, though ye reign not, yet men were
more great in thy reign,
More great, yet I wrong thee, O present, the fruit of the
things that have been,
Man's soul that was high shall be higher, man's heart that God
cleansed shall be clean.
And the blazon shall rest on their bosoms, the soul-star upon
them that flames,
And the child ten times christened shall lead them, the vision
with varying names:
The life that was Mary's shall guard us, the dreams to high
things that belong,

The wonder, the holy, the highest shall stand among men and
be strong,
In its wings they shall dwell, like to children, all words
that revere and forgive,
Pure secrets and kindlier longings in this shall find shelter
and live;
A flower growing high as a star grows, yet fed with the life
of man's roots,
A race of men nearer the spirit, men farther, not nearer to brutes:
Therefore, breathe I a prayer for a moment, at this, the lone
shrine of the past,
Whose face was the sun of the ages, whose soul shall be light
to the last;

For man's hope of high things never faileth, though visions
                               and worships may fail,
O Mary, thou blessed among women, great pureness and
                               motherhood hail!
                    (*The Debater*, Feb. 1893)[1]

AVE MARIA

Hail Mary, thou blessed among women, generations shall rise up to
                               greet:
After ages of wrangle and dogma I come with a prayer to thy feet
Where Gabriel's red plumes were a wind on the lanes of thy lilies
                               at eve.
We love, who have done with the churches, we worship who may not
                               believe.

Shall I reck that the chiefs we revolt with, stern elders with scoff
                               and with frown
Have scourged from thine altar the clingers and reft from thy forehead
                               the crown;
For God's light for the world glimmered through it, the thought
                               whereof thou wert the sign
As a sign for all faiths are as symbols, as human, and man is divine.
We know that men prayed to their image and crowned their own
                               passions as powers
We know that their gods were their shadows, nor are shamed of this
                               queen that was ours;
We know as the people the priest is, as the men are the goddess shall be,
And all harlots were worshipped in Cyprus, all maidens and mothers
                               in thee.

---

[1] This is the revised version that appeared in *The Debater* volume 3, in 1893. The earlier draft, found in typescript with Dorothy Collins' comments, dates from 1891 or '92. The differences are minor as far as the last two lines of verse 3, but from there to the end of the poem is almost entirely changed.

Who shall grumble of dreams or be sad when the tale of thy triumph
is told
When thy star rose a sun and a meteor o'er empires and cities of old.
When against the flushed glories of sirens, the garlands of queens
god-embraced
Came the peace of a poor Jewish maid in the lily-like pride of the
chaste,
Came weak, without swords of the flesh, without splendours of lyre
or of pen
As a naked appeal to things pure in the hearts of the children of men
And e'en as she walked in her dreaming, sweet, pale as the evening-star,
The spell of the wanton was snapt and the revel of gods rolled afar
And she brightened the glens that were gloomy, and softened the
tribes that were wild
Till the world grew a worshipping choir round the shapes of a mother
and child.

O Woman, O Maiden and Mother, now also we need Thee to greet
Now in ages of change and of question I come with a prayer to thy feet
In the earthquake and rending of strata the lives of low passions we see
And the horrors we bound in dark places, rejoice, having hope to be
free
Wild voices from hills half-forgotten laugh scorn on all laws that
restrain
O Queen of all tender and holy, come down and confound them again.
They dream that another shall oust thee, a lower rise strong o'er
our higher
And tread on the stars of thy night, on the rose that was born of
thy brier
A substance of laughter and pleasure, green-robed with the glories
of art
O Mother, thy service was sterner and theirs is more soft than thy part
It is easy, O men, it is easy, this way that is fragrant with flowers;
Less hard than the dream of perfection, the craving for infinite power.
O dead worlds of valour and faith and brave hearts that strove hard
to be pure

O wonderful longing of man the low parts of his spirit to cure,
Was it truth, was it faith, was it madness? I know not; I know it
                                        was high
Something grander than passions that gorge, something prouder than
                                        pleasures that fly.
If indeed these desires be the end: and the visions return not again
Thou shalt know in thy loneliness, Mother, that man was more great
                                        in thy reign
And our flower was most fair for beholders, devourers next come
                                        for the fruit
We grasped at the plumes of the angels, tear you at the grass with
                                        the brute.

Yet need not I turn to despair: shall not man be for ever the same?
He shall fashion a crown for his dreams, for the hope of his spirit a name.
Thou wert goddess and queen, O thou pure one, and what are man's
                                        gods and his kings,
But the changing shifting shadows upon space from unknowable things.
The shadows of One, the unfathomed whom we know not all,
                                        save in this
That we long for the thing that is higher, and turn from the lower
                                        that is
Through all ages to come and all seasons, high hearts of the simple
                                        and true
Shall worship your queenhood in woman as men worshipped woman
                                        in you.
In the house of true passion, unsullied by revels of pleasure or lust
Where Love is brought in half-reluctant, by Honour and Pity and Trust.
If a seed be indeed in our storing, the germ of some fruit-bearing tree
Of the flower of a goodlier union: the crown of a marriage to be
Thou hast watched it and tended it, mother, the dreamer that watched
                                        for a sign
All purity, nobleness in us, O maiden and mother is thine.
For man's hope of high things never faileth, though visions and
                                        worship may fail
O Mary, the blessed among women, sweet Mother of Mysteries, hail!
                                        (earlier, draft version)

THE BALLAD OF GOD-MAKERS

A bird flew out at the break of day
  From the nest where it had curled,
And ere the eve the bird had set
  Fear on the kings of the world.

The first tree it lit upon
  Was green with leaves unshed;
The second tree it lit upon
  Was red with apples red;

The third tree it lit upon
  Was barren and was brown,
Save for a dead man nailed thereon
  On a hill above a town.

That night the kings of the earth were gay
  And filled the cup and can;
Last night the kings of the earth were chill
  For dread of a naked man.

'If he speak two more words,' they said,
  'The slave is more than the free:
'If he speak three more words,' they said,
  'The stars are under the sea.'

Said the King of the East to the King of the West,
  I wot his frown was set,
'Lo, let us slay him and make him as dung,
  It is well that the world forget.'

Said the King of the West to the King of the East,
  I wot his smile was dread,
'Nay, let us slay him and make him a god,
  It is well that our god be dead.'

They set the young man on a hill,
  They nailed him to a rod;
And there in darkness and in blood
  They made themselves a god.

And the mightiest word was left unsaid,
　And the world had never a mark,
And the strongest man of the sons of men
　Went dumb into the dark.

Then hymns and harps of praise they brought,
　Incense and gold and myrrh,
And they throned above the seraphim,
　The poor dead carpenter.

'Thou art the prince of all,' they sang,
　'Ocean and earth and air,'
Then the bird flew on to the cruel cross,
　And hid in the dead man's hair.

'Thou art the sun of the world,' they cried,
　'Speak if our prayers be heard.'
And the brown bird stirred in the dead man's hair,
　And it seemed that the dead man stirred.

Then a shriek went up like the world's last cry
　From all nations under heaven,
And a master fell before a slave
　And begged to be forgiven.

They cowered, for dread in his wakened eyes
　The ancient wrath to see;
And a bird flew out of the dead Christ's hair,
　And lit on a lemon-tree.

(ca. 1900)

BATTLE

Be this thing written, e'er I write
　The record of the Evil time:
That day my soul repented not
　One idle hour, one braggart rhyme.

The grass brought up its million spears
    Aye—for the honour of our star,
Write that no thorn or thistledown,
    Failed me when I went forth to War.

Old tunes of revelry and sport
    Danced on my deafening drums of fight
The hoarded sunlight of spring days
    Blazed for my beacon all the night

After, the days were grey and long
    But for that hour Life battled well,
And all the Trumpets of her tower
    Answered the horns of Azrael

We fought, although our dearest fell—
    We stood, although the planets reeled—
No sullen doubts, no empty days
    Can wipe that blazon from our shield.

And yet—to me, doubtless to me—
    The miracle of time shall come
My thoughts grow light as thistledown
    Once more: but after years in sum

God keep some mark upon my brow
    Though song be loud, though wine be red,
Of one who met Man's oldest foe
    And did not faint till he had fled.

                (ca. 1900)

A BENEDICTION

Wrapped in the windy rains that pelt and blow
When thunders shook the crazy tavern-shed
When pealing skies were bowed about my head
I bent my ear to hear the daisies grow.

Yea: in that dim lost corner where he trod,
In rain like deluge, darkness like eclipse,
A Son of Adam took upon his lips
The love which is the loneliness of God.

Like some blind giant blessed I where I stood
Virtue and vileness, penury and pelf
Man, brute and devil, yea and death itself;
It is so darkly sealed it must be good.

On babes unborn, on nameless brows and dim
The mystic star of one man's love be seen
Nor shall man flee, in wandering ways unclean
The glory of this crown that follows him.

And no wild tyrant, with almighty ban
Who in strong madness dreams himself divine
But hears through fires of flattery and of wine
The thunder of my blessing name him man.

Hush: is it True, the old wild whisper blown,
Are heaven and earth one mighty man? then I
Lift up my head in starry blasphemy
And bless him on his everlasting throne.

                                    (mid to late 1890s)

A BENEDICTION

When wind and rain were like a cloak a-blow
    When thunder shook the crazy tavern shed
When shouting skies were bowed about my head
    I bent it lower and heard the daisies grow.

In that dim hour and corner, where I trod
    In rain like deluge, darkness like eclipse
A Son of Adam took upon his lips
    The love which is the loneliness of God.

A Benediction

For one great hour strong as the world I stood
  And blessed all wholly: penury and pelf
Man, brute and devil: yea, and death itself
  It is so darkly sealed, it must be good.

When from the womb cometh the Son of Scorn
  Naked and shameful: shall be great amaze
Where on his brow a star shall stand ablaze
  The love of one man dead ere he was born.

And no blind tyrant, with almighty ban
  Who in strong madness dreams himself divine
But hears through fumes of flattery & of wine
  The thunder of my blessing name him Man

———

There in my madness blessed I where I stood
  Virtue and vileness, penury and pelf
Man, brute and devil: aye and death itself
  It is so darkly sealed: it must be good

On babes unborn: on brows unmade and dim,
  The mystic star of one man's love be seen
Nor shall man flee, in wandering ways unclean
  The glory and the crown that follows him.

And no wild tyrant, with almighty ban
  Who in strong madness dreams himself divine
But hears through fume of flattery and of wine
  The thunder of my blessing name him man.

Hush: is it true, the old wild whisper blown
  Are earth and heaven one mighty man: then I
Lift up my head in starry blasphemy
    And bless him on his everlasting throne.
                (early to mid 1890s)

THE BLACK VIRGIN

One in thy thousand statues we salute thee
On all thy thousand thrones acclaim and claim
Who walk in forest of thy forms and faces
Walk in a forest calling on one name
And, most of all, how this thing may be so
Who know thee not are mystified to know—
That one cries "Here she stands" and one cries
                    "Yonder"
And thou wert home in heaven long ago.

Burn deep in Bethlehem in the golden shadows,
Ride above Rome upon the horns of stone,
From low Lancastrian or South Saxon shelters
Watch through dark years the dower that was thine
                      own:

Ghost of our land, White Lady of Walsinghame,
Shall they not live that call upon thy name
If an old song on a wild wind be blowing
Crying of the holy country whence they came?

Root deep in Chartres the roses blown of glass
Burning above thee in the high vitrailles,
On Cornish crags take for salute of swords
O'er peacock seas the far salute of sails,
Glooming in bronze or gay in painted wood,
A great doll given when the child is good,
Save that She gave the Child who gave the doll,
In whom all dolls are dreams of motherhood.

I have found thee like a little shepherdess
Gay with green ribbons; and passed on to find
Michael called Angel hew the Mother of God
Like one that fills a mountain with a mind:
Molten in silver or gold or garbed in blue,
Or garbed in red where the inner robe burns
                                    through,
Of the King's daughter glorious within:
Change thine unchanging light with every hue.

Clothed with the sun or standing on the moon
Crowned with the stars or single, a morning star,
Sunlight and moonlight are thy luminous shadows,
Starlight and twilight thy refractions are,
Lights and half-lights and all lights turn about thee.
But though we dazed can neither see nor doubt thee,
Something remains. Nor can man live without it
Nor can man find it bearable without thee.

There runs a dark thread through the tapestries
That time has woven with all the tints of time.
Something not evil but grotesque and groping,
Something not clear; not final; not sublime;

Quaint as dim pattern of primal plant or tree
Or fish, the legless elfins of the sea,
Yet rare as this thine image in ebony
Being most strange in its simplicity.

Rare as the rushing of the wild black swans
The Romans saw; or rocks remote and grim
Where through black clouds the black sheep runs
accursed
And through black clouds the Shepherd follows him.
By the black oak of the aeon-buried grove
By the black gems of the miner's treasure-trove
Monsters and freaks and fallen stars and sunken —
Most holy dark, cover our uncouth love

From thine high rock look down on Africa
The living darkness of devouring green
The loathsome smell of life unquenchable,
Look on low brows and blinking eyes between:
On the dark heart where white folk find no place,
On the dark bodies of an antic race,
On all that fear thy light and love thy shadow,
Turn thou the mercy of thy midnight face.

This also is in thy spectrum; this dark ray:
Beyond the deepening purples of thy Lent
Darker than violet vestment; dark and secret
Clot of old night yet cloud of heaven sent:
As the black moon of some divine eclipse,
As the black sun of the Apocalypse,
As the black flower that blessed Odysseus back
From witchcraft; and he saw again the ships.

In all thy thousand images we salute thee,
Claim and acclaim on all thy thousand thrones
Hewn out of multi-coloured rocks and risen
Stained with the stored-up sunsets in all tones —

If in all tones and shades this shade I feel,
Come from the black cathedrals of Castille
Climbing these flat black stones of Catalonia,
To thy most merciful face of night I kneel.

(ca. 1920)

A CHRISTMAS CAROL

At Bethlehem, that city blest
Did Our Lady take her rest
Mary, fair and undefiled
There conceived and bore a Child
    Mater sanctissima
    Ora pro nobis

And Saint Joseph, when he saw
Christ asleep upon the straw,
In great love he worshipped there
Mary and the Child she bore
    Ave plena gratia
    Ave Rosa Mundi

And the beasts that were around
Knelt upon the holy ground
And in dumb amazement they
Praised the Lord on Christmas Day
    Omnia O Opera
    Benedicite Dominum

But the ox that kneelèd down
Nearest to the manger-throne,
When Our Lady stroked his head,
He the Holy Credo said
    "De Maria Virgine
    Et est Homo factus"

And the shepherds that had heard
Of the coming of the Word
From the mouth of Gabriel
On their knees before Him fell
 Sunt beati pauperi
 Quorum Dei Regnum

Then the kings from out the east
Started to the Birthday feast
Came and knelt, and, as is told,
 (unfinished, ca. 1896–98)

A XMAS CAROL

The Christ-child lay on Mary's lap
 His hair was like a light
(O Weary Weary were the world
 But here is all aright)

The Christ child lay on Mary's breast
 His hair was like a star
(O stern and cunning are the Kings
 But here the true hearts are)

The Christ-child lay on Mary's heart
 His hair was like a fire
(O Weary Weary is the World
 But here the world's desire)

The Christ-child stood at Mary's knee
 His hair was like a crown
And all the flowers looked up at him
 And all the stars looked down.
   (late 1890s)

A Christmas Carol.

At Bethlehem, that city blest
Did Our Lady take her rest
Mary, fair and undefiled
There conceived and bare a Child
      Mater sanctissima
      Ora pro nobis

And Saint Joseph, when he saw
Christ asleep upon the straw,
In great love he worshipped there
Mary and the Child she bare
      Ave plena gratia
      Ave Rosa Mundi

And the beasts that were around
Knelt upon the holy ground
And in dumb amazement they
Praised the Lord on Christmas Day

      Omnia O Opera
      Benedicite Dominum

A CHRISTMAS RHYME

When God was born in Bethlehem
He drank the milk of man.
And Mary asking "Is it fit?"
He bowed and clung and whispered it
"Mother, I say a dreadful thing
Save for my strange and swift coming
At last, even mortal mothers would
Have wearied of all motherhood,
When the babe was but a span."

When God was gone through Galilee,
The water turned to wine,
They questioned of the crimson freak,
He said, "Because all wine grows weak,
Yea, man grows colder than a cow,
They turn the wine to water now.
Alone I lift the feasting face,
For Bacchus, on the hills of Thrace,
Is weary of the vine."

When God was in Jerusalem,
The wine was turned to blood.
They wept. He said "Without this strife
Death had grown even as dull as life.
The sages stare and can but spy
Blue devils in the good blue sky,
But only God in agony
Can look on all good things that be,
And see that they are good."

Then do we bid a blessing down
On milk and blood and wine.
All huge and humble things we bless,
For man's great thought is grown a guess,
And woman's smile is grown a snare,
And power is in the creeds of fear,

And praise is on the thrones of theft,
And there are no things human left,
But those He made divine.
                    (*The Nation*, 1907 or 1908)

THE CREATOR

Far in the sunlit eastward
    Toil is heavy as ours
And a lonely man stood toiling
    Through the yellow evening hours.

Afar in the ancient twilight
    Man's life was a task as here
And a patient man stood working
    Though the wheels of the night drew near.

By the roof and bench of the workshop
    The mallet's weight he wields
And the ring of his blows in measure,
    Ring over the lonely fields

A tattered youth of the village
    A child of the sons of Shem
Three roods of stones and thistle
    From the streets of Bethlehem.

The fiery fragrant lilies
    Like banners broaden and flame
But he reads not in them a legend
    He sees not in them a claim

The ravens thicken, thronging
    The bleak blue skies with noise
But he sees not in them the simple
    In God's broad barns rejoice.

The throats of the west yawn burning
    The eve, like a race of crimes
Drowns blood in blood for a sunset
    But he sees not the signs of the times.

The cornfields seethe, unrolling
    Their golden treasuries
But he sees not tares nor harvest
    Only his work he sees

His brow with sweat is stainèd
    With the sweat that burns and drips
But not in the windy garden
    With the fire-cup at his lips

His hands with nails are wounded
    But not with the nails that rend
When the sun is masked by darkness
    And a great cry speaketh the end:

He sees not the empires breaking
    The floods of the world's new birth
Nor the deathless purpose in heaven
    Nor the golden city on Earth

His thoughts and eyes look downward,
    Down on the lifeless wood
He looks on the thing he maketh
    And beholds that it is good.

                          (ca. 1896–97)[1]

---

[1] This appears to be a revised and composite version of two earlier and shorter poems with this title.

The Creator

The utmost sign of the inmost
The type of the space untrod
Where the wings of the four winds mingle
Guarding the throne of God.

Far in the sunbit eastland
Men's toil was heavy as ours
And a patient man stood toiling
through the yellow evening hours
Far in the dead world's shade
Man's toil was better as here
And a lonely man stood working
Though the wheels of the night were dead

THE CREATOR

The utmost type of the inmost.
　The sign of the place untrod,
Where the winds of the four winds mingle
　That guard the throne of God.

In the great dead days of the eastward
　Men's toil was heavy as ours,
And a man stood at a working bench
　Through the yellow evening hours

The fragrant fiery lilies
　As banners beckon and flame
But he reads not in them a legend,
　He sees not in them a claim.

The ravens flap and dapple
　The gold with a moving cloud,
But he hears them not in the heavens
　Though a thousand throats be loud.

The lips of the clouds are burning
　The eve, like a race of crimes
Drowns blood in blood for a setting
　But he sees not the signs of the times.

His brow with sweat is stainèd
　With sweat that darkens and drips
But not in the windy garden
　With the fire-cup at his lips

His hands with nails are bloody,
　But not in his hour, not then
When a cry told the day-light was darkened
　And man was rejected of men.

He looketh down to his labour
　Down on the lifeless wood
He looks on the thing he fashions
　And beholds that it is good.

　　　　　　　　　(before 1896)

THE CREATOR

The utmost sign of the inmost
   The type of the space untrod
Where the wings of the four winds mingle
   Guarding the throne of God.

Far in the sunlit east-land
   Mens' toil was heavy as ours
And a patient man stood toiling
   Through the yellow evening hours

Far in the dead world's strata,
   Man's toil was bitter as here
And a lonely man stood working
   Though the wheels of the night were near.

The lips of the clouds are burning
   The eve, like a race of crimes
Drowns blood in blood for a setting
   But he sees not the signs of the times.

His brow with sweat is stainèd
   With sweat that darkens and drips
But not in the windy garden
   With the fire-cup at his lips

His hands with nails are bloody,
   But not in his hour, not then,
When a cry told the daylight was darkened
   And man was rejected of men.

He looketh down to his labour
   Down on the lifeless wood
He looks on the things he fashions
   And beholds that it is good.

                         (before 1896)

THE DONKEY

When fishes flew and forests walked
   And figs grew upon thorn
Some moment when the moon was blood
   Then surely I was born.

With monstrous head and sickening cry
   And ears like errant wings
The devil's walking parody
   On all four-footed things.

The tattered outlaw of the earth
   Of ancient crooked will
Starve, scourge, deride me; I am dumb
   I keep my secret still.

Fools! for I also had my hour,
   One far fierce hour and sweet
There was a shout about my ears
   And palms before my feet.

                (ca. 1895–98)

DOUBT

Methought I saw a dark and lonely tower,
   In the blue, silent night abyss alone,
And on its ramparts stood two figures dim
   By the grey starlight strewn.

One sat below in silence, pale and sad,
   With dim eyes pouring o'er an ancient tome,
Whose page was faintly lit with silver glint,
   From the wide starry dome.

One towered above with wild and fiery eyes
   For gazing down the fathomless abyss,
Cleaving with golden gaze the purple gloom,
   Fearful to know, or miss!

Then, while the eyes of one still pored the page,
 And while the other searched the vast unknown,
Their words came faint, borne on the midnight wind,
 Mocking its mystic moan:

"Sister, come down, come down!" The Reader spake,
 "Nor seek to see what by this book we know,
Nor seek to doubt what we may thus believe."
 The other said, "Not so!

If there be that within you, gloomy, vast,
 Hidden be that which it were life to find,
Aye, deeper still my winging gaze must search,
 Leaving all else behind."

"Sister, come down!" again the Reader spake,
 "Lest you should see what it were death to know—
O Horror huge, to swallow all our hope,
 From out yon gloom may grow!"

"I dare not come," again the Watcher spake
 "Nor Death nor Life shall take me unaware.
I, in whatever law yon darkness holds,
 Will see and take my share."

"Sister, come down!" the Reader said again,
 "Nor dare to doubt that which is written here;
Thou could'st not pry into His secrets vast,
 Did'st thou the eternal fear!"

"Do thou arise," the Watcher straight replied,
 "Nor dare to doubt God's truth in high and low:
Didst thou believe, thou could'st not fear to ask;
 Sister, look up to know!"

"Sister, I dare not," she who read replied,
 Bending her pale head trembling o'er the book
"I dare not upward gaze, I know not why,
 Sister, I dare not look."

"Doubter!" the Watcher thundered from above,
  "Blinded blasphemer of the things of God—
See—the dawn breaks, the long red ranks of flame
  The brightening clouds have trod.

See the dawn breaks, and in the purpled vault
  Behold the mystic, the eternal name
Anger to Reader's, and to Watcher's doubt,
  In characters of flame.

Slowly the Reader rose, with features pale,
  'Gainst the sky's violet reared in stern relief,
Spake with bowed head, "Lord, I do now believe,
  Help thou mine unbelief."

                    (*The Debater*, 1891–92)

ECCLESIASTES

There is one sin: to call a green leaf grey,
  Whereat the sun in heaven shuddereth.
There is one blasphemy: for death to pray,
  For God alone knoweth the praise of death.

There is one creed: 'neath no world-terror's wing
  Apples forget to grow on apple-trees.
There is one thing is needful—everything—
  The rest is vanity of vanities.

                    (1890s)

EVEN UNTO THE END OF THE WORLD

A night when wastes of uplands wan were grey with silvering snow,
A shed that shouldered back the blast one dark night long ago
When panted on his mother's breast the little life and new.
Shepherds and kings kneel here alike, and shall I not kneel too

I see no formless temple-god white pontiffs laud and pray,
I only see the happy face look out among the hay,
O son of Mary, starry-eyed,
Hear but my cry, my heart has cried,
   I find thee thus today.

A night when stormy midnight heard the jar of staves and swords,
A night that past all mortal ken, was darkness and the Lord's
When coward kings and hierarchs bore down a lonely man.
And shall I fail him in his need, that slave and sophist can.
I cannot meter the ages trend, the kingdom's gain or loss,
I only hear the pale priests shout, I see the dim crowds toss,
By rich men sold, by kings denied,
O carpenter, O crucified
Count on one striver at thy side,
One watcher at thy cross.

A night, tonight, a thousand nights be ages mad or mild
Shall man show reason to the sage from love of man or child
     (unfinished, ca. 1892)[1]

GLORIA IN PROFUNDIS

(Chorus from an Unfinished Play)

There has fallen on earth for a token
A god too great for the sky.
He has burst out of all things and broken
The bounds of eternity:
Into time and the terminal land
He has strayed like a thief or a lover,
For the wine of the world brims over,
Its splendour is spilt on the sand.

Who is proud when the heavens are humble,
Who mounts if the mountains fall,

[1] Written on rough grey paper.

If the fixed suns topple and tumble
And a deluge of love drown all—
Who rears up his head for a crown,
Who holds up his will for a warrant,
Who strives with the starry torrent
When all that is good goes down?

For in dread of such falling and failing
The Fallen Angels fell
Inverted in insolence, scaling
The hanging mountain of hell:
But unmeasured of plummet and rod
Too deep for their sight to scan,
Outrushing the fall of man
Is the height of the fall of God.

Glory to God in the Lowest
The spout of the stars in spate—
Where the thunderbolt thinks to be slowest
And the lightning fears to be late:
As men dive for a sunken gem
Pursuing, we hunt and hound it,
The fallen star that has found it
In the cavern of Bethlehem.

(ca. 1920)[1]

[1] There exists, in typescript, an earlier version of three stanzas. The first two differ little from the later, published text, but the final one is of twelve lines and reads:

> Our god that is more than immortal
> Is mortal and made; is there;
> Thrust through an unthinkable portal
> And escaped out of everywhere.
> With the falling stars descending
> We descend in the deluge of all
> To find where a thing unending
> Has slipped into space and is small.
> Pursuing we hunt and hound it
> As man hunts for a stolen gem,
> For the fallen star that has found it
> In the cavern of Bethlehem.

GOD

I saw amid the sunshine and the dews
A strange wild boy sit like a stone, astare
Till the brown birds have nested in his hair
And moss and lichen grown upon his shoes.

So still he sits the snail seems hurrying by
Like fire that catches, flower and fruitage pass
And in his ears the noise of growing grass
Roars upwards like a wave towards the sky.

Like hills and heavens he abides the same
In his strange folly, lest a fly be spilled
Only his eyes with slow fire orbed and filled
Spell from a face of night a heart of flame.

"Lift but thy hand, although it hold a rod"
"A sign; a lawless thing" the clamour came
"Show forth thine ancient thunder and thy flame"
"Yea, though thou slay us, stir thyself, O God."

In sunny fields I saw him sitting there
In an awful mercy, lest one life he lose
The golden mosses growing on his shoes
And all the sparrows nesting in his hair.

(1890s)

THE HOUSE OF CHRISTMAS

There fared a mother driven forth
Out of an inn to roam;
In the place where she was homeless
All men are at home.
The crazy stable close at hand,
With shaking timber and shifting sand,
Grew a stronger thing to abide and stand
Than the square stones of Rome.

For men are homesick in their homes,
And strangers under the sun,
And they lay their heads in a foreign land
Whenever the day is done.
Here we have battle and blazing eyes,
And chance and honour and high surprise,
But our homes are under miraculous skies
Where the yule tale was begun.

A Child in a foul stable,
Where the beasts feed and foam;
Only where He was homeless
Are you and I at home;
We have hands that fashion and heads that know,
But our hearts we lost—how long ago!
In a place no chart nor ship can show
Under the sky's dome.

This world is wild as an old wives' tale,
And strange the plain things are,
The earth is enough and the air is enough
For our wonder and our war;
But our rest is as far as the fire-drake swings
And our peace is put in impossible things
Where clashed and thundered unthinkable wings
Round an incredible star.

To an open house in the evening
Home shall men come,
To an older place than Eden
And a taller town than Rome.
To the end of the way of the wandering star,
To the things that cannot be and that are,
To the place where God was homeless
And all men are at home.

(1905–14)

A HYMN

O God of earth and altar,
　Bow down and hear our cry,
Our earthly rulers falter,
　Our people drift and die;
The walls of gold entomb us,
　The swords of scorn divide,
Take not thy thunder from us,
　But take away our pride.

From all that terror teaches,
　From lies of tongue and pen,
From all the easy speeches
　That comfort cruel men,
For sale and profanation
　Of honour and the sword,
From sleep and from damnation,
　Deliver us, good Lord.

Tie in a living tether
　The prince and priest and thrall,
Bind all our lives together,
　Smite us and save us all;
In ire and exultation
　Aflame with faith, and free,
Lift up a living nation,
　A single sword to thee.

(1907)

A HYMN FOR THE CHURCH MILITANT

Great God, that bowest sky and star,
　Bow down our towering thoughts to thee,
And grant us in a faltering war
　The firm feet of humility.

Lord, we that snatch the swords of flame,
  Lord, we that cry about Thy car,
We too are weak with pride and shame,
  We too are as our foemen are.

Yea, we are mad as they are mad,
  Yea, we are blind as they are blind,
Yea, we are very sick and sad
  Who bring good news to all mankind.

The dreadful joy Thy Son has sent
  Is heavier than any care.
We find, as Cain his punishment,
  Our pardon more than we can bear.

Lord, when we cry Thee far and near
  And thunder through all lands unknown
The gospel into every ear,
  Lord, let us not forget our own.

Cleanse us from ire of creed or class,
  The anger of the idle kings;
Sow in our souls, like living grass,
  The laughter of all lowly things.

                              (ca. 1905–14)

THE HYMN OF THE POOR

Late thou comest, little one
  Snow is on the stones.
Earth is bitter, little one,
  Grey with mists and moans.
Thou art cold as we are cold,
  Huddled with the lost.
Star of winter, star of want,
  Crownéd with the frost.

When the dim woods dream with heat
　When the meadows shine
Sea-borne Aphrodite comes,
　Earth-born Proserpine.
Pomps and pageants flower and fade
　Revels stagger by,
Myth on myth like blossoms close,
　Songs with summer die.

Tales no more can cheer us,
Streets are white and drear,
　　　Son of Mary, hear us,
　　　Seed of David, hear!

Bare thou comest, blessed one,
　Clean of rod or crown.
Stark and poor, beloved one,
　As God sends us down.
Thou art bare, as we are bare.
　Bare as death and birth.
Naked as the stars and snows
　We come upon the earth.

Princes kindle crowns with gems,
　Garments load with gold.
Hunger's rags at least can show
　Man's eternal mould.
Sins and secrets in their robes
　Tyrants hide and hoard.
Hind and babe and angel stand
　Bare before the Lord.

Rulers strike and shear us.
Spoil us, prince and peer.
　　　Son of Mary, hear us,
　　　Seed of David, hear!

Mild thou comest, mighty one,
　Brave and undefiled

As, within the eternal man
  Lies the eternal child.
Thou art kind as we are kind,
  Knowing press and pain,
Bearing one another's loads,
  Girt in common strain.

Kings are pale with scorn and wine,
  Gibe at sweat and worth.
Priest and clowns and atheist
  Join a cultured mirth.
Though we narrow be and dull,
  Darkened though we be,
Let the wise men snarl and sneer,
  We have love, and thee.

Arts come never near us,
Sages jest and jeer.
        Son of Mary, hear us,
        Seed of David, hear!

New thou comest, nascent one,
  Little hands astray,
Where life formless lies, and void
  As creation day.
Though our hopes for man be wild,
  Starry, frantic, free,
All things now are possible
  Unto God and thee.
                    (early or mid 1890s)[1]

---

[1] Written in thick pencil on large sheets of coarse grey paper.

JEALOUSY

The Roman Catholic Church has never forgiven us for converting Sir Arthur Conan Doyle from his agnosticism; when men like Mr Dennis Bradley can no longer be content with the old faith, a spirit of jealousy is naturally roused.

— A Spiritualist Paper

She sat upon her Seven Hills
She rent the scarlet robes about her,
Nor yet in her two thousand years
Had even grieved that men should doubt her;
But what new horror shakes the mind
Making her moan and mutter madly;
Lo! Rome's high heart is broken at last
Her foes have borrowed Dennis Bradley.

If she must lean on lesser props
Of earthly fame or ancient art,
Make shift with Raphael and Racine
Put up with Dante and Descartes,
Not wholly can she mask her grief
But touch the wound and murmur sadly,
"These lesser things are theirs to love
Who lose the love of Mr Bradley."

She saw great Origen depart
And Photius rend the world asunder,
Her cry to all the East rolled back
In Islam its ironic thunder,
She lost Jerusalem and the North
Accepting these arrangements gladly
Until it came to be a case
Of Conan Doyle and Dennis Bradley.

O fond and foolish hopes that still
In broken hearts unbroken burn,

What if, grown weary of new ways,
The precious wanderer should return
The Trumpet whose uncertain sound
Has just been cracking rather badly
May yet within her courts remain
His Trumpet—blown by Dennis Bradley.

His and her Trumpet blown before
The battle where the good cause wins
Louder than all the Irish harps
Or the Italian violins
When, armed and mounted like St. Joan
She meets the mad world riding madly
Under the Oriflamme of old
Crying "Montjoie St. Dennis Bradley!"

But in this hour she sorrows still,
Though all anew the generations
Rise up and call her blessed, claim
Her name upon the new-born nations
But still she mourns the only thing
She ever really wanted badly:
The sympathy of Conan Doyle
The patronage of Dennis Bradley.

(1926)

THE NATIVITY

The thatch of the roof was as golden,
Though dusty the straw was and old,
The wind was a peal as of trumpets,
Though blowing and barren and cold.
The mother's hair was a glory,
Though loosened and torn,
For under the eaves in the gloaming—
    A child was born.

Oh! if man sought a sign in the deepest,
That God shaketh broadest His best;
That things fairest, are oldest and simplest,
In the first days created and blest.
Far flush all the tufts of the clover,
Thick mellows the corn,
A cloud shapes, a daisy is opened—
    A child is born.

Though the darkness be noisy with systems,
Dark fancies that fret and disprove;
Still the plumes stir around us, above us,
The wings of the shadow of love.
Still the fountains of life are unbroken,
Their splendour unshorn;
The secret, the symbol, the promise—
    A child is born.

In the time of dead things it is living,
In the moonless grey night is a gleam;
Still the babe that is quickened may conquer,
The life that is new may redeem.
Ho! princes and priests, have ye heard it?
Grow pale through your scorn;
Huge dawns sleep before us, stern changes—
    A child is born.

And the mother still joys for the whispered
First stir of unspeakable things;
Still feels that high moment unfurling
Red glories of Gabriel's wings.
Still the Babe of an hour is a master,
Whom angels adorn,
Emmanuel, Prophet, Anointed—
    A child is born.

To the rusty barred doors of the hungry,
To the struggle for life and the din;

Still with brush of bright plumes and with knocking,
The kingdom of God enters in.
To the daughters of patience that labour,
That weep, and are worn;
One moment of love and of laughter—
    A child is born.

And till man and his riddle be answered,
While earth shall remain and desire;
While the flesh of a man is as grass is,
And the soul of a man as a fire.
While the daybreak shall come with its banner,
The moon with its horn;
It shall stay with us, that which is written—
    A child is born.

And for him who shall dream that the martyr
Is vanished, and love but a toy;
That life lives not through pain and surrender,
Living only through self and its joy.
Shall the Lord God erase from the body
The oath he hath sworn?
Bend back to thy work, saying only—
    A child is born.

                (*The Parents' Review*, Dec. 1897)[1]

THE NATIVITY

The thatch on the roof was as golden,
    Though dusty the straw was and old,
The wind had a peal as of trumpets,
    Though blowing and barren and cold,

---

[1] The version in *Collected Poems* is so much revised that it must count as a separate poem.

The mother's hair was a glory
  Though loosened and torn,
For under the eaves in the gloaming
  A child was born.

Have a myriad children been quickened,
  Have a myriad children grown old,
Grown gross and unloved and embittered,
  Grown cunning and savage and cold?
God abides in a terrible patience,
  Unangered, unworn,
And again for the child that was squandered
  A child is born.

What know we of aeons behind us,
  Dim dynasties lost long ago,
Huge empires, like dreams unremembered,
  Huge cities for ages laid low?
This at least—that with blight and with blessing,
  With flower and with thorn,
Love was there, and his cry was among them,
  "A child is born."

Though the darkness be noisy with systems,
  Dark fancies that fret and disprove,
Still the plumes stir around us, above us
  The wings of the shadow of love:
Oh! princes and priests, have ye seen it
  Grow pale through your scorn;
Huge dawns sleep before us, deep changes,
  A child is born.

And the rafters of toil still are gilded
  With the dawn of the stars of the heart,
And the wise men draw near in the twilight,
  Who are weary of learning and art,

And the face of the tyrant is darkened,
   His spirit is torn,
For a new king is enthroned; yea, the sternest,
   A child is born.

And the mother still joys for the whispered
   First stir of unspeakable things,
Still feels that high moment unfurling
   Red glory of Gabriel's wings.
Still the babe of an hour is a master
   Whom angels adorn,
Emmanuel, prophet, anointed,
      A child is born.

And thou, that art still in thy cradle,
   The sun being crown for thy brow,
Make answer, our flesh, make an answer,
   Say, whence art thou come — who art thou?
Art thou come back on earth for our teaching
   To train or to warn — ?
Hush — how may we know? — knowing only
      A child is born.

                                   (ca. 1902)

THE NEGLECTED CHILD

(Dedicated, in a glow of Christmas charity,
      to a philanthropic society)

   The Teachers in the Temple
      They did not lift their eyes
   For the blazing star on Bethlehem
      Or the Wise Men grown wise.

   They heeded jot and tittle,
      They heeded not a jot

The rending voice of Ramah
  And the children that were not.

Or how the panic of the poor
  Choked all the field with flight,
Or how the red sword of the rich
  Ran ravening through the night.

They made their notes; while naked
  And monstrous and obscene
A tyrant bathed in all the blood
  Of men that might have been.

But they did chide Our Lady
  And tax her for this thing,
That she had lost Him for a time
  And sought Him sorrowing.
                    (1907–14)

THE NURSE'S SONG

Another and still another
As surf rolls in of the sea
And each to each is a brother
And each is a babe to me.

In a poor child's hair the sunshine
As to children all sufficed,
As a crown of glory for ever,
The kiss of the living Christ.

And I sent a blessing upon him
And wished it carried the powers
To flood the ways with sunlight
And choke the fields with flowers.
                    (mid 1890s)

THE OUTLAW

Priest, is any song-bird stricken
   Is one leaf less on the tree?
Is the wine less red and royal
   That the hangman waits for me?

He upon your cross that hangeth,
   It is writ of priestly pen,
On the night they built His gibbet,
   Drank red wine among His men.

Quaff, like a brave man, as He did,
   Wine and death as heaven pours—
This is my fate: O ye rulers,
   O ye pontiffs, what is yours?

To wait trembling, lest yon loathly
   Gallows-shape whereon I die,
In strange temples yet unbuilded,
   Blaze upon an altar high.
                  (mid to late 1890s)

"THE PAGANS"

If these dried hearts indeed forget
That holy dew on dusty floor,
The Four Saints strong about the bed,
The God that dies above the door;

Such mysteries as might dwell with men,
The secret like a stooping face
Dim but not distant; and the night
Not of the abyss, but the embrace;

That only dream that ever dared
To carve upon the face of fate,
The colossal face that fills the sky,
A grief that was compassionate—

If these dear riddles seem but dumb
That once were rather loved than known,
The awful cry of God to God
Mad echoes round a man alone.

The Cross a trinket and a trick,
That blinding triangle of truth
Turning through aeons unbegun
Reverberant loves of age and youth.

Let them go forth, go far, and fling
Deserts between them and desire,
Drop down the past and find the first
Cold chaos ere that seed of fire.

Go where the graven gods of fear
Flat-eyed like fishes glare and gape,
Or dim against the revolving void
The shapeless took a shameful shape.

Grope through a sunless dawn and see,
Heaved high against the bursting blue
In piles the heavens might hardly hold,
The huge half-truth the heathens knew.

From the high terraces of the dead
Look on the dead discoloring dawn,
The flat-faced rocks, the livid land,
Where the scrawled likeness first was drawn.

Only the comfort shall be taken
Only the mysteries shall remain;
When in blunt blinded scripts of eld
Your nursery riddle speaks again.

Where choked by hairy cactus-fingers
Or sea-blue weeds like crakens curled,
One sculptured scene of sacrifice
Betrays the password of the world.

Carved as one awful threefold flower
Triple and cloven and yet alone,
The priest, the victim and the god
Wear the same smiling face of stone.

(1929)

THE PARADOX

These wells that shine and seem as shallow
    as pools,
These tales that, being too plain for the fool's eyes,
Incredibly clear are clearly incredible —
Truths by their depth deceiving more than lies.

When did the ninety and nine just men perceive
A far faint mockery in their title's sense
In the strange safety of their flocks and herds
And all the impenitence of innocence?

The sons of reason sin not and throw stones,
Nor guess where burn behind the battered door,
In the shining irony of Candlemas,
A hundred flames to purify the pure.

(early 1920s)

THE PARDON OF CHRISTMAS

Roofed in with the snows of December
  It returns, it is left to us yet
— A day: with one day to remember.
  A day: with long days to forget.

Undeterred, recurring, soft-footed
  It comes down o'er the world, as today.
To the work, unfulfilled, uncompleted,
  The house where the builders delay.

It sinks from the stars and sits throned
  On the roofs, as the angel of snow,
Watching pale, as the prophets are stoned
  With the stones that were red long ago.

Though our evangel hedges and palters,
  Though the earth-land be rooted in hate,
Though Caiaphas stand at our altar
  And Lazarus gasp at our gate.

Though the gold still clings for our cursing,
  It returns: it remains to us yet
— A day, with one day to remember,
  — A day with dark days to forget.

To forget eighteen centuries wasted
  Thick squandered in madness and guilt,
With the wine of love standing half-tasted,
  The city of promise half-built.

Join hands. Still we surely may gain it.
  The King does redeem and renew.
O Kings ye have lauded and slain it!
  Ye have failed Him: and have we been true?

Ye have shackled and guarded the door
   Ye have hoarded the key in your grips.
Ye have taken the hope from the poor
   And the word of God from his lips.

Ye have spat on and stricken the meek,
   Ye have fenced in and rented his way.
Ye are red with the blood of the weak—
   —Join hands; join hands for today.

Though church councils betray and out-vote Him;
   Though his little ones gasp for our gain;
Though the rich, that cried "traitor" and smote him
   Cry "Holy", and smite him again.

We have all done the sin: we have spoiled him,
   Thorn-crowned him, and mocked and defiled,
—Join hands, join hands—do it softly,
   To-night he is glad, and a child.

                    (early ca. 1892–94)[1]

REGINA ANGELORUM

Our Lady went into a strange country,
        Our Lady, for she was ours,
And had run on the little hills behind the houses
        And pulled small flowers;
But she rose up and went into a strange country
        With strange thrones and powers.

And there were giants in the land she walked in,
        Tall as their toppling towns,
With heads so high in heaven, the constellations
        Served them for crowns;

---

[1] Pencilled on large sheets of coarse grey paper. First sheet illustrated.

And their feet might have forded like a brook the abysses
      Where Babel drowns.

They were girt about with the wings of the morning and evening,
      Furled and unfurled,
Round the speckled sky where our small spinning planet
      Like a top is twirled;
And the swords they waved were the unending comets
      That shall end the world.

And moving in innocence and in accident,
      She turned the face
That none has ever looked on without loving
      On the Lords of Space;
And one hailed her with her name in our own country
      That is full of grace.

Our Lady went into a strange country
      And they crowned her for a queen,
For she needed never to be stayed or questioned
      But only seen;
And they were broken down under unbearable beauty
      As we have been.

But ever she walked till away in the last high places,
      One great light shone
From the pillared throne of the king of all that country
      Who sat thereon;
And she cried aloud as she cried under the gibbet
      For she saw her son.

Our Lady wears a crown in a strange country,
      The crown he gave,
But she has not forgotten to call to her old companions
      To call and crave;
And to hear her calling a man might arise and thunder
      On the doors of the grave.

               (1925)

Reparation

God is great : Through the tangle of scorns
In ordered seasons of suns & snows :
Slowly the thousand crowns of thorns
Shall break & redden to crowns of rose.

God is great : with a myriad throats
Doubt's grey seas rise high & throng.
Yet all their noise is a note 'mid notes
Struck in the chords of his own World-song

God is great : but not most for these
For heavens in chaos & moons in blight.
I see his glory ; as one that sees
Measureless forces he reins aright.

At the roots of my heart lies brown & dry,
Bitter and fragrant, an old "too late".
The dark dumb heat of a buried cry.
And God shall answer it — God is great.

REPARATION

God is great: through the tangle of scorns
In ordered seasons of suns and snows;
Slowly the thousand crowns of thorns
Shall break and redden to crowns of rose.

God is great: with a myriad throats;
Doubt's grey seas rise high and throng,
Yet all their noise is a note 'mid notes
Struck in the chords of his own world-song.

God is great: but not most for these
For heavens in chaos and moons in blight
I see his glory, as one that sees
Measureless forces he reins aright.

At the roots of my heart lies brown and dry,
Bitten and fragrant, an old "too late"
The dark dumb heat of a buried cry,
And God shall answer it—God is great.

(late 1890s)

RESURRECTION

Against a sunset gold and red
A crucifix upon a hill
Came a Blasphemer grinning by
And on the figure worked his will.

He set his own hat on the head
And a rude pipe all coarsely graved
Then screamed the priests and ran, "the dead
Is risen and the world is saved".

(late 1890s)

THE RETURN OF EVE

When Man rose up out of the red mountains
  Of which Man was made
A giant ribbed out of the red mountains
  Reared and displayed.
Of him was not posterity nor parent
  Future or past
But the sun beheld him for a beauteous
        monster
  The first and last.

When God arose upon the red mountains
  Man had fallen prone
Flat and flung wide like a continent, capes
      and headlands,
  The vast limbs thrown.
And the Lord lamented over Man, saying
      "Never
  Shall there be but one
For no man born shall be mighty as he was
      mighty
  To amaze the sun.

"Not till I put upon me the red armour
  That was man's clay
And walk the world with the mask of man for
      a vizor
  Not till that day.

For on God alone shall the image of God be
      graven
  Which Adam wore
Seeing I alone can lift up this load of ruin
  To walk once more."

But the Lord looked down on the beauty of
    Woman shattered,
  A fallen sky,

Crying "O crown and wonder and world's
                    desire".
    Shall this too die?
Lo, it repenteth me that this too is taken;
    I will repay,
I will repair and repeat of the ancient pattern
    Even in this clay.

"And this alone out of all things fallen and
                  formless
    I will form anew,
And this red lily of all the uprooted garden
    Plant where it grew,
That the dear dead thing that was all and only
                a woman
    Without stain or scar
Rise, fallen no more with Lucifer Son of
              Morning,
    The Morning Star."

The cloud came down upon the red mountains
    Long since untrod,
Red quarries of incredible creation
    Red mines of God.
And a dwarfed and dwindled race in the dark
             red deserts
    Stumbled and strayed,
While one in the mortal shape that was once
             for immortals
    Made, was remade.

Till a face looked forth from a window in one
             white daybreak
    Small streets above
As the face of the first love of our first father,
    The world's first love.
And men looked up at the woman made for
            the morning

When the stars were young,
For whom, more rude than a beggar's rhyme
                              in the gutter,
These songs are sung.
                              (early 1920s)

A RIVAL

While I can watch the gusty grass at play,
And hear the wind crash through the pinewood bars,
I envy not to God the crown of stars—
With which He crowned Him on Creation day.

But once she swung, a child, in woods alone
In days no sun or moon shall make again
And when about her came the finch and wren,
God sat and laughed upon a great white throne.

Bent o'er a thousand trifles, low and high
He saw her face, lonely and grave and good
On all the mysteries of her Womanhood
Sleeping and waking, was the unsleeping eye.

Haply some eve she looked through lattice-bars,
Some smile I know not stirred her quaint sweet eyes
Then in a nameless envy I arise
And as a blind brute giant smite the stars.

A fallen star burns on the brow I nod
Huge and obscure I stand of loin and limb,
My name is Lucifer, the name of him
Alone of things that knoweth that God is God.
                              (mid 1890s)

ST. FRANCIS OF ASSISI

In the ancient Christian ages, while a dreamy faith and wonder
    Lingered, like the mystic glamour of the star of Bethlehem,
Dwelt a monk that loved the sea-birds as they wheeled about his chapel,
    Loved the dog-rose and the heath-flower as they brushed his gar-
           ment hem;

Did not claim a ruthless knowledge of the bounds of grace eternal,
    Did not say, "Thus far, not further, God has set the hopes of life."
Only knew that heaven had sent him weaker lives in earth's communion,
    Bade him dwell and work amongst them, not in anger nor in strife.

Aye, though far and faint the story, his the tale of mercy's triumph,
    Through the dimmest convent casements men have seen the stars
           above;
Dark the age and stern the dogma, yet the kind hearts are not cruel,
    Still the true souls rise resistless to a larger world of love.

Is there not a question rises from his word of "brother, sister,"
    Cometh from that lonely dreamer what today we shrink to find?
Shall the lives that moved our brethren leave us at the gates of darkness,
    What were heaven if ought we cherished shall be wholly left
           behind?

Is it God's bright house we dwell in, or a vault of dark confusion,
    Yonder sunlit April meadows, with the singing brooks at play,
With God's daisies clustering wide-eyed o'er the breezy fields of
           morning,
    And God's skylarks whirring westward to the cloudless deeps of
           day?
Laugh aloud, O death and darkness, grin the skulls of crypt and
           charnel,
    All God's glorious flowers of being flame and fade upon a tomb;
Mystic woods and aureoled blossoms, spirit-birds and goblin lizards,
    All that faerie-world goes downward, sloping darkly into doom.

Is it so, one half of nature choked beneath the breath of ruin,
     Does death tread at last a victor on the lives we loved so well?
Take us, too, devouring chaos, hide us from the vast injustice,
     Dust to dust be ours for ever, with the world wherein we dwell.

While the flush of kindred feeling at the cursed wrong and violence,
     Done amid our human brothers, on the helpless and infirm,
Throbs, though fainter, to our being, down the cycles of creation,
     For the shrivelling of the night-moth and the writhing of the
                               worm.

While from things of field and forest, eyes of tenderness and trusting
     Look to ours and link them to us, as we journey side by side
Shall we lift a blind denial to the brotherhood of nature,
     Shall we break the bonds of kinship in the madness of our pride?

Shall not rather hope be with us: noble, broadened, undefined,
     Since all life is as a riddle, since all faith is but a guess:
Hope that every life that liveth has a nobler way before it,
     Has a deathless purpose founded on the everlasting yes.

He that in his mighty gardens shakes the meanest seed of nature,
     Soweth with the seed a promise whence no power can make him
                               free,
He that on his lonely summits feeds the narrowest stream of being,
     Dooms its way through fields and forests on its eternal sea.
                     (*The Debater*, Nov. 1892)

ST. FRANCIS XAVIER
(Prize poem written at St. Paul's)

St. Francis Xavier
The Apostle of the Indies

He left his dust, by all the myriad tread
Of yon dense millions trampled to the strand,
Or 'neath some cross forgotten lays his head
Where dark seas whiten on a lonely land:
He left his work, what all his life had planned,
A waning flame to flicker and to fall,
Mid the huge myths his toil could scarce withstand,
And the light died in temple and in hall,
And the old twilight sank and settled over all.

He left his name, a murmur in the East,
That dies to silence amid older creeds,
With which he strove in vain: the fiery priest
Of faiths less fitted to their ruder needs:
As some lone pilgrim, with his staff and beads,
Mid forest-brutes whom ignorance makes tame,
He dwelt, and sowed an Eastern Church's seeds
He reigned, a teacher and a priest of fame:
He died and dying left a murmur and a name.

He died: and she, the Church that bade him go,
Yon dim Enchantress with her mystic claim,
Has ringed his forehead with her aureole-glow,
And monkish myths, and all the whispered fame
Of miracle, has clung about his name:
So Rome has said: but we, what answer we
Who in grim Indian gods and rites of shame
O'er all the East the teacher's failure see,
His Eastern Church a dream, his toil a vanity.

This then we say: as Time's dark face at last
Moveth its lips of thunder to decree
The doom that grew through all the murmuring past
To be the canon of the times to be:
No child of truth or priest of progress he,
Yet not the less a hero of his wars
Striving to quench the light he could not see,
And God, who knoweth all that makes and mars,
Judges his soul unseen which throbs among the stars.

God only knows, man failing in his choice,
How far apparent failure may succeed,
God only knows what echo of His voice
Lives in the cant of many a fallen creed,
God only gives the labourer his meed
For all the lingering influence widely spread,
Broad branching into many a word and deed
When dim oblivion veils the fountain-head;
So lives and lingers on the spirit of the dead.

This then we say: let all things further rest
And this brave life, with many thousands more,
Be gathered up in the eternal's breast
In that dim past his Love is bending o'er:
Healing all shattered hopes and failure sore:
Since he had bravely looked on death and pain
For what he chose to worship and adore,
Cast boldly down his life for loss or gain
In the eternal lottery: not to be in vain.

(1892)[1]

---

[1] This is the only version I have been able to find. Across the top is written in another hand: "This is not exactly the same as given in the prize poem." The difference is probably slight.

SECRECY

Laughter is sacred, secret unalloyed.
The dark irrational gaiety of things
The boyish valour of the world that swings
The stars exultant in a sickening void.

They say he never laughed, whose anguish deep
Redeemed us on the mountain of the Skull
Who over Salem, neither being dull
Nor cowardly, was man enough to weep.

Grief grows like grass: nor need he, though he can
With sudden pity make a pompous strife
Death is so plain upon the face of life
Tears may be plain upon the face of man.

But mirth is sacred: when from all his own
He sundered, going up a mount to pray
Under the terrible stars in stern array
Upon the lonely peak he laughed alone.[1]

SILENCE

Thou art silent: nailed high in the darkness
Left alone from a sea that recedes
On thy gaunt gibbet lashed, and beyond thee
The blare of victorious creeds
Bowed down with the crown of thy choosing,
Caught up on thine hideous throne
O hast thou no charge for thy people
          No word for thine own.

---

[1] The fancy that His laughter was the one thing hidden by God from mankind occurs more than once in Chesterton's writing. See, especially, the closing pages of *Orthodoxy*.

Five words show upon thee: five voices
More burning than blessing or ban
Words and fickle soothing; but bitter
Five wounds on the limbs of a Man
Five stars of thy royalty: real
And mighty for evil or good
Five seals of apocalypse, speaking
        In silence and blood.

Words clamour and flatter and fool us;
They picture and falter and mask:
Men speak them, and do not the saying
Men hear them, and seek not the task.
We vision and rant for our pleasure
We question and double and allow.
Words are cheap, from the lips: it is dearer
The blood from the brow.

                  (mid 1890s)

THE SONG OF THE CHILDREN

The world is ours till sunset,
   Holly and fire and snow;
And the name of our dead brother
   Who loved us long ago.

The grown folk mighty and cunning,
   They write his name in gold;
But we can tell a little
   Of the million tales he told.

He taught them laws and watchwords,
   To preach and struggle and pray;
But he taught us deep in the hayfield
   The games that the angels play.

Had he stayed here for ever,
　　Their world would be wise as ours—
And the king be cutting capers,
　　And the priest be picking flowers.

But the dark day came: they gathered:
　　On their faces we could see
They had taken and slain our brother,
　　And hanged him on a tree.

(late 1890s)

THE SONG OF THE CRADLE

'Neath a shed-roof that shouldered the tempest
Behind doors that were sealed with the snow.
In the dusty dim straw of the stable
A mother kept watch long ago.
From the nostrils of night came a whirlwind
Like horn beyond horn
And in cloud drift and snow drift and darkness
　　—A child was born.

Need we grope for a fugitive secret
Need we whirl on a mystical quest,
While God setteth plainest his fairest
While God shaketh broadest his best,
Far flush all the crowns of the clover
Thick mellows the corn
A cloud shapes: a daisy is opened
　　—A child is born.

With raw mists of the red earth about them,
Risen stark from the ribs of the earth
Wild and huddled, the man and the woman,
Gazed dumb on the earliest birth
E're the first roof was hammered above them,
The first skin was worn

Before codes, before creed, before conscience
    — A child was born.

What know we of aeons behind us
Dim dynasties lost long ago
Huge empires like dreams unremembered
High cities for ages laid low.
This we know: that with pain and with blessing
With flower and with thorn
Love was there: and his cry was among them
    — A child is born.

And to us, though we wrestle and travail
Though we fancy and fret and disprove
Still the plumes stir around us, above us
The wings of the shadow of Love
Still the fountains of life are unshattered
Their splendour unshorn
The secret, the marvel, the promise
    — A child is born.

Have a myriad children been quickened
Have a myriad children grown old
Grown coarse and unloved and untutored
Grown cunning and savage and cold,
God sits, in a terrible patience
Unangered, unworn
And again, for the child that is squandered
    — A child is born.

And so long is the sign in heavens
In the east the unquenchable gleam
Still the babe that is quickened may conquer
The life that is new may redeem,
Ho, princes and priests, have ye heard it?
Grow pale through your scorn,
Huge dawns sleep before us, stern changes,
    — A child is born.

And the thatch-roof of toil still is gilded,
In the dawn of the star of the heart.
And the wise men draw near in the twilight
Who are weary of learning and art,
And the face of the tyrant is darkened
His spirit is torn,
For a new king is throned of the nation
    — A child is born.

And the mother still joys for the whispered
First stir of unspeakable things
Still feels that high moment unfurling
Red glories of Gabriel's wings
Still the babe of an hour is a master
Whom angels adorn
Emmanuel, prophet, anointed
    — A child is born.

To the rusty barred doors of the hungry
To the houses of sorrow and sin
Still with brush of bright plumes and with knocking
The Kingdom of God enters in
To the daughters of patience that labour
That weep and are worn
The moment of love and of laughter
    — A child is born.

To the gardens of rumour and pleasure
Of fashion and song-swimming nights
Cometh down hope's obscure crucifixion,
The birth-fire that quickens and bites
To the daughters of fame that are idle
That smile and that scorn
With the measure of darkness and travail
    — A child is born.

And till man and his riddle be answered
While earth holdeth lower and higher

While the flesh of a man is as grass is,
The soul of a man as a fire
While the day-break shall come with its banner,
The moon with its horn,
It shall stay with us: that which is written
— A child is born.

Thou, little one, light of the cradle,
The sun making crowns for thy brow.
Thou art flesh of the flesh of Thy mother,
— But whence art thou come: who art thou?
Art thou come back on earth, for our teaching
To train and to warn!
Hush we know not, nor may: knowing only
        — A child is born.

                              (early 1890–92)

SONNET

High on the wall that holds Jerusalem
I saw one stand under the stars like stone.
And when I perish it shall not be known
Whether he lived, some strolling son of Shem,
Or was some great ghost wearing the diadem
Of Solomon or Saladin on a throne:
I only know, the features being unshown,
I did not dare draw near and look on them.

Did ye not guess . . . the diadem might be
Plaited in stranger style by hands of hate . . .
But when I looked, the wall was desolate
And the grey starlight powdered tower and tree
And vast and vague beyond the Golden Gate
Heaved Moab of the mountains like a sea.

                              (1920)

SPILTH

Where those stone waterpots stood round the wall
Slaves that came scurrying from their mills and querns
Cast casual pools and splashed the floor by turns
In light lustration and no fault at all;
But when deep Nature heard the Vine-King call
The fire that feeds us and the blood that burns
Gathering great wine in those almighty urns
Men bore them brimming; and let no drop fall.

Ah not for us the random streams and rash
Of slaves that stand indifferent and depart
Not yet being called to the high thrift of kings
Where for deep draughts, and not for spilth or splash
God gave us beauty and the burning heart
The body built for everlasting things.

(1935)

THE SWORD OF SURPRISE

Sunder me from my bones, O sword of God,
Till they stand stark and strange as do the trees;
That I whose heart goes up with the soaring woods
May marvel as much at these.

Sunder me from my blood that in the dark
I hear that red ancestral river run,
Like branching buried floods that find the sea
But never see the sun.

Give me miraculous eyes to see my eyes,
Those rolling mirrors made alive in me,
Terrible crystal more incredible
Than all the things they see.

Sunder me from my soul, that I may see
The sins like streaming wounds, the life's brave beat;
Till I shall save myself, as I would save
A stranger in the street.

(1915–22)

TO ST. MICHAEL, IN TIME OF PEACE

Michael, Michael: Michael of the Morning,
Michael of the Army of the Lord.
Stiffen thou the hand upon the still sword, Michael,
Folded and shut upon the sheathed sword, Michael,
Under the fullness of the white robes falling,
Gird us with the secret of the sword.

When the world cracked because of a sneer in heaven,
Leaving out of all time a scar upon the sky,
Thou didst rise up against the Horror in the highest,
Dragging down the highest that looked down on the Most High:
Rending from the seventh heaven the hell of exaltation
Down the seven heavens till the dark seas burn:
Thou that in thunder threwest down the Dragon
Knowest in what silence the Serpent can return.

Down through the universe the vast night falling,
(Michael, Michael: Michael of the Morning!)
Far down the universe the deep calms calling,
(Michael, Michael: Michael of the Sword!)
Bid us not forget in the baths of all forgetfulness,
In the sigh long drawn from the frenzy and the fretfulness,
In the huge holy sempiternal silence,
In the beginning was the Word.

When from the deeps a dying God astounded
Angels and devils who do all but die,
Seeing Him fallen where thou couldst not follow,
Seeing Him mounted where thou couldst not fly,

Hand on the hilt, thou hast halted all thy legions,
Waiting the Tetelestai and the acclaim,
Swords that salute Him dead and everlasting
God beyond God and greater than His Name.

Round us and over us the cold thoughts creeping,
(Michael, Michael: Michael of the battle-cry!)
Round us and under us the thronged worlds sleeping,
(Michael, Michael: Michael of the Charge!)
Guard us the Word; the trysting and the trusting
Edge upon honour and the blade unrusting.
Fine as the hair and tauter than the harpstring,
Ready as when it rang upon the targe.

He that giveth peace unto us; not as the world giveth:
He that giveth law unto us; not as the scribes:
Shall He be softened for the softening of the cities
Patient in usury; delicate in bribes?
They that come to quiet us, saying the sword is broken,
Break men with famine, fetter them with gold,
Sell them as sheep; and He shall know the selling,
For He was more than murdered. He was sold.

Michael, Michael: Michael of the Mastering,
Michael of the marching on the mountains of the Lord,
Marshal the world and purge of rot and riot,
Rule through the world till all the world be quiet:
Only establish when the World is broken,
What is unbroken is the Word.

(ca. 1929)

TO THE JESUITS[1]

(SPAIN, 1936)

Flower-wreathed with all unfading calumnies
Scarlet and splendid with eternal slander
How should you hope, where'er the world may wander,
To lose the long laudation of its lies?

The yellow gods of sunrise saw arise
Your tilted towers that housed the moons and suns,
The red sons of the sunset, not with guns
But with guitars, you ambushed for surprise.

You bade the Red Man rise like the Red Clay
Of God's great Adam in his human right,
Till trailed the snake of trade, our own time's blight,
And Man lost Paradise in Paraguay.

You, when wild sects tortured and mocked each other
Saw truth in the wild tribes that tortured you
Slurred for not slurring all who slurred or slew,
Blamed that your murderer was too much your brother

You hailed before its dawn Democracy
Which in its death bays you with demagogues
You dared strong kings that hunted you with dogs
To hide some hunted king in trench or tree.

When Calvin's Christ made Antichrist had caught
Even the elect and all men's hearts were hardened,
You were called profligates because you pardoned,
And tools of ignorance because you taught.

All that warped world your charity could heal
All the world's charity was not for you;

---

[1] This was the last poem to be written by Chesterton. The manuscript was given to Father Corbishley, S.J., and hangs in Campion Hall, Oxford.

How should you hope deliverance in things new
In this the last chance twist of the world's wheel?

One while that wheel as a vast top is twirled
With every age, realm, riot, pomp or pact,
Thrown down in thunder like a cataract,
Said, "Fear not; I have overthrown the world".
                    (*G. K.'s Weekly*, Mar. 26, 1936)

THE TOWERS OF TIME

Under what withering leprous light
The very grass as hair is grey,
Grass in the cracks of the paven courts
Of gods we graved but yesterday
Senate, republic, empire, all
We leaned our backs on like a wall
And blessed as strong and blamed as stolid—
Can it be these that waver and fall?
    And what is this like a ghost returning,
    A dream grown strong in the strong daylight?
    The all-forsaken, the unforgotten,
    The ever-behind and out of sight.
    We turned our backs and our blind flesh felt it
    Growing and growing, a tower in height.

Ah, not alone the evil splendour
And not the insolent arms alone
Break with the ramrod, stiff and brittle,
The sceptre of the nordic throne:
But things of manlier renown
Reel in the wreck of throne and crown,
With tyrannous tyranny, tyrannous loyalty,
Tyrannous liberty, all gone down.

(There is never a crack in the ivory tower
Or a hinge to groan in the house of gold
Or a leaf of the rose in the wind to wither
And She grows young as the world grows old.
A Woman clothed with the sun returning
To clothe the sun when the sun is cold.)

Ah, who had guessed that in a moment
Great Liberty that loosed the tribes,
The Republic of the young men's battles
Grew stale and stank of old men's bribes;
And where we watched her smile in power
A statue like a starry tower
The stone face sneers as in a nightmare
Down on a world that worms devour
   (Archaic incredible dead dawns breaking
   Deep in the deserts and waste and wealds,
   Where the dead cry aloud on Our Lady of Victories,
   Queen of the Eagles, aloft on the shields,
   And the sun is gone up on the Thundering
                              Legion
On the roads of Rome to the battlefields.)

Ah, who had known who had not seen
How soft and sudden on the fame
Of my most noble English ships
The sunset light of Carthage came
And the thing I never had dreamed could be
In the house of my fathers came to me
Through the sea-wall cloven, the cloud and dark,
A voice divided, a doubtful sea.
   (The light is bright on the Tower of David,
   The evening glows with the morning star
   In the skies turned back and the days returning
   She walks so near who had wandered far
   And the heart of the swords, the seven times
                              wounded,
   Was never wearied as our hearts are.)

How swift as with a fall of snow
New things grow hoary with the light.
We watch the wrinkles crawl like snakes
On the new image in our sight.
The lines that sprang up taut and bold
Sag like primordial monsters old,
Sink in the bas-reliefs of fossil
And the slow earth swallows them, fold on fold.
   But light are the feet on the hills of the morning
   Of the lambs that leap up to the Bride of the
                      Sun,
   And swift are the birds as the butterflies flashing
   And sudden as laughter the rivulets run
   And sudden for ever as summer lightning
   The light is bright on the world begun.

Thou wilt not break as we have broken
The towers we reared to rival Thee.
More true to England than the English
More just to freedom than the free.
O trumpet of the intolerant truth
Thou art more full of grace and ruth
For the hopes of the world than the world that made
                      them,
The world that murdered the loves of our youth.
   Thou art more kind to our dreams, Our Mother,
   Than the wise that wove us the dreams for
                      shade.
   God is more good to the gods that mocked Him
   Than men are good to the gods they made.
   Tenderer with toys than a boy grown brutal,
   Breaking the puppets with which he played.

What are the flowers the garden guards not
And how but here should dreams return?
And how of hearths made cold with ruin
The wide wind-scattered ashes burn—

What is the home of the heart set free,
And where is the nesting of liberty,
And where from the world shall the world take
                                        shelter
And man be master, and not with Thee?
  Wisdom is set in her throne of thunder,
  The Mirror of Justice blinds the day—
  Where are the towers that are not of the City,
  Trophies and trumpetings, where are they?
  Where over the maze of the world returning
  The bye-ways bend to the King's highway.
                                        (1925)

TRINITY

Where choked by hairy cactus-fingers
Or sea-blue weeds like crakens curled,
One sculptured scene of sacrifice
Betrays the password of the world,

Carved as one awful threefold flower
Triple and cloven and yet alone,
The priest, the victim and the god
Wear the same smiling face of stone.
                                        (1929)

THE TRINKETS

A wandering world of rivers,
A wavering world of trees,
If the world grow dim and dizzy
With all changes and degrees,

It is but Our Lady's mirror
Hung dreaming in its place,
Shining with only shadows
Till she wakes it with her face.

The standing whirlpool of the stars,
The wheel of all the world,
Is a ring on Our Lady's finger
With the suns and moons empearled
With stars for stones to please her
Who sits playing with her rings
With the great heart that a woman has
And the love of little things.

Wings of the whirlwind of the world
From here to Ispahan,
Spurning the flying forests,
Are light as Our Lady's fan:
For all things violent here and vain
Lie open and all at ease
Where God has girded heaven to guard
Her holy vanities.

(1916–21)

THE TRUCE OF CHRISTMAS

Passionate peace is in the sky—
And in the snow in silver sealed
The beasts are perfect in the field,
And men seem men so suddenly—
  (But take ten swords and ten times ten
  And blow the bugle in praising men;
  For we are for all men under the sun;
  And they are against us every one;
  And misers haggle and madmen clutch,
  And there is peril in praising much,

And we have the terrible tongues uncurled
That praise the world to the sons of the world.)

The idle humble hill and wood
Are bowed upon the sacred birth,
And for one little hour the earth
Is lazy with the love of good—
　　(But ready are you, and ready am I,
　　If the battle blow and the guns go by;
　　For we are for all men under the sun,
　　And they are against us every one;
　　And the men that hate herd all together,
　　To pride and gold, and the great white feather,
　　And the thing is graven in star and stone
　　That the men who love are all alone.)

Hunger is hard and time is tough,
But bless the beggars and kiss the kings;
For hope has broken the heart of things,
And nothing was ever praised enough.
　　(But hold the shield for a sudden swing
　　And point the sword when you praise a thing,
　　For we are for all men under the sun,
　　And they are against us every one;
　　And mime and merchant, thane and thrall
　　Hate us because we love them all;
　　Only till Christmastide go by
　　Passionate peace is in the sky.)

(1904)

THE TWO MAIDENS

"Robin loved Our Dear Lady
And for doubt of deadly sin
Would never hurt a company
That any woman was in."
                        — Old Ballad of Robin Hood

The wind had taken the tree-tops
  Upon Sherwood, the noble wood,
Two maidens met in the windy ways
  Held speech of Robin Hood.

And the first maid to the second said
  "He keeps not tryst to-day."
And the second said to the first maiden,
  "Mayhap he is far away."

And far away on the upland
  The last trees broke in the sky
As they brought him out of grey Kirkleas
  To bend his bow and die.

High on the moors above Kirkleas
  The mighty thief lay slain,
The woman that had struck him down
  He would not strike again.

And the maid cried as the high wind
  In the broken tree-tops cries,
"They have taken him out of the good greenwood,
  And I know not where he lies.

"The world is a wind that passes
  And valour is in vain
And the tallest trees are broken
  As the bravest men are slain.

"Deep in the nettles of a ditch
  He may die as a dog dies
Or on the gallows, to be the game
  Of the lawyers and the lies.

"The wood is full of wicked thieves,
  Of robbers wild and strong,
But though he walked the gallows way,
  Of him I had no wrong.

"Because he scorned to do me scathe
  I walked forth clean and free
And I call my name Maid Marian
  Because he honoured me."

"I too am only a simple maid,
  Our stories are the same.
As your green gown to my blue gown
  Your name is like my name.

"The world is full of wicked men,
  Of robbers rich and strong,
To plot against my maiden fame,
  But of him I had no wrong.

"And because he scorned to do me scathe
  I have travelled many a mile
To bring you a word out of his mouth
  To lift your face and smile.

"He is not dead in the ditch-nettles,
  Or on the gallows-tree;
But a great king has taken him
  To ride with his chivalry.

"And made him a master of bowmen
  For the memory of the day
When one that died at the king's right hand
  Was a thief on the king's highway.

"And I have travelled many a mile
From a city beyond the sea
To give you news of your true-love
Because he honoured me."

(1918–26)

VERSES MADE UP IN A DREAM
(which you won't believe)

People, if you have any prayers
Say prayers for me.
And bury me underneath a stone
In the stones of Battersea.

Bury me underneath a stone,
With the sword that was my own;
To wait till the holy horn is blown
And all poor men are free.

(ca. 1905)[1]

THE WHITE WITCH

The dark Diana of the groves
Whose name is Hecate in hell
Heaves up her awful horns to heaven
White with the light I know too well.

The moon that broods upon her brows
Mirrors the monstrous hollow lands
In leprous silver; at the term
Of triple twisted roads she stands.

---

[1] These lines appear, slightly altered, in "The Ballad of the White Horse".

Dreams are no sin or only sin
   For them that waking dream they dream;
But I have learned what wiser knights
   Follow the Grail and not the Gleam.

I found One hidden in every home,
   A voice that sings about the house,
A nurse that scares the nightmares off,
   A mother nearer than a spouse,

Whose picture once I saw; and there
   Wild as of old and weird and sweet,
In sevenfold splendour blazed the moon
   Not on her brow; beneath her feet.

                (1916–25)

THE WISE MEN

Step softly, under snow or rain,
   To find the place where men can pray,
The way is all so very plain
   That we may lose the way.

Oh we have learnt to peer and pore,
   On tortured puzzles from our youth,
We know all labyrinthine lore,
We are the three Wise Men of yore,
   And we know all things but the truth.

We have gone round and round the hill,
   And lost the wood among the trees,
And learnt long names for every ill,
And served the mad gods, naming still
   The Furies the Eumenides.

The gods of violence took the veil
   Of visions and philosophy,

The Serpent that brought all men bale,
He bites his own accursed tail,
  And calls himself Eternity.

Go humbly . . . it has hailed and snowed . . .
  With voices low and lanterns lit,
So very simple is the road,
  That we may stray from it.

The world grows terrible and white,
  And blinding white the breaking day;
We walk bewildered in the light,
For something is too large for sight,
  And something much too plain to say.

The Child that was ere worlds begun —
  (. . . We need but walk a little way . . .
We need but see a latch undone . . .)
The Child that played with moon and sun
  Is playing with a little hay.

The house from which the heavens are fed,
  The old strange house that is our own,
Where tricks of words are never said,
And Mercy is as plain as bread,
  And Honour is as hard as stone.

Go humbly; humble are the skies,
  And low and large and fierce the Star,
So very near the Manger lies
That we may travel far.

Hark! Laughter like a lion wakes
  To roar to the resounding plain,
And the whole heaven shouts and shakes
  For God Himself is born again
And we are little children walking
  Through the snow and rain.

                              (1913)

III

I WONDER NOT . . .

Apocalypse.

In seas and stones and painful lore of weeds
In twisted runes of all things made that are
I gained a knowledge wilder than the creeds
The mightiest message trusted to a star.

Unsealing glory as a sevenfold sun
Tongued with seven thunders that adore or damn
I gained it: Tell it not to anyone.
I say the secret in your ear: I am.

G. K. Chesterton.

THE ANCIENT OF DAYS

A child sits in a sunny place,
   Too happy for a smile,
And plays through one long holiday
   With balls to roll and pile;
A painted wind-mill by his side,
   Runs like a merry tune,
But the sails are the four great winds of heaven,
   And the balls are the sun and moon.

A staring doll's-house shows to him
   Green floors and starry rafter,
And many-coloured graven dolls
   Live for his lonely laughter.
The dolls have crowns and aureoles,
   Helmets and horns and wings,
For they are the saints and seraphim,
   The prophets and the kings.

                (ca. late 1890s)

APOCALYPSE

In seas and stones and painful lore of weeds
In twisted runes of all things made that are
I gained a knowledge wilder than the creeds
The mightiest message trusted to a star.

Unsealing glory as a sevenfold sun
Tongued with seven thunders that adore or damn
I gained it: Tell it not to anyone
I say the secret in your ear: I am.

                (ca. 1895–98)

APOCALYPSE

The first of the seals was opened; the gold
                    of the dawn unsealed
The last of the seals was opened, the red day
                    tottered and reeled
The clouds that are bridled like dragons, the
                    stars that are shaken like swords
Daily they come and nightly: are they not great
                    and the Lord's?

But the people behold them always
    They pass them and cry without fear
"If the sun be dark we will listen
    If the moon be blood we will hear"
But the pomp of the suns goes onward
And the race of the moons goes by:
And we stand in the heart of a marvel
    You and the earth and I.

The hands of the Lord still fashion, with fire, with
                    blood and with earth
And measureless wheels go even in the twilight
                    house of birth
And the life comes fair as sunrise, and the lives
                    roll in like a sea
A babe, O Lord, from thy palace: is not each
                    a prophet of thee?

But the people receive them always
    They pass them and cry without fear
"If one come in the cloud, we will listen
    If one rise from the dead we will hear"
And, like star on star, they are rising
Bright clouds in the night drift by
And we dwell in the thick of a gospel
    Thou and the world and I.

                            (ca. 1890–92)

AS THE TREE FALLETH

"Down in a pale plain dry as chaff
  "Thou shalt come to a place called 'Traitor's Staff' "

I went and found but a flowering tree
  Round which the maids ran merrily.

"Down in the marsh that boulders bruise
  Thou shalt come to the place called 'Traitor's Shoes' "

I went and found two pools shine there
  By rushes and lilies and fish made fair.

"Down in the valley where black clouds brood
  Thou shalt come to the place called 'Traitor's Blood' "

I came: the valley from tail to head
  Like a sunset burned with roses red

"Whither, O wanderer, lies your goal?"
"I go to the place called 'Traitor's Soul' "

"What will you find when you are there?"
"I shall find this too grown passing fair."

                              (ca. 1897–98)

AT NIGHT

How many million stars there be,
That only God hath numberéd;
    But this one only chosen for me
In time before her face was fled.
Shall not one mortal man alive
    Hold up his head?

                      (ca. 1899)[1]

---

[1] For Frances.

AUTUMN

The woods are bronzed with autumn
When all the leaves are gold
The year grows old around me
And I am passing old
The walls are gilt with mosses
Leaves are a golden sea
The world is fair and ancient
And all is sweet to me.

When I was young and yearning
I chased a drifting dream
I saw a world's ideal
Through mere and tangle gleam
But now the common millions
That trust and toil and grieve
Are flushed in one great sunset
The light I soon must leave.

The young heart, wild and windy
May chase the fresh-blown seed
May seek the lonely blossom
That burns upon the mead.
But stricken hearts grow gentle
And I am passing old
And now I sit in autumn
When all the leaves are gold.

(ca. 1894–96)

THE BABE UNBORN

If all the sky were full of stars
And all the hills of grass,
And all the roofs of chimney-pots
How well the time would pass.

If there were streets where folk went by
    And fields were flowers grew
And roads ran up against the hill
    I know what I shall do.

I think that if they gave me leave
    Within that world to stand
I would be good for all the day,
    I spent in fairyland

They should not hear a word from me
    Of selfishness or scorn
If only I could find the way,
    If only I were born.

                    (ca. 1894)[1]

THE BEATIFIC VISION

Through what fierce incarnations, furled
    In fire and darkness, did I go,
Ere I was worthy in the world
    To see a dandelion grow?

Well, if in any woes or wars
    I bought my naked right to be,
Grew worthy of the grass, nor gave
    The wren, my brother, shame for me.

But what shall God not ask of him
    In the last time when all is told,
Who saw her stand beside the hearth,
    The firelight garbing her in gold?

                    (late 1890s)

[1] See "By the Babe Unborn", a later version, on page 197.

BEHIND

I saw an old man like a child,
His blue eyes bright, his white hair wild,
Who turned for ever, and might not stop,
Round and round like an urchin's top.

'Fool,' I cried, 'while you spin round,
'Others grow wise, are praised, are crowned.'
Ever the same round road he trod,
'This is better: I seek for God.'

'We see the whole world, left and right,
'Yet at the blind back hides from sight
'The unseen Master that drives us forth
'To East and West, to South and North.

'Over my shoulder for eighty years
I have looked for the gleam of the sphere of spheres.'
'In all your turning, what have you found?'
'At least, I know why the world goes round.'
                                    (late 1890s)

A BOOK OF WILD PICTURES

The Unseen

A world of snowy hills set aloft in a golden sky
And up to the highest peak, from the lowest root of valley
A long, long, strange procession, toil and totter and rally
A line of huge strange beasts of burden marching by

And the highest furthest beasts half lost in the mist aloft
Are vast fantastic things of the morning of the world
But all are straining in bonds, twisted and strained and furled
Winding through hamlet and pasture, forest and slope and croft.

And dragged by all, at the tail, a chariot rich and rare
Where sits a man, rich clad and haughty and lord of all
And at the head of all, some brute, out of sight out of call
Strong, tremendous, forgotten, breaking the mountains bare

A moment comes: and a stagger, and the King and the pomp I ween
Hang on the great steep slopes over a naked abyss
And the whole dead weight of the chain and man in his pride I wis
Hangs on the one great creature that no man hath ever seen.

(late 1890s)

BOOTLACES

Once I looked down at my bootlaces
    Who gave me my bootlaces?
The bootmaker? Bah!
Who gave the bootmaker himself?
What did I ever do that I should be
    given bootlaces?
("The Notebook", ca. 1894–97)

BY THE BABE UNBORN

If trees were tall and grasses short,
    As in some crazy tale,
If here and there a sea were blue
    Beyond the breaking pale,

If a fixed fire hung in the air
    To warm me one day through,
If deep green hair grew on great hills,
    I know what I should do.

In dark I lie: dreaming that there
   Are great eyes cold or kind,
And twisted streets and silent doors,
   And living men behind.

Let storm-clouds come: better an hour,
   And leave to weep and fight,
Than all the ages I have ruled
   The empires of the night.

I think that if they gave me leave
   Within the world to stand,
I would be good through all the day
   I spent in fairyland.

They should not hear a word from me
   Of selfishness or scorn,
If only I could find the door,
   If only I were born.

                 (ca. 1897)[1]

THE CHILD

When earth and all her seers were sad
   The child rose from the floor
He tossed his newspaper cocked hat
   And drumming, passed the door.

His crest was but a feather, such
   For seraph' wings sufficed:
His sword was but a cross of wood:
   So was the cross of Christ.

---

[1] See "The Babe Unborn", an earlier version, on page 195.

Above the roofs, above the woods
  His ragged regiment curled,
Upon the great white road that is
  The girdle of the world.

Not for years was the idle child
  Seen by his peoples' eyes,
But strange things done in a distant sea
  Came to the ears of the wise.

And the sages stared and ceased to weep —
  In the dawn of an ancient light
For the dragon that ate the sun and moon
  Lay dead by the seas of night.

                              (ca. 1895)[1]

CHORUS FOR A PLAY

For the children is the challenge of the giant
And the valley hath the vision of the hills
And they cry of things unconquered and defiant
Where the hunter of tomorrow hunts and kills
And well for them the dream of faerie fills
And the children of the twilight if they learn
The children of the twilight that discern not
The light that is the last of human ills

But none hath seen the mountain from the mount
And none hath found the tree-top in the tree.
Though the sea goes soaring sky-ward like a fount,
For the flat and goggling fishes of the sea

---

[1] Written in pencil on a blank fly-leaf of G. K. C's copy, given him by his Aunt Kate and Uncle Sidney, of Robert Louis Stevenson's *Virginibus Puerisque*, Christmas 1894. The book is held at the G. K. Chesterton Study Centre, Bedford.

But to us the wave is level with the lea
And the sea is like a pool in barren places
Where we at evening find our fallen faces
And know they are no wearier than we.

(ca. 1910)

THE CROWN OF WOMAN

In a house between the sunrise and the sunset
In the twilight of a mighty house and old,
Sits a woman 'mid the treasuries of her tresses
Like the fountains of a living sea of gold,
And she weaves the golden legend of the ages
With the braids of her own tresses thereunto
And only with that tracery for the pages
Is the story ever old and ever new.
> For the hair of a woman is her glory
> It weaveth all of secret and renown
> Through all chivalry and mystery and story
> The glory of a woman and her crown.

When the giant limbs of Adam stirred primeval
From the sudden sleep that smote him on the hills
When the sparrows scattered at his vast upheaval
And his blinded gropings rent the daffodils
On his mighty twilight broke a windy splendour
Round eyes that were as suns upon his sleep
The burning halo passionate with colours
The leaping locks that call the heart to leap
> For the hair of a woman is her glory
> It weaveth all of secret and renown
> Through all chivalry and mystery and story
> The glory of a woman and her crown.

The sunshine of the Lord that crowns and quickens
The brows and breasts of all the lives that toil.
The cornfield of the Lord that nods and shimmers
The stirring of the splendour of the soil
The harp-strings of the Lord that ring and crackle
With the song of all the stars and their desire
The war-flame of the Lord, to scourge the Evil
The fangs thereof consuming as a fire
  For the hair of a woman is her glory.
  It weaveth all of secret and renown
  Through all chivalry and mystery and story
   The glory of a woman and her crown.
      (ca. 1896)

THE DAISY

  Colossal leagues of powers
  Went to make one daisy.
  And colossal choirs of angels
  Could not give thanks for it.
    ("The Notebook", mid 1890s)

THE DELUGE

Though giant rains put out the sun,
 Here stand I for a sign.
Though Earth be filled with waters dark,
 My cup is filled with wine.
Tell to the trembling priests that here
 Under the deluge rod,
One nameless, tattered, broken man
 Stood up and drank to God.

Sun has been where the rain is now,
   Bees in the heat to hum,
Haply a humming maiden came,
   Now let the deluge come:
Brown of aureole, green of garb,
   Straight as a golden rod,
Drink to the throne of thunder now!
   Drink to the wrath of God.

High in the wreck I held the cup,
   I clutched my rusty sword,
I cocked my tattered feather
   To the glory of the Lord.
Not undone were the heaven and earth,
   This hallow world thrown up,
Before one man had stood up straight,
   And drained it like a cup.

                     (early 1900s)

THE DELUGE

When dark and deafening skies are bowed
   About my head I stand
Straight, ere the tavern rafters fall,
   With the wine cup in my hand.
Drink, ere the thunder rend the roof,
   Drink, ere it break the bars,
The toast that maketh him that drink
   Stronger than all the stars.

To the farthest bird of the heavens
   To the smallest fish of the sea,
To the sign of the falling turret
   To the sign of the flowering tree.

Wrapped in the dark rains cloak of night
　　Under the dark rain's rod,
A nameless man: a broken man
　　Stands up and drinks to God.

High in the wreck I held the cup,
　　I clutched my rusty sword.
I cocked my tattered feather
　　For the glory of the Lord.
Bodies and souls,
　　Evil things and divine
Seas and stars and systems,
　　I drank them with the wine.

Brute and devil and death itself,
　　Even death, where I stood
It is so darkly sealed and hid
　　It must be passing good.

　　　　　　　　　　　　(late 1890s)[1]

THE DESECRATERS

Witness all: that unrepenting,
　　Feathers flying, music high,
I go down to death unshaken
　　By your mean philosophy.

For your wages, take my body,
　　That at least to you I leave;
Set the sulky plumes upon it,
　　Bid the grinning mummers grieve.

---

[1] Unfinished, probably abandoned. The latter part is heavily altered, with several lines struck out. The theme, and many lines, are similar to the later version with the same title.

Stand in silence, steep your raiment
   In the night that hath no star;
Don the mortal dress of devils,
   Blacker than their spirits are.

Since ye may not, of your mercy,
   Ere I lie on such a hearse,
Hurl me to the living jackals
   God had built for sepulchres.
              (late 1890s)

EARTH'S CHAMPION

About my brow I bind the black crow's wings
A pine my spear is and a thorn my spur
I bear the blazon of the grasshopper
And ride, the champion of the fame of things

My sword is loyal to the old earth's crown
Her primrose crown, for which I wage my wars
I shake my spear at the eternal stars,
And dare them to despise the thistledown.

Passionate red and gorgeous gold encrust
Fruit forests and fields: fair women walk like day,
Prophets and poets—ah the heart can say
What pride I have in this divine old dust.
              (mid 1890s)

THE EARTH'S SHAME

Name not his deed: in shuddering and in haste
  We dragged him darkly o'er the windy fell:
That night there was a gibbet in the waste,
  And a new sin in hell.

Be his deed hid from commonwealths and kings,
  By all men born be one true tale forgot;
But three things, braver than all earthly things,
  Faced him and feared him not.

Above his head and sunken secret face
  Nested the sparrow's young and dropped not dead,
From the red blood and slime of that lost place
  Grew daisies white, not red.

And from high heaven looking upon him,
  Slowly upon the face of God did come
A smile the cherubim and seraphim
  Hid all their faces from.

(ca. 1896–97)[1]

THE EARTH'S VIGIL

The old Earth keepeth her watch the same,
  Alone in a voiceless void doth stand,
Her orange flowers in her bosom flame,
  Her gold ring in her hand,
The surfs of the long gold-crested morns
  Break evermore at her great robe's hem,
And evermore come the bleak moon-horns,
  But she keepeth not watch for them.

---

[1] This, from *Collected Poems*, is very slightly revised from the version in *The Speaker*, August 1897.

She keepeth her watch through the æons,
But the heart of her groweth not old,
For the peal of the bridegroom's pæans,
And the tale she once was told.

The nations shock and the cities reel,
The empires travail and rive and rend,
And she looks on havoc and smoke and steel,
And knoweth it is not the end.
The faiths may choke and the powers despair,
The powers re-arise and the faiths renew,
She is only a maiden, waiting there,
For the love whose word is true.

She keepeth her watch through the æons,
But the heart of her groweth not old,
For the peal of the bridegroom's pæans,
And the tale she once was told.

Through the cornfield's gleam and the cottage shade,
They wait unwearied, the young and old,
Mother for child and man for maid,
For love that once was told.
The hair grows grey under thatch or slates,
The eyes grow dim behind lattice panes,
The earth-race wait as the old earth waits,
And the hope in the heart remains.

She keepeth her watch through the æons,
But the heart of her groweth not old,
For the peal of the bridegroom's pæans,
And the tale she once was told.

God's gold ring on her hand is bound,
She fires with blossom the grey hill-sides,
Her fields are quickened, her forests crowned,
While the love of her heart abides,

And we from the fears that fret and mar
  Look up in hours and behold awhile
Her face, colossal, mid star on star,
  Still looking forth with a smile.

  She keepeth her watch through the æons,
    But the heart of her groweth not old,
  For the peal of the bridegroom's pæans,
    And the tale she once was told.

                                  (1905–14)

THE EARTH'S VIGIL[1]

  The old Earth keepeth her watch the same
  Alone in a voiceless void doth stand
  Her orange-flowers on her bosom flame
  Her gold ring on her hand
  Her cheek has colours from all the dawns
  And her eyes have all the dreams of the sea
  And her brow is set 'mid the naked stars
  And all alone sits she
      She keepeth her watch through the æons
      But the heart of her groweth not old,
      For the peal of the bridegroom's pæans
      And the tale she once was told.

[1] This is an early draft, of one verse only. The second half of this stanza differs from that in *Collected Poems*.

THE END OF FEAR

Though the whole heaven be one-eyed with
    the moon,
  Though the dead landscape seem a thing
    possessed,
As one that singeth through the flowers of June.
  Yet I go singing through that land oppressed

No more, with forest-fingers crawling free
  O'er dark flint wall that seems a wall of eyes,
  Shall evil break my soul with mysteries
Of some world-poison maddening bush and tree.

No more shall leering ghosts of pimp and king
  With bloody secrets veiled before me stand.
  Last night I held all evil in my hand
Closed; and behold it was a little thing.

I broke the infernal gates and looked on him
  Who fronts the strong creation with a curse;
  Even the gods of a lost universe,
Smiling above his hideous cherubim.

And pierced far down in his soul's crypt unriven
  The last black crooked sympathy and shame,
  And hailed him with that ringing rainbow name
Erased upon the oldest book in heaven.

Like emptied idiot masks, sin's loves and wars
  Stare at me now: for in the night I broke
  The bubble of a great world's jest, and woke
Laughing with laughter such as shakes the stars.
               (1890s)

THE ETERNAL HEART

A great steam-station full of folk,
  A crowd that swayed and seethed and broke.
    God set me on his burning throne
  Seraphs and saints were all my own.

And I saw all things with his Eye.
And as the maids and men went by,
  It seemed ten million heavens went past
Each one of them the best and last.

For my one heart was charmed and torn
  With loves of all the lovers born.

(late 1890s)

ETERNITIES

I cannot count the pebbles in the brook.
  Well hath He spoken: 'Swear not by thy head,
  Thou knowest not the hairs,' though He, we read,
Writes that wild number in His own strange book.

I cannot count the sands or search the seas,
  Death cometh, and I leave so much untrod.
  Grant my immortal aureole, O my God,
And I will name the leaves upon the trees.

In heaven I shall stand on gold and glass,
  Still brooding earth's arithmetic to spell;
  Or see the fading of the fires of hell
Ere I have thanked my God for all the grass.

(mid to late 1890s)

A FAIRY TALE

All things grew upwards, foul and fair:
The great trees fought and beat the air
With monstrous wings that would have flown;
But the old earth clung to her own,
Holding them back from heavenly wars,
Though every flower sprang at the stars.

But he broke free: while all things ceased,
Some hour increasing, he increased.
The town beneath him seemed a map,
Above the church he cocked his cap,
Above the cross his feather flew,
Above the birds: and still he grew.

The trees turned grass; the clouds were riven;
His feet were mountains lost in heaven;
Through stange new skies he rose alone,
The earth fell from him like a stone,
And his own limbs beneath him far
Seemed tapering down to touch a star.

He reared his head, shaggy and grim,
Staring among the cherubim;
The seven celestial floors he rent,
One crystal dome still o'er him bent:
Above his head, more clear than hope,
All heaven was a microscope.

(late 1890s)

THE FANATIC

We have thought long enough and talked long enough
    And the world is weary of words.
And the sword itself is clockwork now —
    A sullen wheel of swords.

Like sickening steams before the sun
    The fumes of culture creep—
And the wise men laugh more sadly
    Than the strong men used to weep.

And I know that clouds are alive and cling
    And the dusty path is rough
But I know that the least grain of the dust
    Has never been praised enough.

A single grain of the drifting dust
    If we took it and loved it well
We could blow the trumpet North and South
    And fight with the world and hell.

And find the truth of an ancient thing
    Lost in the oldest lyre
It was the man who burnt his ships
    Who set the Thames on fire.

                  (1920)

FEMINA CONTRA MUNDUM

The sun was black with judgment, and the moon
    Blood: but between
I saw a man stand, saying, 'To me at least
    The grass is green.

'There was no star that I forgot to fear
    With love and wonder.
The birds have loved me'; but no answer came—
    Only the thunder.

Once more the man stood, saying, 'A cottage door,
    Wherethrough I gazed
That instant as I turned—yea, I am vile;
    Yet my eyes blazed.

'For I had weighed the mountains in a balance,
          And the skies in a scale,
I come to sell the stars—old lamps for new—
          Old stars for sale.'

Then a calm voice fell all the thunder through,
          A tone less rough:
'Thou hast begun to love one of my works
          Almost enough.'

                              (mid to late 1890s)

THE FISH

Dark the sea was: but I saw him,
   One great head with goggle eyes,
Like a diabolic cherub
   Flying in those fallen skies.

I have heard the hoarse deniers,
   I have known the wordy wars;
I have seen a man, by shouting,
   Seek to orphan all the stars.

I have seen a fool half-fashioned
   Borrow from the heavens a tongue,
So to curse them more at leisure—
   —And I trod him not as dung.

For I saw that finny goblin
   Hidden in the abyss untrod;
And I knew there can be laughter
   On the secret face of God.

Blow the trumpets, crown the sages,
   Bring the age by reason fed!
('He that sitteth in the heavens,
   'He shall laugh'—the prophet said).
                    (late 1890s)

FRAGMENT FROM DANTE

Then Bernard smiled at me, that I should gaze
  But I had gazed already; caught the view,
Faced the unfathomable ray of rays
  Which to itself and by itself is true.

Then was my vision mightier than man's speech;
  Speech snapt before it like a flying spell;
And memory and all that time can teach
  Before that splendid outrage failed and fell.

As when one dreameth and remembereth not
  Waking, what were his pleasures or his pains,
With every feature of the dream forgot,
  The printed passion of the dream remains: —

Even such am I; within whose thoughts resides
  No picture of that sight nor any part,
Nor any memory: in whom abides
  Only a happiness within the heart,

A secret happiness that soaks the heart
  As hills are soaked by slow unsealing snow,
Or secret as that wind without a chart
  Whereon did the wild leaves of Sibyl go.

O light uplifted from all mortal knowing,
  Send back a little of that glimpse of thee,
That of its glory I may kindle glowing
  One tiny spark for all men yet to be.

                    (1905-15)

THE GATE OF EVERYWHERE

When the dawn split with sudden gold
  A solid terror blocked the skies
With star-defying stone that told
    Where some mad king in ages old
      To Chaos offered sacrifice.

A gateway gods might have begun
  (A man had dreamed of it and died)
Around waste flats: this huge deed done
    Stared useless, shameless at the sun
      An art's colossal suicide.

But through the arch the earth seemed bright
  The still fields sweeter than a song,
A happy little world framed right
    And through the arch the long roads white
      Dragged me like silver chords along.

I pass beneath: I turn, descry
  Back through the gateway e'er the same
Sweet baffling broken glimpse: then I
    Stood, and thanked God with a great cry
      For one man dead without a name.

One man who saw the old world's worth
  And here for all the brave unfurled
The ancient banner of our earth
    And reared in monstrous midnight birth
      A portal worthy of the world.

                    (ca. 1900)

GLENCOE

The star-crowned cliffs seem hinged upon the sky,
The clouds are floating rags across them curled,
They open to us like the gates of God
Cloven in the last great wall of all the world.

I looked, and saw the valley of my soul
Where naked crests fight to achieve the skies,
Where no grain grows nor wine, no fruitful thing,
Only big words and starry blasphemies.

But you have clothed with mercy like a moss
The barren violence of its primal wars,
Sterile although they be and void of rule,
You know my shapeless crags have loved the stars.

How shall I thank you, O courageous heart,
That of this wasteful world you had no fear;
But bade it blossom in clear faith and sent
Your fair flower-feeding rivers: even as here

The peat burns brimming from their cups of stone
Glow brown and blood-red down the vast decline
As if Christ stood on yonder clouded peak
And turned its thousand waters into wine.

(1905–14)

GOOD NEWS

In scudding cloud on high steep meadows shed,
  In blaze and thunder, in desire and fear
I learned a secret: hearken in your ears—
  "Behold, the daisy has a ring of red."

Then waxed I like the wind because of this
    And ran, like gospel and apocalypse
From door to door with new anarchic lips
    Crying the very blasphemy of bliss.

I snap the spear and break the guarded gate
    For death and I fear not the face of Kings
I left behind the wild swan's failing wings
    Whipped by a whirling love more wild than hate.

In the last wreck of Nature: dark and dread
    Shall in eclipse's hideous hieroglyph
One wild form reel on the last rocking cliff
    And shout "The daisy has a ring of red."

                      (1901–6)

GOOD NEWS

Between a meadow and a cloud that sped
    In rain and twilight, in desire and fear,
    I heard a secret—hearken in your ear,
'Behold the daisy has a ring of red.'

That hour, with half of blessing, half of ban,
    A great voice went through heaven and earth and hell,
    Crying, 'We are tricked, my great ones, is it well?
Now is the secret stolen by a man.'

Then waxed I like the wind because of this,
    And ran, like gospel and apocalypse,
    From door to door, with new anarchic lips,
Crying the very blasphemy of bliss.

In the last wreck of Nature, dark and dread,
    Shall in eclipse's hideous hieroglyph,
    One wild form reel on the last rocking cliff,
And shout, 'The daisy has a ring of red.'

                      (late 1890s)

GREEN LEAVES

The little fields of green and gold
   Wherein my feet go lovingly
   And past the thatches and the wold
   The sea-grey meadows by the sea
   How should the thistle-downs that flies
   Give back my love or hear my rhyme
   Or all the daisy elfin-eyes
   Have looked on me at anytime:
   Only a man unknown, unseen,
   Who finds the green leaves truly green.

How should the men that busy rove
   Have heard my feet amid the din
   Or vision know my lonely love
   At every casement looketh in.
   And woman knows how full of air
   Thy care for earth's divine old dust
   For who shall kiss for flower the sun
   That warns the just and the unjust
   Even I: a man unknown, unseen
   That finds the green leaves truly green.

Fair-blooded faces, maiden-brows
   Blue eyes adrift as dreaming sea
   But not for me the sea-star shows,
   Nor any fair face flames for me.
   For could a man enwrap his arms
   About the whole earth fierily
   Through seas and seasons, snows and calms
   Then as death cometh, I were he
   Only a man, unknown, unseen
      Who finds the green leaves truly green.
                (late 1890s)

THE HEIRS OF THE AGES

Young was the green world's chart
Young did the pearl clouds part
Young was the hate in my heart
    This my bow bending—
Struck I my spear in the ground
    Hush: was there magic round?
Was the world's law discrowned
        Was the world ending?

Shot I my shafts: I heard
    Each wave wings as it whirred
    Each bolt turn to a bird
        Sped, singing so—
Turned I my spear to behold
Branching it stood in the mould
    Blossomed a fruit tree old
        Where was my foe?

Chattered the birds in bands
"Lost in the ancient sands
Ruined his sepulchre stands."
        "Mute is his mirth"
Out of the leaves of the tree.
    Entered the cry into me
"We are the meek—yea we
        Inherit the Earth."
                (mid 1890s)

THE HERITAGE OF WONDER

I have loved my land yet hailed it as a stranger
When birth-wracks wrecked me on a faerie shore:
I have kept the Faith yet hardly grasped it more
Than groping shepherds when they found the Manger.
I have loved my friends yet feared them more than
    foes
Lest they should ask the name God only knows;
And in long years of mating have been blest
Restlessly wondering why I was at rest.

                        (ca. 1933)

THE HOPE OF THE YEAR

Earth's icy dome, the skull that wears
    Terrible crystals for a crown,
    Is billed at last with Cook's renown.
And Peary's personal affairs.

Like clockwork angels up the blue,
    Air-ships arise and prophesy
    That purer time when pigs shall fly
Yet these be stately trifles too.

Not on these lads the lip be curled
    Who ride as well as fly their kites;
    Nor those, that count the best of sights
The bald spot of the poor old world.

Let Fakirs die for faith, and kill,
    But Christian man can die for fun.
    'Tis something yet that things are done
And man is but a schoolboy still.

But while they brake the North; and clove
  The adamant of ice with ease,
  I found less high in Northern seas
The foolish island that I love.

And while they floated like a spark
  With all their engines in the sky,
  I only dreamed some time that I
Might stroll across an English Park.

Surely the drums of laughter roll,
  As the great winter gathers nigh
  We may do better things than fly,
And find more places than the Pole.

Do death to usurer and spy,
  And find again our native towns,
  And break the battle-line of crowns
With Europe in her yeomanry.

Lord! not too late a nation learns
  God! say we have not grown too old!
  But through the fog and filth and gold,
The trumpet of that time returns,

When Boston was a splash of tea,
  And Paris was a cry for bread,
  And London raised a doubtful head
And heard the guns of liberty.
            ("The Wonderful Year", 1909)

THE HUMAN TREE

Many have Earth's lovers been
Tried in seas and wars, I ween;
Yet the mightiest have I seen
   Yea, the best saw I.
One that in a field alone
Stood up stiller than a stone
   Lest a moth should fly.

Birds had nested in his hair,
On his shoon were mosses rare,
Insect empires flourished there,
   Worms in ancient wars;
But his eyes burn like a glass,
Hearing a great sea of grass
   Roar towards the stars.

From them to the human tree
Rose a cry continually,
'Thou art still, our Father, we
   Fain would have thee nod.
Make the skies as blood below thee,
Though thou slay us, we shall know thee
   Answer us, O God!

'Show thine ancient fame and thunder,
Split the stillness once asunder,
Lest we whisper, lest we wonder
   Art thou there at all?'
But I saw him there alone,
Standing stiller than a stone
   Lest a moth should fall.

               (late 1890s)

THE HUNTING OF THE DRAGON

When we went hunting the Dragon
In the days when we were young,
We tossed the bright world over our shoulder
As bugle and baldrick slung;
Never was world so wild and fair
As what went by on the wind,
Never such fields of paradise
As the fields we left behind:

    For this is the best of a rest for men
    That men should rise and ride
    Making a flying fairyland
    Of market and country-side,
    Wings on the cottage, wings on the wood,
    Wings upon pot and pan,
    For the hunting of the Dragon
    That is the life of a man.

For men grow weary of fairyland
When the Dragon is a dream,
And tire of the talking bird in the tree,
The singing fish in the stream;
And the wandering stars grow stale, grow stale,
And the wonder is stiff with scorn;
For this is the honour of fairyland
And the following of the horn;

    Beauty on beauty called us back
    When we could rise and ride,
    And a woman looked out of every window
    As wonderful as a bride:
    And the tavern-sign as a tabard blazed,
    And the children cheered and ran,
    For the love of the hate of the Dragon
    That is the pride of a man.

The sages called him a shadow
And the light went out of the sun:
And the wise men told us that all was well
And all was weary and one:
And then, and then, in the quiet garden,
With never a weed to kill,

   We knew that his shining tail had shone
   In the white road over the hill:
   We knew that the clouds were flakes of flame,
   We knew that the sunset fire
   Was red with the blood of the Dragon
   Whose death is the world's desire.

For the horn was blown in the heart of the night
That men should rise and ride,
Keeping the tryst of a terrible jest
Never for long untried;
Drinking a dreadful blood for wine,
Never in cup or can,
The death of a deathless Dragon,
That is the life of a man.

            (1915–20)

I AM

There is a Knowledge wilder than the creeds
Of this, though all hope scatter like the seeds
Am I more proud than any tongue can tell
On this, though all hope scatter like the chaff
Would I abide as on a mighty staff—
Yea for this thing lift up my head and laugh
      In everlasting hell.

"I am": men lightly utter it: but I
Saying "I am" to any sod or sky
Raise a new self, vaster yet the same
Stars crown my head: imperial and alone
In my own ears my voice is not my own
And he that sitteth on the last great throne
      Sayeth his own name.

           (mid 1890s)

KING'S CROSS STATION

This circled cosmos whereof man is god
  Has suns and stars of green and gold and red,
And cloudlands of great smoke, that range o'er range
  Far floating, hide its iron heavens o'erhead.

God! shall we ever honour what we are,
  And see one moment ere the age expire,
The vision of man shouting and erect,
  Whirled by the shrieking steeds of flood and fire?

Or must Fate act the same grey farce again,
  And wait, till one, amid Time's wrecks and scars,
Speaks to a ruin here, 'What poet-race
  Shot such cyclopean arches at the stars?'

           (mid 1890s)

THE LAMP POST

Laugh your best, O blazoned forests,
   Me you shall not shift or shame
With your beauty: here among you
   Man hath set his spear of flame.

Lamp to lamp we send the signal,
   For our lord goes forth to war;
Since a voice, ere stars were builded,
   Bade him colonise a star.

Laugh ye, cruel as the morning,
   Deck your heads with fruit and flower,
Though our souls be sick with pity,
   Yet our hands are hard with power.

We have read your evil stories,
   We have heard the tiny yell
Through the voiceless conflagration
   Of your green and shining hell.

And when men, with fires and shouting,
   Break your old tyrannic pales;
And where ruled a single spider
   Laugh and weep a million tales.

This shall be your best of boasting:
   That some poet, poor of spine,
Full and sated with our wisdom,
   Full and fiery with our wine,

Shall steal out and make a treaty
   With the grasses and the showers,
Rail against the grey town-mother,
   Fawn upon the scornful flowers;

Rest his head among the roses,
  Where a quiet song-bird sounds,
And no sword made sharp for traitors,
  Hack him into meat for hounds.

                              (late 1890s)

LAUGHTER

Say to the lover when the lane
Thrills through its leaves to feel her feet
"You only feel what smashed the slime
When the first monstrous brutes could meet."
Shall not the lover laugh and say
(Whom God gives season to be gay)
"Well for those monsters long ago
If that be so; but was it so?"

Say to the mother when the son
First springs and stiffens as for fight
"So under that green roof of scum
The tadpole is the frog's delight,
So deep your brutish instincts lie."
She will laugh loud enough and cry
"Then the poor frog is not so poor.
O happy frog! But are you sure?"

Ye learned, ye that never laugh,
But say "Such love and litany
Hailed Isis; and such men as you
Danced by the cart of Cybele,"
Shall I not say "Your cart at least
Goes far before your horse, poor beast.
Like Her! You flatter them maybe,
What do you think you do to me?"

                              (1918–25)

LILIES OF THE VALLEY

Lean and listen: lean and listen:
    If our ears were very keen
If we heard the little noises
    Of the growing things of green
If we heard the blossom breaking
    Like the tongues of every tree
If we heard the grass a-growing
    Like the roaring of the sea
If we heard these little lilies
    We should know and understand
They are ringing for our bridal
    On the bells of fairy-land.

Lean and listen: lean and Listen.
                    (unfinished, mid
                     to late 1890s)

A MAN

Starry, Colossal, blinding, bare
Look down out of thine Everywhere
Lo: I am dust: dust too is fair.

A Man: yet all men are the same
Striving and stammering to proclaim
Thy deafening and confounding Name.

A man; unfathomed Fatherhood,
Only a man of bone and blood
Who found thy good earth Passing Good.
                    (mid 1890s)

A MAN AND HIS IMAGE

All day the nations climb and crawl and pray
  In one long pilgrimage to one white shrine,
Where sleeps a saint whose pardon, like his peace,
  Is wide as death, as common, as divine.

His statue in an aureole fills the shrine,
  The reckless nightingale, the roaming fawn,
Share the broad blessing of his lifted hands,
  Under the canopy, above the lawn.

But one strange night, a night of gale and flood,
  A sound came louder than the wild wind's tone;
The grave-gates shook and opened: and one stood
  Blue in the moonlight, rotten to the bone.

Then on the statue, graven with holy smiles,
  There came another smile — tremendous — one
Of an Egyptian god. 'Why should you rise?'
  Do I not guard your secret from the sun?

'The nations come; they kneel among the flowers
  Sprung from your blood, blossoms of May and June
Which do not poison them — is it not strange?
  Speak!' And the dead man shuddered in the moon.

'Shall I not cry the truth?' — the dead man cowered —
  'Is it not sad, with life so tame and cold,
That earth should fade into the sun's white fires
  With the best jest in all its tales untold?

'If I should cry that in this shrine lie hid
  Stories that Satan from his mouth would spew;
Wild tales that men in hell tell hoarsely — speak!
  Saint and Deliverer! Should I slander you?'

Slowly the cowering corse reared up its head,
  'Nay, I am vile . . . but when for all to see,
You stand there, pure and painless — death of life!
  Let the stars fall — I say you slander me!

'You make me perfect, public, colourless;
   You make my virtues sit at ease—you lie!
For mine were never easy—lost or saved,
   I had a soul—I was. And where am I?

'Where is my good? the little real hoard,
   The secret tears, the sudden chivalries;
The tragic love, the futile triumph—where?
   Thief, dog, and son of devils—where are these?

'I will lift up my head: in leprous loves
   Lost, and the soul's dishonourable scars—
By God, I was a better man than This
   That stands and slanders me to all the stars.

'Come down!' And with an awful cry, the corse
   Sprang on the sacred tomb of many tales,
And stone and bone, locked in a loathsome strife,
   Swayed to the singing of the nightingales.

Then one was thrown: and where the statue stood
   Under the canopy, above the lawn,
The corse stood; grey and lean, with lifted hands
   Raised in tremendous welcome to the dawn.

'Now let all nations climb and crawl and pray;
   Though I be basest of my old red clan,
They shall not scale, with cries or sacrifice,
   The stature of the spirit of a man.'

                                   (late 1890s)

A MAN BORN ON THE EARTH

Perhaps there has been some mistake.
How does he know he has come to the right place?
But when he finds friends
He knows he has come to the right place.

You say it is a love affair
Hush: it is a new Garden of Eden
And a new progeny will people a new earth.
God is always making these experiments.
                    ("The Notebook", mid 1890s)

MAN'S DIVINE EQUALITY

Nigh on twice a thousand springs
Now have passed on golden wings
Since over Bethlehem's starlit snow,
Pealed the angel anthem slow
To Man's goodwill from God on high
To Man's divine equality.

As the green spring seed is born
As grows slow the golden corn
Slow and sure, and manifold
Creepeth in the age of gold
To Man's goodwill from God on high
To Man's divine equality.

Not at once doth it appear
"Lo, 'tis there" nor "lo, 'tis here."
Like a thief beneath the night
Like slow dawn's rose-red light.
To Man goodwill from God on high.
To Man divine equality.

Lo, dry bones a valley fill
All, is desolate and still,
"Can these live?" the Voice hath cried
"Lord, thou knowest," the seer replied.
And the four strong winds of God
Fire them hot with life and blood,
To Man goodwill from God on high
To Man divine equality.
                    (late 1890s)

THE MARINER

The violet scent is sacred
   Like dreams of angels bright;
The hawthorn smells of passion
   Told in a moonless night.

But the smell is in my nostrils,
   Through blossoms red or gold,
Of my own green flower unfading,
   A bitter smell and bold.

The lily smells of pardon,
   The rose of mirth; but mine
Smells shrewd of death and honour,
   And the doom of Adam's line.

The heavy scent of wine-shops
   Floats as I pass them by,
But never a cup I quaff from,
   And never a house have I.

Till dropped down forty fathoms,
   I lie eternally;
And drink from God's own goblet
   The green wine of the sea.
               (1890s)

MEMORY

If I ever go back to Baltimore,
The City of Maryland,
I shall miss again as I missed before
A thousand things of the world in store,
The story standing in every door
That beckons on every hand.

I shall not know where the bonds were riven,
And a hundred faiths set free,
Where a wandering cavalier had given
Her hundredth name to the Queen of Heaven,
And made oblation of feuds forgiven
To Our Lady of Liberty.

I shall not travel the tracks of fame
Where the war was not to the strong;
Where Lee the last of the heroes came
With the Men of the South and a flag like flame,
And called the land by its lovely name
In the unforgotten song.

If ever I cross the sea and stray
To the City of Maryland,
I will sit on a stone and watch or pray
For a stranger's child that was there one day:
And the child will never come back to play,
And no one will understand.

(1920s)

THE MIRROR OF MADMEN

I dreamed a dream of heaven, white as frost,
The splendid stillness of a living host;
Vast choirs of upturned faces, line o'er line.
Then my blood froze; for every face was mine.

Spirits with sunset plumage throng and pass,
Glassed darkly in the sea of gold and glass.
But still on every side, in every spot,
I saw a million selves, who saw me not.

I fled to quiet wastes, where on a stone,
Perchance, I found a saint, who sat alone;

I came behind: he turned with slow, sweet grace,
And faced me with my happy, hateful face.

I cowered like one that in a tower doth bide,
Shut in by mirrors upon every side;
Then I saw, islanded in skies alone
And silent, one that sat upon a throne.

His robe was bordered with rich rose and gold,
Green, purple, silver out of sunsets old;
But o'er his face a great cloud edged with fire,
Because it covereth a world's desire.

But as I gazed, a silent worshipper,
Methought the cloud began to faintly stir;
Then I fell flat, and screamed with grovelling head,
'If thou hast any lightning, strike me dead!

'But spare a brow where the clean sunlight fell,
The crown of a new sin that sickens hell.
Let me not look aloft and see mine own
Feature and form upon the Judgment-throne.'

Then my dream snapped: and with a heart that leapt
I saw across the tavern where I slept,
The sight of all my life most full of grace,
A gin-damned drunkard's wan half-witted face.
                                        (mid to late 1890s)

MODERN ELFLAND

I cut a staff in a churchyard copse,
    I clad myself in ragged things,
I set a feather in my cap
    That fell out of an angel's wings.

I filled my wallet with white stones,
  I took three foxgloves in my hand,
I slung my shoes across my back,
  And so I went to fairyland.

But lo, within that ancient place
  Science had reared her iron crown,
And the great cloud of steam went up
  That telleth where she takes a town.

But cowled with smoke and starred with lamps,
  That strange land's light was still its own;
The word that witched the woods and hills
  Spoke in the iron and the stone.

Not Nature's hand had ever curved
  That mute unearthly porter's spine.
Like sleeping dragon's sudden eyes
  The signals leered along the line.

The chimneys thronging crooked or straight
  Were fingers signalling the sky;
The dog that strayed across the street
  Seemed four-legged by monstrosity.

'In vain,' I cried, 'though you too touch
  The new time's desecrating hand,
Through all the noises of a town
  I hear the heart of fairyland.'

I read the name above a door,
  Then through my spirit pealed and passed:
'This is the town of thine own home,
  And thou hast looked on it at last.'

                              (late 1890s)

THE MONSTER

"The degenerate Greek intellect wasted itself in futile debates about the dual nature of Christ." — Magazine Article.

One with the golden eagle of the morning,
Flat and flung wide above the spinning plains,
It seemed my spirit sprang and wheeled and flew.
The world went under us like a river of light,
An ectasy of order, where each life,
Rejoicing in its law, rushed to its end:
To break itself and breed; the embattled vines,
Grassland and grainland waved their thousand spears
In one wild rhythm as they swept along,
A map of marching armies, all one way;
And ploughmen on their uplands ribbed with gold,
Went forward happy, with their backs to heaven.
Only the sacred eagle up the stream
Strove back to his beginnings; left behind

The white archaic dawns on herbless hills,
The first cold hues of chaos; like a stair
Mounted the soundless cataracts of the sun,
Seeking the sun of suns; till suddenly
The last heavens opened; for one flash I saw
Something too large and calm for sight or reason,
The Urns of Evil and Good, vast as two worlds,
And over them a larger face than Fate's
Of that first Will that is when all was not.
But that unblinded burning eagle soared
And perched upon His thunderous right hand.
I cowered, and heard a cry torn out of me
In an unknown tongue older than all my race,
"O Father of Gods and Men"; and saw no more.

The vulture from his dark and hairy nest
Far down the low-browed cliffs of the abyss
Stood black against the sun; a shape of shame:

A plumed eclipse; and all the ways of men
Were paved with upturned faces; masks of hate:
For that hooked head was like a horrible tool,
An instrument of torture made alive
With creaking pinions; for what end they knew:
The vulture of the vengeance of the gods.

For a red under-light on all that land,
A hell that is the underside of heaven,
Glowed from men's struggling fires; and as I followed
That evil bird over lost battle-fields,
Where panoplied and like fallen palaces
The great and foolish kings who warred with doom
Lay sunken with their star; I saw far off,
Misshapen, against the dark red dome of sky,
A mountain on a mountain. As I gazed
The shape seemed changed: the upper mountain moved.
It heaved vast flanks ribbed like the red-ribbed hills,
Thrust down an uprooted forest with one heel
And stretched a Titan's arm to touch the sky.

"You slay for ever, but you slay too late;
A stolen secret turns not home again.
While I lie lifted high against your wrath,
Hanged on this gibbet of rock, far down below
The fire is spreading on the earth's dark plains
And my red stars come forth like flowers of night
And my red sun burns when your white sun dies.
See where man's watchfire dances and derides,
The sickly servile sunset crawling away:
Lo; my red banner thrashes through the air,
Nor dare your vulture peck it if he pass."

The vulture passed, a shadow on the fire,
And the dark hills were loud with dreadful cries.

I woke; the skies were empty of the eagle,
And empty of the vulture all the abyss:
And something in the yawning silence cried

Giants and gods were dying in new dawns:
Daylight itself had deepened; there opened in it
New depths or new dimensions; stone and tree
In that strange light grew solid; as does a statue
Or many-sided monument set beside
The flattened fables on a bas-relief.
Only in dark thin lines against the dawn
The last and lingering monsters limped away,
The boys with crooked legs and cries of goats
Ran as from one pursuing; amid the weeds
Wailed the strange women, neither fish nor flesh,
And from the hoary splendours of the sea
Rose Triton with the limbs that curled like whirlpools,
Stonily staring at some sign afar.

For a new light in a new silence shone
From some new nameless quarter of the sky
Behind us on the road; and all strange things
Looked back to something stranger than themselves
And, towering still and trampling, the Last Centaur
Cried in a roar that shook the shuddering trees,
"We rode our bodies without bridle at will,
We hurled our high breasts forward on flying hooves:
But these two bodies are a simple thing
Beside that Fear that comes upon the world.
A Monster walks behind." I dared not turn;
A shape lay like a shadow, on the road.
I saw not but I heard; a sound more awful,
Then from the blackest cypress-close the call
Of some dark Janus shouting with two mouths:
"I am Prometheus. I am Jupiter.
In ravening obedience down from heaven,
Hailed of my hand and by this sign alone,
My eagle comes to tear me. Touch me not."

I lay there as one dead. But since I woke
This single world is double till I die.

                                        (1920s)

THE MORTAL ANSWERS[1]

" . . . Come away—
With the fairies, hand in hand,
For the world is more full of weeping
Than you can understand."
                    —*W. B. Yeats*

From the Wood of the Old Wives' Fables
  They glittered out of the grey,
And with all the armies of Elf-land
  I strove like a beast at bay;

With only a right arm wearied,
  Only a red sword worn,
And the pride of the house of Adam
  That holdeth the stars in scorn.

For they came with chains of flowers
  And lilies' lances free,
There in the quiet greenwood
  To take my grief from me.

And I said, "Now all is shaken
  When heavily hangs the brow,
When the hope of the years is taken,
  The last star sunken. Now—

"Hear, you chattering cricket,
  Hear, you spawn of the sod,
The strange strong cry in the darkness
  Of one man praising God,

---

[1] There is an early version of this poem entitled "Thieves", which has 3 stanzas. The only difference is in the first line of the 3rd stanza.

"That out of the night and nothing
    With travail of birth he came
To stand one hour in the sunlight
    Only to say her name.

"Falls through her hair the sunshine
    In showers; it touches, see,
Her high bright cheeks in turning;
    Ah, Elfin Company,

"The world is hot and cruel,
    We are weary of heart and hand,
But the world is more full of glory
    Than you can understand."

                                        (1905–15)

MUSIC

Then the strong trumpets like the guns of God
Burst, dealing life more terrible than death
The beautiful terror that the tube of brass
    Made of man's breath;
And drums that shake the heart and wake the soul
    Rolled like deep seas
But no gun followed. And the silence drank
    Thunders of peace.

And trumpet over trumpet overtopping
    The purple trees
Made upon earth and all the reeling forests
    Earthquakes of peace
Earth that had heard the hundred horns of war
    And none like these.
Peace upon earth: peace on one piece of earth
    Came down that day;

When to the wild melodies like wintry weather
When to the crack of thunder-clouds together
Broke the broad daybreak on Paraguay.

(early 1900s)

THE MYSTERY

If sunset clouds could grow on trees
It would but match the may in flower;
And skies be underneath the seas
No topsyturvier than a shower.

If mountains rose on wings to wander
They were no wilder than a cloud;
Yet all my praise is mean as slander,
Mean as these mean words spoken aloud.

And never more than now I know
That man's first heaven is far behind;
Unless the blazing seraph's blow
Has left him in the garden blind.

Witness, O Sun that blinds our eyes,
Unthinkable and unthankable King,
That though all other wonder dies
I wonder at not wondering.

(1916–21)

NIGHTMARE

The silver and violet leopard of the night
Spotted with stars and smooth with silence sprang;
And though three doors stood open, the end of light
Closed like a trap; and stillness was a clang.

Under the leopard sky of lurid stars
I strove with evil sleep the hot night long,
Dreams dumb and swollen of triumphs without wars,
Of tongueless trumpet and unanswering gong.

I saw a pale imperial pomp go by,
Helmet and hornèd mitre and heavy wreath;
Their high strange ensigns hung upon the sky
And their great shields were like the doors of death.

Their mitres were as moving pyramids
And all their crowns as marching towers were tall;
Their eyes were cold under their carven lids
And the same carven smile was on them all.

Over a paven plain that seemed unending
They passed unfaltering till it found an end
In one long shallow step; and these descending
Fared forth anew as long away to wend.

I thought they travelled for a thousand years;
And at the end was nothing for them all,
For all that splendour of sceptres and of spears,
But a new step, another easy fall.

The smile of stone seemed but a little less,
The load of silver but a little more:
And ever was that terraced wilderness
And falling plain paved like a palace floor.

Rust red as gore crawled on their arms of might
And on their faces wrinkles and not scars:
Till the dream suddenly ended; noise and light
Loosened the tyranny of the tropic stars.

But over them like a subterranean sun
I saw the sign of all the fiends that fell;
And a wild voice cried "Hasten and be done,
Is there no steepness in the stairs of hell?"

He that returns, He that remains the same,
Turned the round real world, His iron vice;
Down the grey garden paths a bird called twice,
And through three doors mysterious daylight came.
                                        (1916–21)

A NOVELTY

Why should I care for the Ages
    Because they are old and grey?
To me, like sudden laughter,
    The stars are fresh and gay;
The world is a daring fancy,
    And finished yesterday.

Why should I bow to the Ages
    Because they were drear and dry?
Slow trees and ripening meadows
    For me go roaring by,
A living charge, a struggle
    To escalade the sky.

The eternal suns and systems,
    Solid and silent all,
To me are stars of an instant,
    Only the fires that fall
From God's good rocket, rising
    On this night of carnival.
                        (mid to late 1890s)

ON RIGHTEOUS INDIGNATION

When Adam went from Paradise
 He saw the sword and ran;
The dreadful shape, the new device.
The pointed end of Paradise,
And saw what Peril is and Price,
 And knew he was a man.

When Adam went from Paradise,
 He turned him back and cried
For a little flower from Paradise;
There came no flower from Paradise;
The woods were dark in Paradise,
 And not a bird replied.

For only comfort or contempt,
 For jest or great reward,
Over the walls of Paradise,
The flameless gates of Paradise,
The dumb shut doors of Paradise,
 God flung the flaming sword.

It burns the hand that holds it
 More than the skull it scars;
It doubles like a snake and stings,
Yet he in whose hand its swings
He is the most masterful of things,
 A scorner of the stars.

    (1913)

THE PESSIMIST

You that have snarled through the ages, take your answer and
    go —
I know your hoary question, the riddle that all men know.
You have weighed the stars in the balance, and grasped the
    skies in a span:
Take, if you must have answer, the word of a common man.

Deep in my life lies buried one love unhealed, unshriven,
One hunger still shall haunt me — yea, in the streets of heaven;
This is the burden, babbler, this is the curse shall cling,
This is the thing I bring you; this is the pleasant thing.

'Gainst you and all your sages, no joy of mine shall strive,
This one dead self shall shatter the men you call alive.
My grief I send to smite you, no pleasure, no belief,
Lord of the battered grievance, what do you know of grief?

I only know the praises to heaven that one man gave,
That he came on earth for an instant, to stand beside a grave,
The peace of a field of battle, where flowers are born of blood.
I only know one evil that makes the whole world good.

Beneath this single sorrow the globe of moon and sphere
Turns to a single jewel, so bright and brittle and dear
That I dread lest God should drop it, to be dashed into stars
    below.
                . . . .

You that have snarled through the ages, take your answer
    and go.

                                (mid to late 1890s)

THE PILLAR BOX

A stranger garbed outlandishly
  Came to our town beside the sea
"In mine own city" thus he said—
  "There stands a little man in red
Who in the steep street standeth still
  And morn and even eats his fill
Of tales untold, wild truths and lies
  Small wars and secret chivalries
You may walk round him as may be
  He guards his secrets soldierly—
A quaint red tower not three feet wide
  And thousands of mens' souls inside."

Some, hearing mocked the tale aloud
  And chased the liar with a crowd
Some smote and scattered cruelly
  His blood upon the stones, but he
Still wore his happy sunset smile
  Till after rambling many a mile
He met a man beside the sea
  Who answered very quietly
"A common pillar-box: accord
  I ready credence" at that word
The gentle stranger frail of limb
  In still scorn laid a hand on him
With eyes that blazed like magic stones
  And shook him like a bag of bones.
             (ca. 1900)

POST-RECESSIONAL

A reply to Kipling's "Recessional"

God of your fathers, known of old,
    For patience with man's swaggering line,
He did not answer you when told
    About you and your palm and pine,
Though you deployed your far-flung host
And boasted that you did not boast.

Though drunk with sight of power and blind,
    Even as you bowed your head in awe,
You kicked up both your heels behind
    At lesser breeds without the law;
Lest they forget, lest they forget,
That yours was the exclusive set.

We fancied heaven preferring much,
    Your rowdiest song, your slangiest sentence,
Your honest banjo banged, to such
    Very recessional repentance;
Now if your native land be dear,
Whisper (or shout) and we shall hear.

Cut down, our navies melt away.
    From ode and war-song fades the fire,
We are a jolly sight to-day
    Too near to Sidon and to Tyre
To make it sound so very nice
To offer ancient sacrifice.

Rise up and bid the trumpets blow
    When it is gallant to be gay,
Tell the wide world it shall not know
    Our face until we turn to bay.
Bless you, you shall be blameless yet,
For God forgives and men forget.

(1920s)

THE PRAISE OF DUST

'What of vile dust?' the preacher said.
  Methought the whole world woke,
The dead stone lived beneath my foot,
  And my whole body spoke.

'You, that play tyrant to the dust,
  And stamp its wrinkled face,
This patient star that flings you not
  Far into homeless space.

'Come down out of your dusty shrine
  The living dust to see,
The flowers that at your sermon's end
  Stand blazing silently.

'Rich white and blood-red blossom; stones,
  Lichens like fire encrust;
A gleam of blue, a glare of gold,
  The vision of the dust.

'Pass them all by: till as you come
  Where, at a city's edge,
Under a tree—I know it well—
  Under a lattice ledge,

'The sunshine falls on one brown head.
  You, too, O clod of clay,
Eater of stones, may haply hear
  The trumpets of that day.

'When God to all his paladins
  By his own splendour swore
To make a fairer face than heaven,
  Of dust and nothing more.'

                                    (mid 1890s)

THE RAIN

The dark and deafening skies are bowed
  About my brows again—
But drunk with darkness as with wine
  I laugh against the rain.

If I brought sunshine with a song—
  And rain clouds with a wish
If forests bore for me their fruit
  And seas for me their fish.

There were a fury in my heart
  Through all Eternity—
At the base world that could not hold
  —A greater thing than I.
                  (ca. 1900)

RE-BORN

A strange new youth is on me: not of song
Nor fiery wine, nor woman's kisses dim
But of the long night's strife I strove with him
Whose face is secret and whose hands are strong.

There is a joy too keen for common thought
This: that whoe're has slowly scaled and spelled
Cycles of starry suffering: may be held,
Worth, at last to learn that he is naught.

Now and for one great moment, not in me
Nor any crown I hope for, I rejoice
But in a meadow-game of girls and boys
Some sunset in the centuries to be.
                  (mid 1890s)

A RHYME OF DUST

Dust and a blast soon broken,
  This is the song I sing,
Systems gather and sever,
  Suns upon suns roar over
But crowned with disdain for ever
  Dust and a blast is King.

Dust that designs and clamours
  Dust that makes and that mars
Dust that is girt with graces
  Builder, breaker and healer
Darer of all the spaces
  Scorner of all the stars.

Filled of a frantic wisdom,
  Fierce with a childish trust,
Kings and crowds in alliance,
  Priests and people and princes,
Long may it dance defiance,
  The glad old dance of dust.

"Dust and a breath soon broken"
  A sneer is the sages ban:
But glory, O thou that criest,
  More than all flowers and forests
Glory to God in the highest
  For the dust of the earth made man.
                    (late 1890s)

A SECOND CHILDHOOD

When all my days are ending
And I have no song to sing,
I think I shall not be too old
To stare at everything;
As I stared once at a nursery door
Or a tall tree and a swing.

Wherein God's ponderous mercy hangs
On all my sins and me,
Because He does not take away
The terror from the tree
And stones still shine along the road
That are and cannot be.

Men grow too old for love, my love,
Men grow too old for wine,
But I shall not grow too old to see
Unearthly daylight shine,
Changing my chamber's dust to snow
Till I doubt if it be mine.

Behold, the crowning mercies melt,
The first surprises stay;
And in my dross is dropped a gift
For which I dare not pray:
That a man grow used to grief and joy
But not to night and day.

Men grow too old for love, my love,
Men grow too old for lies;
But I shall not grow too old to see
Enormous night arise,
A cloud that is larger than the world
And a monster made of eyes.

Nor am I worthy to unloose
The latchet of my shoe;

Or shake the dust from off my feet
Or the staff that bears me through
On ground that is too good to last,
Too solid to be true.

Men grow too old to woo, my love,
Men grow too old to wed:
But I shall not grow too old to see
Hung crazily overhead
Incredible rafters when I wake
And find I am not dead.

A thrill of thunder in my hair:
Though blackening clouds be plain,
Still I am stung and startled
By the first drop of the rain:
Romance and pride and passion pass
And these are what remain.

Strange crawling carpets of the grass,
Wide windows of the sky:
So in this perilous grace of God
With all my sins go I:
And things grow new though I grow old,
Though I grow old and die.

(1916–21)

THE SKELETON

Chattering finch and water-fly
Are not merrier than I;
Here among the flowers I lie
Laughing everlastingly.
No: I may not tell the best;
Surely, friends, I might have guessed
Death was but the good King's jest,
    It was hid so carefully.

(late 1890s)

SOLITUDE CALLS THE MAN

When I was young with mysteries
    I went into the wilderness
My fiery tears and nameless dreams
    To cool on Nature's callousness

Where her meek children, one-eyed flowers
    And one-legged trees, in sane surprise
Saw me a monster many-limbed
    The first man made under the skies

When I was old with memories
    I went into the wilderness
There to unload my pack of tales
    And my life's lesson to confess.

Into the vast void ruined land
    That I might leap and dance and sing
And no man know my foolishness
    Save my old crony who is King.
                              (1898–99?)

THE SONG OF THE WHEEL

Wheels within wheels, the wheels for ever turning
Wheels within wheels, a rising and a roaring,
Axles enkindled like to suns in burning
Circles unending like to seas in pouring
Wheels within wheels, the wheels for ever turning.

Wheel of the flax, the wheel for ever turning,
'Neath thatch and casement tingling and humming
Gold hair grown grey, and faces pale in yearning,
Weaving the raiment, watching for the coming,
Wheel of the flax, the wheel for ever turning.

Wheel of the ship's helm, wheel for ever turning,
Under grey seas with lips of thunder glooming,
Under bleak stars the bleaker face discerning,
Land's fitful lights a shifting and a looming:
Wheel of the helm: the wheel for ever turning.

Wheel of the potter, wheel for ever turning,
From the red furnace giant shadows flinging
Pots for all homesteads hardening and burning,
Pots for all homes and still the wheel is singing,
Wheel of the potter: wheel for ever turning.

Wheel of the pulley, wheel for ever turning,
Loading, unloading still and never ceasing,
High on gaunt walls his wage the builder earning,
Up through blue day the naked house increasing
Wheel of the pulley, wheel for ever turning.

Wheel of the engine, wheel for ever turning,
Livid and huge, through iron Kingdoms ranging,
Clashing and groaning, battering and spurning,
Ever the same: and is there nothing changing?
Wheel of the engine: wheel for ever turning.

Wheel of the world, the wheel for ever turning,
Golden with daybreaks, red with every setting,
Thronging with lives, with all the planets burning,
What is it weaving, what is God begetting,
Wheel of the world, the wheel for ever turning.

Wheel of my work, the wheel for ever turning,
Cheerful or toilful, ever still renewing,
Morn after morn, the circling lesson learning,
Knowing is past me: I am here for doing:
Wheel of my work: the wheel for ever turning.

                                   (late 1890s)

SONNETS IN SUMMER HEAT

I

I too have dreamed of dark titanic roses
Hot in the Hanging Gardens of the Sun,
Grass-blanched and blasted where the Unspeakable One
Blazed in the mirror of the face of Moses,
Or goblin gourds the slow green dawn discloses
Enormous in quiet isles no sail has won,
Or purple Persian forests crushed, whereon
Some rock-hewn monster like a realm reposes.

But though I sought dark fruits that thrive in thunder
And dusky sunflowers turned to alien suns,
I did not seek for wonders, but for wonder,
Nor these wild images but more innocent ones:
I looked for my lost eyes: which long ago
Saw one red daisy in the flower-pot grow.

II

Tall tiger rocks striped with the strata stand
Against the devouring glories of the sun,
Dry wells like dragons drink the sands that run,
Red and dark grey and purple and silver sand:
And all the multi-coloured waste is fanned
With fans of dissolution and eclipse
The hollow swells with horror and the hill slips
The changing rocks of this enchanted land.

So moves the Desert; and the whole world's pride
Is dust, yet knew itself for more than mire,
When driven with the blast of all the world's desire
Dry-throated thirst deep as the desert cried
When God ungirt of column of cloud and fire
Came out of Egypt to be crucified.

III

Blue with the bloom of darkest grapes the night,
The fruited night hangs swollen, as some divine
New Deluge not of water but of wine
Might drown us not in death, but in delight:
And purple tropic torrents from the height
Madden the world's weeds from their flat design
And new shapes dance and nameless colours shine
Dizzying deep roots: the Dionysian light.

The heavens are sealed: and though we thrive we thirst
For that most holy Vine that holds the sky,
The clouds the seer called bottles, that do not burst,
Abide the breaking of that ancient cry:
I shall not drink again of the fruit of the vine
Till with dead men I drink a deathless wine.

                                              (1929)

THOU SHALT NOT KILL

I had grown weary of him; of his breath
And hands and features I was sick to death.
Each day I heard the same dull voice and tread;
I did not hate him: but I wished him dead.
And he must with his blank face fill my life—
Then my brain blackened, and I snatched a knife.

But 'ere I struck, my soul's grey deserts through
A voice cried, 'Know at least what thing you do.
'This is a common man: knowest thou, O soul,
'What this thing is? somewhere where seasons roll
'There is some living thing for whom this man
'Is as seven heavens girt into a span,

'For some one soul you take the world away—
'Now know you well your deed and purpose. Slay!'
Then I cast down the knife upon the ground
And saw that mean man for one moment crowned.
I turned and laughed: for there was no one by—
The man that I had sought to slay was I.

(late 1890s)

THE TRIUMPH OF MAN

Say: Who is this that cometh royally,
  Up out of Edom with his garments red
Of sun and star and clay of quick and dead?
  Master and prince and victor: It is I.

A strange new youth is on me not of song
  Nor fiery wine, nor woman's kisses dim
But of the long night's strife I strove with him
  Whose face is secret and whose hands are strong.

Hear! for one great hours triumph. Not in me,
  Nor any hope of mind do I rejoice
But in a meadows-game of girls and boys
  Some sunset in the centuries to be.

(ca. 1895)

THE TRIUMPH OF MAN

I plod and peer amid mean sounds and shapes,
  I hunt for dusty gain and dreary praise,
  And slowly pass the dismal grinning days,
Monkeying each other like a line of apes.

What care? There was one hour amid all these
   When I had stripped off like a tawdry glove
   My starriest hopes and wants, for very love
Of time and desolate eternities.

Yea, for one great hour's triumph, not in me
   Nor any hope of mind did I rejoice,
   But in a meadow game of girls and boys
Some sunset in the centuries to be.

                  (late 1890s)

UBI ECCLESIA

'You must seek for a Castle East of the sun and West of the moon.'
                                — Fairy Tale

'For as the lightning cometh out of the east, and shineth even unto the
west, so shall also the coming of the Son of Man be.' — Matthew 24:27

Our Castle is East of the Sun,
And our Castle is West of the Moon,
So wisely hidden from all the wise
In a twist of the air, in a fold of the skies,
They go East, they go West, of the land where it lies
    And a Fool finds it soon.

Our Castle is East of the Sun
And abides not the law of the sunlight,
The last long shot of Apollo
Falls spent ere it strike the tower
Far East of the steep, of the strong,
Going up of the golden horses,
Strange suns have governed our going,
Strange dials the day and the hour.
With hearts not fed of Demeter,
With thoughts unappeased of Athene,
We have groped through the earth's dead daylight

To a night that is more, not less:
We have seen his star in the East
That is dark as a cloud from the westward,
To the Roman a reek out of Asia,
To the Greeks, foolishness.

For the Sun is not lord but a servant
Of the secret sun we have seen:
The sun of the crypt and the cavern,
The crown of a secret queen:
Where things are not what they seem
     But what they mean.

But our Castle is West of the Moon,
Nor the Moon hath lordship upon it,
The Horns and the horsemen crying
On their great ungraven God:
And West of the moons of magic
And the sleep of the moon-faced idols
And the great moon-coloured crystal
Where the Mages mutter and nod:
The black and the purple poppies
That grow in Gautama's garden
Have waved not ever upon us
The smell of their sweet despair:
And the yellow masks of the Ancients
Looking west from their tinkling temples
See Hope on our hill Mountjoy,
And the dawn and the dancers there.

For the Moon is not lord but a servant
Of the smile more bright than the Sun:
And all they desire and despair of
And weary of winning is won
In our Castle of Joyous Garde
     Desired and done.

So abides it dim in the midmost
The Bridge called Both-and-Neither,
To the East a wind from the westward,
To the West a light from the East:
But the map is not made of man
That can plot out its place under heaven,
That is counted and lost and left over
The largest thing and the least.

For our Castle is East of the Sun,
And our Castle is West of the Moon,
And the dark labyrinthine charts of the wise
Point East and point West of the land where it lies,
And a Fool walks blind on the highway
    And finds it soon.

                          (ca. 1928–29)

UNCREATION

Ye that when surges covered the stars
   Spat at the soaring sea
Captains bold, to a bolder heart
   Gather and bow the knee.

See in his eyes a stranger star
   Of peril and prowess done
Last night he made him a narrow bed
   And laid him down thereon.

He gave his limbs to the starry laws
   To swathe and guard and keep
He gave his soul to the unknown God
   And dared to be asleep.

One long glad day to blow and shine
  Given—and left behind
Hope—look ye that seek a sign—
  Look, ye fools and blind.

                              (mid 1890s)

UNWRITTEN

If on me too came once the mood
  That comes when rain is on the sea
When heaven itself were only stale
  And angels gaudy: write of me

That hour the singer triumphed not
  I sent not honest streets among—
With fingered lute and laurel-crown
  The howling leper of a song.

Though the mood came with sunset words
  I stamped it as a sin that smells
Though it was rich with moons and stars
  I hid it under all the hells.

Some pride remained: though sadder stared
  The face of my good father rime
I spat not at his silence back
  The silly insult of a rhyme.

The vision of a world in vain
  If once it smote me: there it lies—
Still while a soul can hold it down
  And dumb when all the dead shall rise.

                              (1890s)

"VULGARISED"

All round they murmur, 'O profane,
    Keep thy heart's secret hid as gold';
But I, by God would sooner be
    Some knight in shattering wars of old,

In brown outlandish arms to ride,
    And shout my love to every star
With lungs to make a poor maid's name
    Deafen the iron ears of war.

Here, where these subtle cowards crowd,
    To stand and so to speak of love,
That the four corners of the world
    Should hear it and take heed thereof.

That to this shrine obscure there be
    One witness before all men given,
As naked as the hanging Christ,
    As shameless as the sun in heaven.

These whimperers—have they spared to us
    One dripping woe, one reeking sin?
These thieves that shatter their own graves
    To prove the soul is dead within.

They talk; by God, is it not time
    Some of Love's chosen broke the girth,
And told the good all men have known
    Since the first morning of the earth?
                            (late 1890s)

THE WOOD-CUTTER

We came behind him by the wall,
   My brethren drew their brands,
And they had strength to strike him down—
   And I to bind his hands.

Only once, to a lantern gleam,
   He turned his face from the wall,
And it was as the accusing angel's face
   On the day when the stars shall fall.

I grasped the axe with shaking hands,
   I stared at the grass I trod;
For I feared to see the whole bare heavens
   Filled with the face of God.

I struck: the serpentine slow blood
   In four arms soaked the moss—
Before me, by the living Christ,
   The blood ran in a cross.

Therefore I toil in forests here
   And pile the wood in stacks,
And take no fee from shivering folk
   Till I have cleansed the axe.

But for a curse God cleared my sight,
   And where each tree doth grow
I see a life with awful eyes,
   And I must lay it low.

                    (late 1890s)

IV

FRIENDS

A Standing Invitation.

Remember, when the nurses lose you,
 And you have passed from Homes to Home
That all roads lead to Overroads,
 And only some of them to Rome

Come to our beechen field, grown famous
 For putting people on their legs,
Not made of moonshine & of egg-shells,
 But made of sunshine & of eggs.

You know where Frances counts her chickens,
 And still the eggs in millions mount:
Come down & reckon, dear accountant,
 Things for which no one can account.

You know the fish of this aquarium,
 A Carp that waves a friendly fin,
A Winkle that's of Scotch extraction
 And not extracted with a pin.

May to the may-tree comes in glory,
 Sun to the sun-flowers where they flame,
And Rhoda to the rhodadendrons,
 Purple with pride to bear her name

G.C.

ABSENT FRIENDS

In vain anigh the windows high
    The lady doctors wait,[1]
The parents of the world relapse
    Into the savage state.[2]
The books remain unedited
    The books remain unbound
While I in Ludgate Circus
    Lie groaning on the ground.
Lay by, lay by, my waistcoat pink,
    My coat of satin blue,
They're going from Victoria,
    My visions always do.
I never loved a dear gazelle
    To charm me with its glance
It packed its bag, that quadruped
    And went away to France.
            (ca. 1898–1900)

[1] Ethel Oldershaw, one of a departing group of holidaymakers, was secretary to a group of women doctors.

[2] Frances, later to be G. K. C's wife, was secretary to the P.N.E.U, described by Gilbert as

The Parents' National
Highly Rational
Educational Union.

AD AMICOS[1]

By the waters of Boston we sat down and wept
The aerated waters they drink — in hotels
Till they showed us the place where the liquors are kept
In a town like a hive full of cellars for cells.

But though fountains of wine or of water might foam
There flowed in our pockets a fountain of ink;
And we clasped to our bosoms the pens of our home
And licked them when looking for something to drink.

If the pen made the poet, the habit the monk,
What songs of our country had soothed us the while,
When five Prohibitionists, palpably drunk
Scarce raised in the exile one radiant smile.

It is thousands of miles over land, over sea,
From Omaha City to Overroads door
But we said; the great prairies will leave, as they flee,
Like infinite shadows, the things that are sure.

We said, they are certain, the field or the friend
From which we are far or of which we were fond;
That the donkeys still hammer down Aylesbury End,
And a dog is still drinking in Candlemas Pond.

Jock wears the white fur of a blameable life
As misguided he flees from the Captain of Guides;
With the donkey of young convalescents at strife
The Jack of our Beanstalk triumphantly rides.

And the dog and the donkey were dreams of our night
And we pondered the riddle and never could say
Why the donkey is brown when the lady is white,
And the puppy is white when the lady is Gray.

---

[1] Written from America to Mrs. Margaret Halford and other Beaconsfield friends in thanks for a gift of fountain pens.

She first, for whose mad and magnanimous action,
The pen should be turned to a fountain of praise
Our duchess, our Lady, the Queen of Distraction,
The loser of hair-pins, the finder of strays.

And she too, who sent us the pen of her picking,
Whose fairy-like foot made Trotsky[1] trot,
Is she not also alive—and kicking
Possibly quadrupeds; possibly not.

But too many the memories and names that we number
So returned from the round of the earth and its ends.
We have given one hour out of labour and slumber
To the muse that men serve in the Temple of friends.

(ca. 1930–31)

AN AFTERNOON CALL

Three sisters, and there has been a quarrel.
The eldest is dignified and very uncomfortable.
She talks with an exaggerated friendliness and triviality,
Dealing bravely with the social embarrassment.
Another seems moody and fretful,
But shakes it off bit by bit
And comes to her sister's help,
Smiling against her will.
The third sits and reads Tennyson
As one reads Tennyson when one is very angry,
With no word except when questioned.
Probably they were all wrong in the quarrel.
(In all family quarrels and most other ones
    everyone is wrong).

---

[1] Trotsky was the Chestertons' donkey, so called because he wouldn't runsky.

But would anyone decide for me
Which I felt most for
And should most have liked to assist?
                            ("The Notebook", 1894–97)

APOLOGY[1]

Alas, this Rembrandtesque design
Of you can show but shadowy traces
My portraiture I must confine
Exclusively to Ugly Faces.

My ill-trained pencil never treats
Faces I like or friends I know:
I narrow the fierce light that beats
Upon the harmless Eskimo.

Where for six months the white world sleeps,
Your engine never would grow cold;
Your most Internal Engine keeps
All the Combustion it can hold.

And you whose hooter sang its song
From Tarragona to Brabant,
Who crossed the Alps, taking along,
Like Hannibal, an Elephant.

---

[1] Written after a discussion on Catholicism with a family called Church. Drawing of esqui-
maux gazing with rapt faces at a preacher in winter clothing with halo.

St. Dorothy of Ashtead, known as The Apostle of the Esquimos, after converting Surrey, South
and Mid-Bucks, and Cornwall to the Catholic Faith, formed a view of the British climate
which led her to petition Pope Urban XXX for permission to transfer her missionary activities
to the Arctic: where attired in more suitable clothing, she inspired a universal devotion, un-
disturbed by the scenes of violence that had marked her disputes with the Churches in her
own land. — Acta Sanctorum. [— G. K. C.]

So would your social tact have told,
At first if Nordics were not nice,
Were Arctic social circles cold,
You would contrive to break the ice.

(1928–30)

APOLOGY

Forgive us you, whose pageant flames
With youth and beauty and the morning,
If blows like dust across your stage
The breath of things too stale for scorning;
How should you flout these mummied queens
Or mock them when you never met them—
In lost Victorian scenes, so far
That men forget that they forget them?

How should you guess, of these grey jests,
If mocked or mocker be more silly—
With Maeterlinck a Missing Link
And Willie Yeats a Weary Willie,
Or if Conviction or Convention
Marshalled those fashions long ago
Or if Pinero rhymes to Hero
Or only rhymes to "in a row"?

Cras vobis. Even the fervent youth
Who faintly murmurs, "Rather rotten"
Shall rot with Shelley and St. Paul
These that forget shall be forgotten

Even in Arlen time shall quench
St. Michael's faith, the ecstatic flame
And Mr. Coward toes no more
The crest of his crusading name.

Forgive these Phantasmal things
The ghosts of Ghosts, in Ibsen's day
For he that writes them is a ghost
And as you gaze, he fades away.

(ca. 1925)

This is the prelude to a playlet, "The Tragic Women", written by G. K. C. for
Mrs. Barbara Morley-Horder (*née* Barbara West) and The Garden Players, of St.
Johns Wood. The original is held by the Marion E. Wade Center, Wheaton Col-
lege, Illinois.

AN APOLOGY FOR A LETTER UNPOSTED
(For Clare Nicholl)

He thought he saw the Unicorn, the horned and holy horse,
He looked again and saw it was a Subject for Remorse,
He rushed for what he meant to post—
                        and didn't post, of course.

He thought he saw the Unicorn, the Virgin's wildest pet,
He looked again and saw it was a Long Outstanding Debt.
He wrote and wrote and wrote and wrote—
                        and hasn't written yet.

He thought he saw the Unicorn, her mane a wind of pride,
He looked again and tried again, and worked until he died;
He ordered a Pantechnicon—
                        that's waiting still outside.

He thought he saw the Unicorn, that breaketh curb and bond,
He looked and saw a girl of whom he was extremely fond . . .
The floods rose to the Chilterns when
                        they found him in his pond.

He thought he saw the Unicorn, crowned of the Silver Spear,
He wondered if it was a Stag and saw it was a Dear—
And so he drowned himself—
                        some say in Water—
                                some in Beer.

(1924–26)

BARBARA

Elf-locked, elf-eyed, exquisite Barbara,
Married a pirate: they stationed at Scarborough.
His riches were great and she owns an estate
From Market Bosworth to Market Harborough.
(probably 1920s)

BEERBOHM AND BELLOC

And Max's queer crystalline sense
Lit, like a sea beneath a sea,
Shines through a shameless impudence
As shameless a humility.
Or Belloc somewhat rudely roared
But all above him when he spoke
The immortal battle trumpets broke
And Europe was a single sword.
(ca. 1905)

BELLOCOSE

The furious Frenchman comes with his clarions
    and his drums,
His tactics of Sadowa and his maxims of Jean-Paul,
He is bursting on our flanks, grasp your pikes
    and close your ranks,
For Belloc never comes but to conquer or to fall.
(A fragment, 1902–6)

THE COSMIC FACTORIES

What are little boys made of?
Bentley is made of hard wood with a knot in it, a complete set of
    Browning and a strong spring;
Oldershaw of a box of Lucifer matches and a stylographic pen;
Lawrence of a barrister's wig: files of *Punch* and salt,
Maurice of watch-wheels, three riders and a clean collar.
Vernède is made of moonlight and tobacco,
Bertram is mostly a handsome black walking-stick.
Waldo is a nice cabbage, with a vanishing odour of cigarettes,
Salter is made of sand and fire and an university extension ticket.
But the strongest element in all cannot be expressed; I think it is
    a sort of star.

(ca. 1894–95)[1]

A CURSE IN FREE VERSE

(This is the only rhyme admitted: otherwise the enchanting lyric is
all that the most fastidious fashionable taste could require):

I CURSE PARADOX —
I curse the contradictory inconsistencies of the Modern Mind:
I curse and curse and curse . . .

Those who dogmatise about the folly of dogma:
Those who moralise about the non-existence of morals:
Those who say people are too stupid to educate their children
But not too stupid to educate each other's:
Those who say we can be certain of nothing.
Because we are so certain of all the exploded evolutionary hypotheses
That show we can be certain of nothing . . .

---

[1] This poem was written about members of the Junior Debating Club. See also the poems
J.D.C. below, pp. 286–97.

But what are all these inconsistencies —
Compared with the conduct of Those Who
Deliberately call Their House Christmas Cottage,
And then go away from it at Christmas?

I hate those who wage and win twenty unjust wars
And then say "The World now requires Peace",
Who then make a League for Peace and use it to make another War:
I hate those who intemperately denounce Beer and call it Temperance;
Those who deny what science says about Cancer
And what Christianity says about Calvary
And Call the Contradiction Christian Science.
I hate those who want to Rise out of Barbarism
By running about naked and grubbing up roots and herbs;
But what are all these aversions . . . ?
Compared with the blighting blistering horror and hatred
With which I regard
THOSE WHO CALL THEIR HOUSE CHRISTMAS COTTAGE
AND THEN GO AWAY FROM IT AT CHRISTMAS?

(The Poet is removed, cursing . . .)

(early 1930s?)

DIGBY D'AVIGDOR[1]

His clothes, his elegance, his ease,
The silver music of his sneeze,
I cannot make you understand,
I must employ the artist's hand.

---

[1] D'Avigdor was a friend of G. K. Chesterton at St. Paul's School. This verse was written some years later at a reunion of the J.D.C. Chesterton wrote it, with a sketch, on the back of d'Avigdor's menu-card.

E. C. B.

Before the grass grew over me,
  I knew one good man through and through
And knew a soul and body joined
  Are stronger than the heavens are blue.

A wisdom worthy of thy joy,
  O great heart, read I as I ran;
Now, though men smite me on the face,
  I cannot curse the face of man.

I loved the man I saw yestreen
  Hanged with his babe's blood on his palms.
I loved the man I saw to-day
  Who knocked not when he came with alms.

Hush! — for thy sake I even faced
  The knowledge that is worse than hell;
And loved the man I saw but now
  Hanging head downwards in the well.
                                    (late 1890s)

ENID, AN INVITATION

What, Enid, was your soul's mystic hour?
Was it in childish days when, it is said,
Following the truly Spiritistic aim
You made the sort of noise to wake the Dead?

When you, too, turned the tables upside down
Dear Poltergeist, and threw the chairs about
"Manifestations" sceptics may dispute
But yours it was impossible to doubt.

None shall dispute your Spirits, whence they came,
That they were high and never could be low

Though all the Grays like spectres turn to White
When you start haunting houses, we shall know.

And you and I, like thin and tenuous shades,
Well nigh invisible to mortal eyes
Might meet once more at Top Meadow tomorrow
Before you vanish—and oh materialise!

(1920s)

FRIENDS

Lawrence, with quiet face, scarce lit
With meek maliciousness of wit
Legal and formal: praise the Lord
For one man true as a steel sword.

Frances, with brave brown eyes that go
As straight and sudden as a blow.
Courageous with the generous blood
And wisdom of her womanhood.

Bertram a stately thing to see
Wearing the shape of chivalry
Mighty as some old prince of fray
And simple as a child at play.

Edmund, with visage sad and sane
Yet in the fulness of the brain
A twist, like some great oak of worth
With the old humour of the Earth.

Lizzie, with bright and tangled fence.
And dazzling inconsequence
And all the laughing chords along
A sadness like an Irish song.

Lucian, a god of Eastern lands
Whirling with many heads and hands.
Yet one heart only—let the wise
Guess in what quiet place it lies.

Annie, with still eyes full of Truth
Above my childhood and my youth
Like Nature's face her face is young
Who was before me: yet is young.

And Waldo, tumbled in the press
Who in divine fastidiousness
Chose stars, and stood from out the mire
Alone with his own soul's desire.

Mildred, one face for everyone
Whom God made happier than the sun
Who flashed and fluttered, singing by,
The ribbons of life's bravery.

Vernède: up curled in the dark ease
Of oriental mysteries—
And weaving, for a dreamy sport
His twisted arabesques of thought.

Leila, who carried brave and light
The thoughtful load of rule and right
And let not works nor all things wise
Make dark the laughter of her eyes.

                              (late 1890s)

A HAPPY XMAS

Dear Dorothy, forgive me now,
   If just at Xmas time
—which time, (in fact) is 2 a.m.
   I write so brief a rhyme,

Perhaps the great Twelfth Night will bring
  With the coming of the Kings—
Your book to you, my wits to me,
  And other missing things.

              (1927–35)

A HAPPY XMAS

God rest you, merry gentlemen,
Let nothing you dismay.
I have become a Wandering Wait
That sings on Xmas Day.

It was the carol of a friend,
That roused you from your bed.
It was my voice that reached your ears,
Your boot that reached my head.

God rest you, merry gentlemen,
When thus I yelled and prayed.
You rested not, and it was plain
That something you dismayed.

For shepherds watching flocks by night,
You did not care a pin;
When good King Wenceslas looked out
He hadn't a look in.

So as you scorned my vocal powers,
And all my Xmas capers,
I sank to writing verse, like this,
And working for the papers.

              (1920s)[1]

---

[1] Written beside a drawing of himself singing carols.

A HAPPY XMAS
To the Gray Minstrels

Good King Wenceslas looked out
On the Feast of Friday—
There he saw three charming girls
Trying to look untidy—
Never vagabonds were neater:
Hastily he changed the metre
Asked them in and greeted each
In the Czecho-Slovak speech
So Bohemia's Saints must talk:
Then the three resumed their walk
Neighbours saw them trail along
Boyish hats, barbaric song;
Murmured low "I fear the Grays
Have got into Bohemian Ways."
                    (mid 1920s?)

A HAPPY XMAS

Observe the Convalescent Child
    Upon the box's lid
Observe the Dog who plays the Goat,
    —I know a Dog who did.

He fled, with darts like any hare's,
    And leaps like any frog's,
Out of the Home for Lost—at least,
    The Home for Losing Dogs.

Over the roads of Overroads,
    We chased with feint and shout;
A Dog must have his Day; and his
    Was nearly a night out.

Go then and seek, O Child demure
  And Dog so ill-behaved,
The house where little dogs are lost,
  And little children saved.

             (1926–35)

A HAPPY XMAS

There came to Rhoda's Christmas feast
Catalan plotters; four at least:
And three dictators; dukes of Spain:
And from her ancient League of Rain
— One clerk (who only gave us mists)
And seven Anti-Socialists:

       * * * * * * *

And one Distributist behind
Whom no one really seemed to mind.
          (probably 1920s)[1]

A HAPPY XMAS

This Infant used to howl and yell
Because he was extremely well.
In bursting health, though very small,
And could not Convalesce at all.

He ate the soap and smelt the drains;
He threw himself in front of trains;

---

[1] Written beneath a large (ca. 15" x 9½") pencil drawing of the procession of guests, with G. K. C. at the end of the line.

He swallowed nails, that he might come
Into the Convalescent Home.

At length he found a way to win
His purpose; for they put him in
The Mentally Defective Ward
Along with Your Obedient Bard.
(1930)

A HAPPY XMAS

Upon me and my mackintosh
    Descend the roaring rains
Myself has long been washed away
    Me mackintosh remains.
(1910–20)

THE HYMN OF THE I.D.K.

The Poet
celebrates the
Secretary.

By the old Bath Road Pagoda
    Looking Eastward for her tea
There's a Secretary sitting
    And she don't think much of me.
But she thinks of my subscription
    And from time to time will say,
"Are you coming, harmless creature, coming to the
        I.D.K.?
Coming to the I.D.K.
You might find a word to say,
    Make a timid observation to the listening I.D.K."
When the weary ages say—
    "Who shall light us on our way?"
In a voice resembling thunder I reply "The I.D.K."

The   The Bar, the Stage, the Pulpit,
Avocations   The Battlefield, the Bank,
of the I.D.K.   Have remarked a certain Manner
                       Adorn a certain rank
                   When in streaming tears they ask us
                   We gravely smile and say
                   "This you only gain by coming, coming to the
                       I.D.K."
                   You may know the I.D.K.
                      We have all a certain way
                   An undetermined Something which is the I.D.K.
                   When the weary ages say—
                      "Who shall light us on our way?"
                   In a voice resembling thunder I reply "The I.D.K."

The Debates of   Then some are nuts on Karma
the I.D.K.   And some go blind on Monks
                   And Manners simply stunning
                       And as for Morals—chunks.
                   For there one member hammers
                       And there another Smiles
                   And when I get on ethics—
                       I wreck the town for miles.
                   Mighty Caesar turned to clay—
                       Interests the I.D.K.
                   And other passing aspects of the topics of the day.
                   When the weary ages say—
                      "Who shall light us on our way?"
                   In a voice resembling thunder I reply "The I.D.K."

An Idyll   The furniture is flying—
                       I'm lying in the grate
                   And in the blind confusion
                       I find my necktie straight.
                   Just look behind the sofa
                       There's two Agnostics missed
                   By raking round the fender you'll find a pessimist

O ye toiling sons of clay—
  Kings and Lords whom you obey
Labour long, O labour truly to be like the I.D.K.
When the weary ages say—
  "Who shall light us on our way?"
In a voice resembling thunder I reply "The I.D.K.".

The Poet does   Ship me somewheres west by Chiswick
a Yearn.   Where the low is like the high
Where there ain't no Mrs. Grundy
  And a man can wear a tie
For I'm learning here in Fleet Street
  What the hoary exile tells
If you've heard the Park a-calling you won't never heed
      naught else
No you won't heed nothing else.
But the tales Miss Frances tells
And the theories and the trumpings and the brand-new
               heavens and hells
When the clamourous nations say
  "Who shall guide us on our way?"
In a voice resembling thunder I observe "The I.D.K."
                (mid to late 1890s)[1]

AN IDYLL

Tea is made; the red fogs shut round the house but the gas burns.
I wish I had at this moment round the table
A company of fine people.
Two of them are at Oxford and one in Scotland and two at other
  places.
But I wish they would all walk in now, for the tea is made.
                (mid 1890s)

---

[1] To this, G. K. C. appended a note: "(Will write a better one when I have some leisure. Don't show this to anyone with whom I have a character to lose.)"

IN THE LYME-LIGHT

In the steep street where the sea hangs over the houses,
Hangs with all its fishes like a sky with all its birds,
Are the friends I see and the friend who is far asunder
    To whom I send only words.

Late I have found you, said the great Augustine—
Friends of my Faith, you are young with its ancient youth,
But not too late, for I know though I die, these also
    Go on and die in the truth.

For I know the steep street goes down, but not to destruction
For it fares though it falls, though it dips out of sight, even then
To a living sky like a sea. . . . Good luck to your fishing
    O fishers of men.

Crude. Obscure. Obviously written without stopping to think.
Exactly. But (as I have the honour to remark) quite true.

Finally the conception has been set and arranged so as to be suitable for
Community Singing. The effect is Choral rather than Lyrical and
arranged for thirty thousand voices.

    O where and O where
    Is the quite essential Clare
Dr. Wingrave and the Antiquaries digging everywhere
    Declare they do not know—but O how horribly they care!
They dug up a book of verses and a doubtful tuft of hair
And a soaking pair of shoes that are considered Very Rare
    But O where and O where
    Is all the rest of Clare?
Her remains, if they remain after this terrible affair,
Whatever their defects, we should prefer them as they were:
With the poppy-coloured clothing and the absent-minded air.
We found a London typist with a wild distracted stare
Who, though wrecked by business methods, was enabled to declare
That she lived at Berkeley Something and it wasn't Berkeley
    Square—

So—O Clare and O Clare
I am forced to send it there

(and so on. It has seventy-eight verses in all).

Yours always
G. K.C.

(1920s?)

INSCRIBED IN A COPY OF
"GREYBEARDS AT PLAY"

When all the follies here provoke
  Your old satiric lash,
When the anatomy I draw
  Enrages Dr. Nash,

Yet there is one within your house
  Who here the sense may see
A little—ere she grows too old,
  And far too wise for me.[1]

INSCRIBED IN A COPY OF
"THE RETURN OF DON QUIXOTE"

(For Clare Nicholl)

"All that the thin Knight's thinner shadow here,
Shows forth—the Spaniard's steed, the Spaniard's spear—
Blend in your blazoned sign, dear Unicorn,
Summed up and symbolised in Horse and Horn
Since, white and wild, from the first legends flamed
One lance unbroken and one steed untamed.

Go: teach the doubters what they doubt — that we,
Who smell the wind beyond the world, are free;
That ours, not theirs, the light on lands untrod,
The galloping on the mountain, and the God;
That ours, not theirs, the thunderclap and the cry
When things too huge for fable hurtle by;
That doubts chain up the spirit, and dogmas free;
And, throned on marble, men see Liberty.

Say that the Knight called Errant did not err
To loose wild Honour and to follow her —
Say this: and then with all his friends be free
To burn this book with Quixote's library."

INSCRIPTION FOR RHODA BASTABLE

The book in which these figures grin
Will afterwards be written in
By Kings and Deans & Dukes & Earls
And worthy boys & wicked girls.

Here Mr Hugh Price Hughes ere long
Will write some rattling comic song
And the good ruler of Potsdam
Will write a funny telegram.

But turn at least to page nineteen
Where Li Hung Chang has written in
Chinese as pure as a pagoda
Exactly what I think of Rhoda.
                    (1900–1901)

[1] Dr. Nash married the sister of G. K. C.'s friend, Lucian Oldershaw. This was written during a visit to them and their baby daughter.

INSCRIBED IN A COPY OF
"THE BALLAD OF THE WHITE HORSE"

In this book the pretty pictures[1]
May incur your righteous strictures,
Only do not read the verse
Because you'll find it even worse.

AN INVITATION DECLINED

Prince, Yorkshire holds me now
By Yorkshire hams I'm fed
I can't assist your row
I send ballades instead.

                 (early 1920s)

THE J.D.C.

Eat the crust and drink the water, use the simple homely store,
Cup and crust refused to no man passing by Pagani's door.
None are turned back by Pagani: glance around the table here
You will see that even the basest are admitted to his cheer
All the lowliest, all the meanest of the lower class are there
Every poor man has a seat there and the bankrupt has the Chair
Let us sup with poor Pagani, fall into his simple ways
Bring me five bottles of claret; I would dream of other days.

All the old times come around us, we are girt with ancient rule
Children dancing on the green grass at that simple village school.

---

[1] The only illustrated edition of the Ballad, with small vignette illustrations by Robert Austin, was issued in 1928. The implied jest at the pictures may suggest that G. K. C. had himself drawn in a copy — as was his habit. This verse was published in "C.T.S. Notes", Aug. 1961.

Masters haunt us: round our spirits there is circling, is there not?
All the infant glee of Lupton, all the rude strength of La Motte,
Yes, we hear their antique virtues echoing from forgotten domes,
Manly modesty of Cornish, baby merriment of Holmes
Is it Mr Walker yonder, hoary, just about to roar?
No, on closer observation, it is Waldo d'Avigdor
Is that Mr Barlow Gardiner — no, the features melt and alter
I'm deceived by a resemblance, it is Frederick Gurney Salter.

Are we really growing smaller, are we drinking tea again
No alas, let us put up with claret, burgundy, champagne,
Tell me, are there Eton collars sprouting above all our coats
On my hat-band are there growing three extraordinary goats,
Am I once again discussing all the old entanglements
Education, socialism, papers, pigs, advertisements
Whether fox-hunting is Christian, whether magazines do harm
Whether Kipling has a mission, whether Maidlow has a charm
Whether it is quite in order if a fluent speech and able
Is pronounced by Mr Fordham from beneath the dining table.
Whether Mr Langdon-Davies can be technically right
In addressing the Debaters with a head obscured from sight
What is our true constitution, if a club we really be
Or a mission, or a madhouse or a chartered Company.

Gone are all these ancient questions; o'er the presidential claim
Rise a newer race of tyrants whom I do not dare to name
Yea a newer race of rulers, higher stronger and more fair
Before whom your Chairman trembles, bows and quakes and combs his
    hair
Long I ruled you, o my children, guided every infant prayer.
Kept you in complete obedience, let no whisper stir the air,
Now I yield to newer rulers, ruling [over new][1] estates
Crash the thunder, blare the portent, for your Chairman abdicates.

                                                    (ca. 1895)

[1] In the penultimate line, the two words enclosed in brackets are doubtful.

THE J.D.C.: A CELEBRATION

Water has flowed under the bridges
(or over bridges in this weather)
And storm and war and peace have passed
Since all our brethren met together
If after us the Deluge come
Or London Bridge be broken down
What many waters cannot quench
Our driest summer could not drown

The skies may fall; the expert eye
May see St. Paul's Cathedral lean
Or doubt whether the tile that's loose
Is on the dome or on the dean;
A wiser dean the sainted name
Saved for his school; and started thus
That ever rising scale of fame
That mounts from Milton up to Us.

But here awhile we lay aside
The names by which men know us better
And then when we were little boys
And men of letters by the letter;
And Mr S. and Mr O.
And Mr C. who sings this lay
Always including Mr B.
But not including Mr A.

Though no such princely names are ours,
Trust magnates or cat burglars even,
Nor "Mr B." conceal the large
Financial grasp of Mr Bevan;
Though none of us has made a corner
In which to buy a coronet;
Lord Top of Meadow and Lord Fernley
Are saving for a peerage yet.

At least we stand unstained by knighthood
Save for one unsullied by an O.B.E.
The world found none of us ignoble
Enough for its nobility;
But not unworthy work and workers
Have shared with these, the earliest ones,
A past in whose eternal mirror
Their selves are younger than their sons.

Where an immortal Mr F.
Hurls with a strength that cannot fail
Through howls that never shall be silent
A bun that never shall be stale;
The buns are stale, but not the thrower,
The tea but not the talk is cold;
And we might still, with none to aid us,
Be Junior to a world grown old.

I know not if they err who say
The rising generation rises
More languidly, to meet with doubt
The old unvarying surprises;
But here at least might we debate
And each be riotously right
And if the young are old today
Then let the old be young tonight.

(mid 1920s)

J.D.C.: CHAUNT OF THE
JUNIOR DEBATING CLUB

Come pass the cup, Debaters all
And fill the tea-pot high
The hissing of that holy wind
Makes better song than I.

Let others joy in maddening wine
   Where words and blows go free,
But we in hours of honest talk
   And draughts of honest tea.

Though Evans laughed a heavy laugh,
   And Crocker groans a groan.
Though Berne may adopt a foolish smile
   Peculiarly his own
Though Watson may explain his views
   In sudden howls and neighs,
Do we not feel the scorn of some
   More honour than their praise?

Wher'ere a thoughtful brow grows dark
   To view a thoughtless school
Wher'ere a brow has flushed to list
   The ribald and the fool
He is our comrade in the camp,
   Our brother in the fight
And welcome were he to our board
   On any Friday night.

Though scorn of all may rage without
   Among the mass who saw
An absent-minded president;
   A sombre editor.
Here in the midst there is no scorn
   But trust of friend and friend.
A strong and silent loyalty
   That worketh to an end.

We do not envy certain youths
   With sticks and cigarettes
Who fill their meek companion's ears
   With mythic racing bets.
We do not yearn for a cigar,
   Or for a dog-cart sigh.
We do not think Valetta's tone
   Particularly high.

Then pass the cup, Debaters all
  And fill the tea-pot high,
And in the joy of wild debate
  May hours like moments fly.
As critics quiet and composed
  As brothers kind and free,
Join hand in hand the tea-pot round,
  Joy to the J.D.C.

(1891-93)

J.D.C.: ODE

On the Second Annual Assembly of the Junior Debating Club
1900

When we last met at Pinoli's winter roared with
                    snow and sleet,
Tempests tore the golden orchards all the way down
                    Wardour Street.
Scarcely the last purple heather could to the
                    Criterion cling.
But today the place is shifted: and we meet here
                    in the Spring.

In the Spring a brighter eyeglass shines in Mr Digby's
                    eye,
In the Spring the Secretary gets himself a wilder
                    tie,
In the Spring a livelier polish changes on the burnished
                    Sams,
In the Spring the Dinner calls him and the member comes
                    and crams.

Think not this materialistic: to the philosophic
                    one,
Food itself is full of meaning: there are lessons in
                    a bun,

There are truths hid in a biscuit: and we feel in hours
                   like these,
Lyric passion in the gravy: ancient pathos in
                 the cheese.

Life was ours, we lived it, brothers, life the common
                 and divine,
We have faced the direst perils: we have brought
              them here to dine.
We have seen that we have conquered: high above
              this festive hall
Seen the sombre ghost of Maidlow wave his pardon
             o'er us all.

Yes: tonight our peace be on him: on all ancient things: on them
All the Members, all the speeches less remarkably ad rem
Write but this: our boyhood's follies did not fight us
              nor restrain
Whatsoe'er we said or said not, we arose and we remain.
                 (1900)

THE J.D.C.: A REUNION

We meet again: but all around
   Are changes painful Very—
The meal has many courses now,
   The tea is turned to sherry.
But though the milk to wine be changed
   No tears, no oaths I find
To all these changes you appear
   Courageously resigned.

But since, like brigands in carouse
   We quaffed the maddening tea,
Since first we ate the ardent bun
   And flung the muffin free,

We have not changed: and time may show
   Some of our staid five-coursers
As good at breaking wine glasses
   As once at smashing saucers.

Recorded all: our maiden aunts
               (. . . unfinished)

A RETURN TO ST. PAUL'S SCHOOL[1]

On to the old haunts
Hied I to Hammersmith
Hied unto Valhal
Where over Asas all
Ruleth and roareth
All-father Walker
Come from the Cow.

High in the hall he stood,
Vincent the Volsung,
Prince of the Paulines
Mighty in war
Gave me my place there,
Where in the passage
Gathered Debaters all
Greeting the friends:

[1] This is an unfinished verse, written in the style of an early Scandinavian saga, celebrating a reunion at St. Paul's School, attended by G. K. C. and many of his school-fellows. It has never been published and was clearly intended as a private joke.

It was written in pencil by G. K. C., in two columns, on the blank fly-leaves of a copy of James Sime's 'Life of Goethe' which was given to Chesterton by his father on April 6, 1889, and is now in the possession of the Chesterton Study Centre at Bedford, England. Many of the names in the verse were familiar to me, but for others I had to call on the expertise of Mr. Christopher Deane, the present Archivist and Librarian at St. Paul's School. In deciphering the scrawl I had great help from Professor Denis Conlon. There remains one missing word, indicated by brackets, where G. K. C. obliterated a word and gave no replacement. A glossary follows the poem.

Sams and Vernède there,
Bertram and d'Avigdor,
Lucian the swift one,
Lawrence the wise one,
Bentley the laugh-maker,
Mighty of heart.
Only abode not
Maurice the chess-player,
Youngest of Asas,
Far from the field.

Broad on the benches
Gathered Debaters all
Girded and grave.
Gathered before them
Chumleigh's and Gardeners,
Gathered behind them
Bailies and Magnuses.
Far in the back row
Harris and Ogilvie
Laughed as the elf-folk,
Laughed as the storm-[giants],
Thought not at all.

Spake in his turn then
Chumleigh the [cheerful],
Spake in his order
[   ] the priest man,
Till in his longing
Sewell the scribe spake:
"Long is the speech-making,
Long is the minute-book.
Back to banquet,
Back to the brown mead,
Warriors all".

Heartily shouted then

Asas in Valhal;
Throng through the hall-gates
Broke to the banquet hall,
Girdled the board.
Merrily laughed they
Quaffing the brown mead.
Burden of Bewsher
Rose with his harp then,
Cyril the sagaman
Cunning in concerts,
Sang he his song.

Song upon song then
Chanted the scald-folk,
Songs of the broodmares
Ending in Doodah.

Songs of the beaked ships,
Songs of the swan's bath
Merrily sang I,
Quaffing the brown mead,
Talking with Magnus,
Talking of Leonard,
Brother of Trolls.

Back from the banquet
Back to the battlefield.
              (ca. 1902)

GLOSSARY TO "ST PAUL'S SCHOOL"

1. *Hammersmith*. London borough, on the Thames and adjoining Kensington. The school was situated here until it moved to Barnes.

2. *Asas*. The gods. (From the glossary of Bishop Percy's translation of *Northern Antiquities*. The school library copy was published in 1890.)

3. *Walker*. The High Master in G. K.'s time, Dr. F. W. Walker.

4. *The Cow*. The Red Cow. A public house opposite the School.

5. *Debaters all*. Members of the Junior Debating Club.

6. *Sams*. Hubert A. Sams (later 'Sir' and author of *Pauline and Old Pauline*).

7. *Vernède*. Robert Vernède. Later a poet. He was killed in the 1914–18 war.

8. *Bertram*. F. G. L. (Later Deputy-Director of Civil Aviation, the Air Ministry).

9. *d'Avigdor*. There were two d'Avigdor brothers, Digby and Waldo, both close friends of G. K. C.

10. *Lucian* Oldershaw. Founder and organiser of the J.D.C., later to be G. K.'s brother-in-law.

11. *Lawrence* Solomon. One of the two brothers in the J.D.C. Later Professor of History at London University.

12. *Bentley*, Edmund Clerihew. Inventor of the "Clerihew", and G. K.'s closest friend at St. Paul's. Later wrote detective stories, etc.

13. *Maurice* Solomon, brother to Lawrence.

14. *Chumleighs*. Mr. R. F. Colmeley. Master in charge of the new Senior Form created specially for Bentley, Oldershaw, and a few others. He was very well liked.

15. *Gardiners*. The Rev. Robert Barlow Gardiner, from 1875 Fourth Master of the School. Later became Surmaster (Deputy Head).

16. *Bailies*. Cyril Bailey, school Captain, 1888–90.

17. *Magnuses*. Laurie Magnus, later author and journalist.

18. *Ogilvie*, Harry Hyacinth. Later became Captain of the school's 1st XV (Rugby football) and 1st XI (Cricket).

19. *Sewell*, Archibald Hankey. Another pupil.

20. *The brown mead*. Tea.

21. *Bewsher*, Fred. W., the school Bursar.

THE J.D.C. UNHUNG[1]

Friends, when I think of how we talked and bored and
                                        bawled and banged
I often really wonder why we none of us are hanged

[1] A lady connected by marriage with the J.D.C. observed that it was very remarkable that no member of that society had failed: asked whether she meant that none of them had been hanged, she replied that that, after all, was something.

None really hanged. Attempts, perhaps, some efforts and no more
I knew a Mental Healer who came to the side door
Who said I fired a shot at him and hit; which is absurd.
Police enquiries, too, were made at Fernley, I have heard
When the Chinese Mandarin swotting hard with Oldershaw and staff
Performed the Hara-Kiri to make the children laugh.
And Fordham had a narrow squeak; when reeling from the Troc
He lost his way and lost his wig and strayed into the dock.
Where in ecstatic slumber through the trial he remained
Till half-way through the summing up, the error was explained
And Salter knifed a policeman; but the wound, alas, has healed.
A person selling Burberys who came to Beaconsfield
Saved Lawrence from the gallows by the speed at which he ran.
And Maurice did give orders to electrocute a man:
Only a new assistant, whose diction was at fault,
Electroplated him instead: a technical assault.
And Waldo had a bright idea to put us at our ease
"Be insured against the Gallows and then murder whom you please."
His clients were but half convinced, however he harangued,
They guessed some fallacy; and still were hanged if they'd be hanged.
Beside the paper mill and moat, are publishers regaled?
Moonlight. A publisher. The pond. But better thoughts prevailed.
I know not how in foreign lands fate missed our wandering lambs
How oft the lucky rope has broke for Digby or for Sams.
How Bertram dodged his warders; or if ten times or again
"Reprieve for Langdon-Davies!" rang thundering through the plain
Bentley, who murders every night, escaping every time
He has explained his method in a recent work on crime.
Friends; we are fallen on evil days; wild years are closing in
The awful years when men can die for virtue, not for sin
As in such bloody splendour set the sun of the Gironde
Yet men could still look over it and see a star beyond.
Those young; learned and unnamed, like us in many ways.
Who perished at the palisades, singing the Marseillaise
Well, friends, if you and I should come to dangle on a string
Unless the Sec. has lost the notes, we shall have songs to sing.

(ca. 1900–1902)

JOAN

Steadfast, upstanding, magnanimous Joan
Wed a Brigand to whom the Albanian Throne
Descended by Will:
And she got it: but still
Retained in addition a will of her own.

LAWRENCE [SOLOMON][1]

On Hell's high gates to thunder,
  Befallen to crown and kiss
To strengthen the sick one: this is good,
  But the glory of good is this.

When over the stern soul-battle
  Breaks, like a music-bar
The name of him we need not save,
  Whose soul is strong as a star.

Who goeth his own way ever,
  Whose peace on earth shall abide,
Whose heart is straight and shining and true,
  As the steel sword at the side.

Blessed is he, yea blessed
  Happy is he to be born,
Who has not gone in the gates of sin,
  Or sat in the seat of scorn.

Whose face was bent to the furrow,
  Who ate not the fruit where it hung
On the twilight tree and did not know
  The best and the worst too young.

---

[1] G. K. C. titled it simply 'Lawrence'.

This is the worker's blessing
  The world's first viols played
A flutter of robes and faces
  A heaven and earth new made.

I will sing of the great archangel,
  And the dead Christ hung on tree,
But the great strange song of the second youth,
  Is a song too high for me.

(mid 1890s)

LINES BY THE LATE LORD TENNYSON

(On Miss Spencer being transferred with her typewriter from
the Study to the Dining Room)

Of old sat Freda on the heights
The letters strewn about her feet.
She watched from far the local sights,
She saw the neighbours meet.

She murmured much of fools and worms,
Self-censured in her Christian mind,
And fragments of abusive terms
Came rolling on the wind.

Yet came she down when gongs had pealed
In friendship to our feasting place,
Removed her goggles and revealed
The fulness of her face.

(ca. early 1920s)

LINES INSCRIBED FOR
MR. THOMAS HUTCHINSON

If we two clung to a sad sea-crag
Should we not hail each other's face?
Do we not cling to a flying star
That cleaves the idle seas of space?

If we two dwelt by a village green
Should we not boast it's stream and spire?
Shall we not vaunt the citied earth
Crowned with the stolen star of fire?

If we two danced in a single dance
Should we not touch with hands or feet?
But we in God's red carnival
May dance and die and never meet

But in the grand dark day that comes
When we shall fight for all things fair
Fly the green leaf of earth: and I
Shall know you by the badge you wear.
                              (Oct. 1901)[1]

LINES ON A CRICKET MATCH

How was my spirit torn in twain
When on the field arrayed
My neighbours with my comrades strove,
My town against my trade.

And are the penmen players all?
Did Shakespeare shine at cricket?
And in what hour did Bunyan wait
Like Christian at the wicket?

[1] The poem was reproduced in facsimile holograph in the catalogue of the Chesterton Exhibition at Wahlert Memorial Library, Loras College, Dubuque, Iowa, in 1974.

When did domestic Dickens stand
A fireside willow wielding?
And playing cricket—on the hearth,
And where was Henry Fielding?

Is Kipling, as a flannelled fool,
Or Belloc bowling guns,
The name that he who runs may read
By reading of his runs?

Come all; our land hath laurels too,
While round our beech-tree grows
The shamrock of the exiled Burke
Or Waller's lovely rose.

Who ever win or lose, our flags
Of fun and honour furled,
The glory of the game shall stand
Stonewalling all the world,

While those historic types survive
For England to admire,
Twin pillars of our storied past,
The Burgess and the Squire.

(1922–23)[1]

LINES TO A YOUNG LADY BORN
BEFORE APRIL FOOLS' DAY

When March went out a lion or a lamb,
And you came in, a lamb or lioness
(For which you were, when in the cot or pram,
I do not know although I partly guess),

[1] The match, played at Beaconsfield, was between the village of Knotty Green and The In-
valids—a team of authors, captained by G. K. C.'s friend J. C. Squire.

Knotty Green: 1st innings 28. 2nd innings 21.

The Invalids: 1st innings 61.

They gave you that strong name, with other mercies,
Especially no doubt to suit my verses.

My verses, which were then, as you are, young,
More numerous than now and even worse,
But then were things less glorious to be sung,
And several things more damnable to curse;
And so in rhymes I now find crude and scrappy,
I kicked the pessimists to make them happy.

Thank Heaven you missed, and men need tell you not,
What tosh was talked when you were very small,
When Decadence, which is the French for Rot,
Turned life to an irreverent funeral.
The leaden night of that long peace is dead
And we have seen the daybreak . . . very red.

England, unbroken of the evil kings,
Whose line is breaking in the breaking snow,
Open your ways to large and laughing things
And the young peace be with you where you go,
And far on that new spire, new sprung in space
St Michael of the morning give you grace.

The Spring is with us, whose new-made election
Leaps in the beeches that baptised our Field,
Walks in our woods the ways of resurrection
In a new world washed in the wind and healed;
Young as your ancient name, more strong than death,
Strength of the House of God, Elizabeth.

(March 1916)[1]

---

[1] Written for Frederica Elizabeth Spencer.

LINES TO THE AIR OF "GODOLPHIN HORNE"[1]

Godolphin School was large and cool;
It thought the human race a fool:
And bade its Secretary share
This distant and distinguished air:
And oh, the Girl was deathly proud,
She passed from where, in clotted crowd,
Crouch in the town of the Four Ends
The hovel of her humble friends.
Alas, that such a stately smirk
Should follow on a change of work!
But such was Frederica's case.
. . . Just then, they sought to fill her place
And the forsaken Journalist
Sat mute and goggled at the list:

He runs through a list of names of possible new secretaries with appropriate and disparaging comments, and continues:

Stay, did not she whose fancies soar
On Sarum's spires, on ours no more,
Scarce turning from her high intent,
Cast us a Cousin ere she went?
A Churchman, training now on spec . . .
Come, question the Godolphin Sec!

But scarcely had he said the word
Than murmurs of dissent were heard.
Her Sister found the time to write,
"Would you describe the girl as Bright?"

And even She that was our own
Remarked in her sub-acid tone,
"I doubt if *she* is what you need."
The circle murmured, but agreed;

---

[1] Written for Frederica (Freda) Elizabeth Spencer. See Maisie Ward, *Return to Chesterton* (New York: Sheed and Ward, 1952), pp. 171-72.

The Journalist said, "Well, well, well—
No doubt you're right . . . one cannot tell.
Damn it!" he ended, with a bawl,
"I won't have any Sec at all."

And now a wearier power he wields
As Butler at the Inglefields.

(early 1920s)

LINES WRITTEN IN A PICTURE BOOK

This is the sort of book we like
  (For you and I are very small),
With pictures stuck in anyhow,
  And hardly any words at all.

You will not understand a word
  Of all the words, including mine;
Never you trouble; you can see,
  And all directness is divine—

Stand up and keep your childishness:
  Read all the pedants' screeds and strictures;
But don't believe in anything
  That can't be told in coloured pictures.

(1906–12)

A LIST

I know a friend, very strong and good. He is the best friend in the
  world.
I know another friend, subtle and sensitive. He is certainly the
  best friend on earth.

I know another friend: very quiet and shrewd, there is no friend
so good as he.
I know another friend, who is enigmatical and reluctant, he is the
best of all.
I know yet another: who is polished and eager, he is far better than
the rest.
I know another, who is young and very quick, he is the most beloved
of all friends.
I know a lot more and they are all like that.

Amen.
(early 1890s)[1]

LYME REGIS SED SINE REGINA

When last I went riding
  Through Lyme of the King
I heard the town's Crier
  I heard the bell ring.
But not for the lost King
  That's over the water
It wailed through the West
  For a Queen and a daughter

Ah woe for the townland
  That wails for its queen
For the Unicorn fled
  Where Fame's garland is green.
For in quest of the Laurel
  She went up to town
— Ah, if I were the Lion
  We'd fight for the Crown.

(1920–31)

[1] Written about the J.D.C.

MADGE

Blue garb fluttering gustily,
Brown hair's eddy adrift,
Thou God's gayest gift,
All folk laugh with thee lustily.

Proud little face and clear
While these merrily love thee
Let me bend, and above thee
Whisper my secret — fear.

Lo, I may not make light of thee
Little child as thou art
I am humbled of heart
Stricken still at the sight of thee.

Something challenges, checks
What would fondle or flout thee
Burning and round about thee
The mystical circle of sex.

Mythical immemorial,
Starry, secret of plan,
Woman: and shall a man
Burn his hands in the aureole.

She as low as a star
Straight with an elfin slenderness
These with a taunting tenderness
I, afraid and afar.

(mid 1890s?)

MASTERMAN AND CHESTERTON

Lo: Masterman and Chesterton
  This happy picture shows.
The former is the one whose eye
With a fine pathos glows.
  I am the one with auburn hair
And the finely chiselled nose.

Thus between heaven and earth they passed
  Over the Kentish plain.
The earth was noble English mud,
The heavens were mostly rain.
  If you should see their faces, you
Will know them both again.

                   (1905?)

A MIDSUMMER NIGHT'S DREAM

Midsummer Night, whose dream we knew
Is gone with that great Summer's gleams
And better words could better show
Midwinter has its nights and dreams;

Memories of many friends could bring
Not I alone, the clumsiest,
But better mummers of our masque
  This Tribute to the best.

We never trod that stage again
On narrower boards of Burnham Hall,
But livelier steps the rest might head
To a more punctual bugle-call;
And even more resplendant Moon
Might lead a more obedient Dog
And someone else could act the Duke
And I would act the Log.

But one above us, poised secure
A final act unschooled by time.
The ruler of the elfin stage
The genius of the pantomime,
The winter plays are off; nor yet
Shall Robin Hood exalt his horn
Not yet out of the wood—nor in it.
The Babes are Babes unborn.

Yet, as you bear with lenient laughter,
The clowns that to your portals come,
The waits who will not wait for Christmas,
The Mummers who are far from mum;
Take with such tolerance of these rhymes
Our love, that equals art with art;
You, who in better things than mumming,
Can choose the better part.
     (Christmas, 1921)

MILDRED

Pale face pathetically lit with laughter,
Pure heart and glad, since once my song began,
Man has known, thee pass him but thereafter
Felt his blood stir and knew himself a man.

God, when the world seemed weary and neglected,
Set thee, a silver trumpet, to his lip:
Blew, and we rose a chivalry erected,
Shield on the shoulder, sword hilt on the hip.

Queen of high hearts, I could not love or crave thee,
Kind face and clear, I would not if I could:
Thine is to shine as given of him that gave thee
God's sun that gilds the evil and the good.

Pale face and frank, of its own mirth bewild'red
Love is a new thing: seek it not awhile;
One thing we crave, and of thy mercy, Mildred
Smile on us all still: be thyself and smile.

Nay, what are we, we pass from thee uncounted,
Yet will we hold heads high and gratefully
What of all stars that only God has counted,
He set our feet upon a star with thee.

                                        (early 1890s?)

NAMESAKE

Mary of Holyrood may smile indeed,
    Knowing what grim historic shade it shocks
To see wit, laughter and the Popish creed,
    Cluster and sparkle in the name of Knox.

                            (1925)

ON LUCIAN OLDERSHAW, WHO
INTRODUCED HIM TO FRANCES

For well Thou knowest, O God most wise,
How good on earth was his gift to me.
Shall this be a little thing in thine eyes
That is greater in mine than the whole great sea?
                              (in a letter to Frances,
                                    March 1901)

OUR LADY OF WAIN

(To Mildred Wain)

Low eyelids that cloud like a prison
Grey eyes full of shimmer and shower
And the tremulous mouth and the risen
Pale face like a luminous flower;
Pale face of its own mirth bewild'rèd
What shall fix it at last, what remain?
O anything but sombre Miss Mildred,
                    Our Lady of Wain.

Seven sleepers the Greeks gave their city
But thy sister is sleeping for seven
Thou would'st wake us from hell, or from Kitty
(And she will not haunt us in heaven)
For the songs of thy singing have sounded
Since God bade thy life's song begin
And thine excellent father abounded
                    To furnish the tin.

Dost thou dream in a respite of slumber
In a pause in the rush of thy life
Of Grove House (which is not on the Humber)
Of the room where the dancers were rife

When the conduct of Crocher made fervent
Our friends who were mild in the man,
As one cursed him, his host, and thy servant
        Our Lady of Wain.

They passed and their hatpegs were taken
Those sowers of natural oats
They passed, and without being shaken
Leaving singular things in our coats,
Mildred laughs, poking close and relentless
Her sister, to keep her awake
With a piece in her fingers of scentless
        And edible cake.

Out of Scarboro', heavily laden
Her brothers bring, burdened in youth
A lady, a mortal, a maiden
A Queen over goodness and truth;
She is calm and her raiment is mellow
Dark hair, as the night in a skein,
And yours is decidedly yellow
        Our Lady of Wain.
       (Schoolboy poem,
       according to D. E. C. 1890-91)

OUR SHIP COMES HOME!

Heed not the darkness and the rain
   There grows a passion in the gloam,
There speeds a purpose through the seas—
   Our ship comes home! Our ship comes home.

Within my living soul I know
   Our ship shall save us once for all,
But should it split on rock or reef
   Besieged with breakers: let it fall.

As fits the ship of a man's soul,
  Heaped with the slain and wrecked and red,
But flying flags at every spar
  And on the prow a woman's head.

(1904)[1]

THE PLAYER'S CLUB

Far from the Player's Club but not in play
For many months I have wandered far away
As one man in his time plays many parts
(Bacon) I masquerade in many arts
Disguised as a Reviewer push the pen
And learnedly correct more learned men
Make up just like a literary man
And look as like a poet as I can
Carrying the deception to the point, I fear
Of even writing verse, as I do here

I missed your brightest shows; I cannot tell
How Mr King got on as Ariel
It has not been my privilege to hear
Holloway's Cobweb, Beecroft as King Lear
Or learnt how Maurice Solomon, they say
Romped through Goliath in the Scripture play
But I have not forgotten; and to you
For all your works I yield my thanks anew
You whom, whatever part your fancy plays
We need not judge and we are safe to praise.

(Lines sent to Mrs Halford,
Christmas, 1926)

---

[1] Written for Mrs. Saxon Mills, who typed (refusing payment) *The Napoleon of Notting Hill.* The poem was pasted inside a copy of the book, and the above is incomplete, being the final three verses only.

RHYME FOR A PARLOUR GAME

Written for Clare Nicholl, this is a clue to the "O'Nicholl rubies".
It contains three clues to her name.

To whom in summer long ago
Came the donor with the doe
Comes a doom more like my own
Red as blood and hard as stone;
Yet shall she adorned be
Whose sister's name is Poverty,
Dowering, for those who understand,
A province in my native land.

(1920s?)

SOME REVELATIONS OF JOURNALISM

It is as well that you should know
The truth about that empty show,
That vast and histrionic ruse,
Which calls itself 'the Daily News'.

'Tis a dark truth, if truth be said.
We tried at every other trade
And we have found (with joy I sing)
That we were bad at everything.
When upon any work our wit
We tried, we made a mess of it.
When your Papa, exultant, sailed
A pirate, he distinctly failed.
When Wilson's dancing seemed to pall
Upon the Empire Music Hall,
When Spender found, and also Nash
That were not meant to haberdash,

When simple Bentley first began
To see he was no sandwich man,
When I myself perceived that I
Must work, or I should shortly die,
We all abandoned worldly strife,
And chose this simple mode of life.

One secret more: one person writes
All the whole paper all the nights.
He writes on war and war's redress,
On literature and ladies' dress.
Upon the commerce of Hong Kong
He is particularly strong.
His beard is long, his gestures free,
And his initials G. K. C.

                              (ca. 1905)[1]

SONG OF THE CONSPIRATORS

What do you know about people who go about
Raiding a village like tramps?
Storming the shops for improbable objects,
Buying superflous stamps:
Shouting for anything, mud or mixed pickles,
Stroking a nigerous cat:
What do you know of the way of the Nicholls?
What do you know about that?

What do you know about people who blow about
Lyme, and along the parade,
Where in the solemn sarcophagous shelter
In its funeral shade

---

[1] Written in the autograph album of a daughter of A. G. Gardiner, editor of *The Daily News*. The poem is printed in *Fleet Street Radical*, a biography of Gardiner by Stephen E. Koss (Lane, 1973).

Poor old G. K. (who is perfectly chronic)
Talks through his Horrible Hat—
Under the gloom of the columns Ionic
What do you know about that?

What do you know about what is the Show about
Destined to knock you all flat—
What do you know of . . . .[1]
What do you know about that?

(1900–1910)

A SONG OF WILD FRUIT

To D. E. C. with thanks

The Pineapple knows nothing
Of the Apple or the Pine,
The Grape-Fruit is a fruit: but not
The God's fruit of the Vine;
And Grape-nuts are not even Nuts
For the Hygienic Hut
Where the nut-crank with the nut-crackers
Is cracking his own nut.

Far in the land of Nonsense Names
These antic fruits were born,
Where men gather grapes of thistles
And the figs grow on the thorn.
And Ananias names the fruit
That Frenchmen call Ananas;
And all the Plantains are a plant,
And . . . No! We have Bananas!

(1927–35)

---

[1] "The line left blank has a series of secret symbols—quite impossible to reproduce."
— Maisie Ward, *Return to Chesterton*.

SONG TO AN OLD TUNE

(To a lady desiring communication from South Bucks)

I'll send thee ducks of Aylesbury
And casks of Burnham beer,
Coffee to rouse thee to a cry
And toffee to a cheer —
And Turkish Delight shall on thee break,
And fine French pastry rise:
And all my soul shall strive to make
More and yet more mince pies.
For these rich cakes when hunger wakes,
A hush shall fall on all,
And chocolate pudding shall arrive
And cocoa pudding pall;
And tons of pork unpacked in class
May cause some faint surprise,
But all my soul shall strive to wake
Such wonder in thine eyes.

(ca. 1917)

A STANDING INVITATION

Remember, when the nurses lose you,
    And you have passed from Homes to Home,
That all roads lead to Overroads,
    And only some of them to Rome.

Come to our beechen field, grown famous,
    For putting people on their legs,
Not made of moonshine and of egg-shells,
    But made of sunshine and of eggs.

You know where Frances counts her chickens,
    And still the eggs in millions mount:
Come down and reckon, dear accountant,
    Things for which no-one can account.

You know the fish of this aquarium,
    A Carp that waves a friendly fin,
A Winkle that's of Scotch extraction
    And not extracted with a pin.[1]

May to the may-tree comes in glory,
    Sun to the sun-flowers where they flame,
And Rhoda to the rhodadendrons,
    Purple with pride to bear her name.
                    (1914–18)

A 'THANK-YOU' FOR COMING TO TEA

To the Nicholls sisters

Saint Nicholas Patron of Nicholls
And also of Children and Thieves
(For he burgles our houses at Christmas
As every good Christian believes).

But he comes not to take but to give,
And his Nicholls are even as he:
For they bring us the Wine of their Youth in exchange
For a chemical puddle called Tea.
                    (1920s or earlier?)

[1] "Carp" was the family nickname for Frances, G. K. C.'s wife. "Winkle" was their Scotch terrier.

THE THREE CONQUISTADORS

Stanzas from a book made for Sheila Matier,
a little girl in California, 1930–31

From Mexico, where people drink
Wild wine, the brew of shame,
Came Juan to California, where
The people do the same.

        *   *   *

Quong, who (unlike your father's friend)
    Was not a Buddhist monk,
As Chinese pirate spoiled the ships
    And filled his junk with junk.

        *   *   *

But when they came to Sheila's house,
    Those wild, marauding three,
They felt her softening touch and grew
    Quite as polite as she.

Red Bison climbed to Sheila's house,
    As Goats that scale an Alp,
But though he much admired her hair
    He did not take her scalp.

And Juan, he murdered nobody
    For days and days; and Quong
Found out, with tears, that he belonged
    To Mr. Matier's tong.

'For oh,' they cried, 'we come in peace
    To walk the sunset strand
Far from that bleak but boiling sea
    That breaks on eastern land.

'That swings and sways with dizzy tides
    Since first the ocean drank
Atlantis to the dregs, and left
    A whirlpool where she sank.

'Of storms, armadas, Vikings, tars,
   That make the tides terrific.
But Sheila need not shrink from us,
   For we are all Pacific.'

                    (1930–31)

TO A CATHERINE WHEEL

Child of St. Catherine—none shall groan
If to your gain and our great loss
You turn the wheel of all the world
And heave to sight the southern cross.
Though o'er the nether pole of night
Southward the southern signals burn,
Catherine, hold tryst and keep the faith,
And wheels revolve but wheels return.

TO A POETESS

I heard a maid on a godolphin's back
Uttering such dulcet and harmonious breath
That G. K. C. grew civil at her song.
      Midsummer Night's Dream, Act II, Scene 3.

Those friends thou hast, and their adoption tried,
Grapple them to thy soul with whoops . . .
      Hamlet, Act I, Scene 3.

Dear Sappho of satiric flight—
Deem not it does your kindness wrong,
If such delay on such delight
Keeps silent him that heard your song:

And you that know our dreams undying
While all the dying days go by
Forgive me first for not replying,
And then forgive me the reply.

Nor bend that dark didactic brow,
From your scholastic seat who stoop
To our old lyre of laughter, now
Mute as the harp of Tara (whoop).
Save for some chord that whoops at night—
—Or bannered trumpets dumb and drooping,
Whoop, bugles, whoop—in echo's flight
Hear horns of elfland faintly whooping.

Forgive if effort and fatigue,
Be spent on slighter occupations
On sports like the New Witness League,
Or trifles like the League of Nations.
Whether I wrote of Art or Air,
The War, the Nation, the New Age;
Whether at Lady Stopford's Fair
I played the fool to play the sage—

None but the brave deserve the Fair,
And at the Fair I dared to tread,
Equipped with Johnson's hat and hair,
But not, I grieve to say, his head.
The part of Mrs. Thrale was thrown
(Who wed a fiddler and a brewer)
On Mrs. Commeline—though her own
Husbands were more refined—and fewer.

Though round the ladies as they stood
Crinolines kept the crowd at bay,
My whoops did more than their hoops could
To wave the shrieking world away.

No tyrant with his armed troop
Could wield my terrors or could win them.
— Alas for those that never whoop
But die with all their whooping in them!

Pray that we dream not wholly wrong
Such drivel makes the strife less dreary,
And any light and foolish song
May be a war-song for the weary.
Loans may be War-loans, and not lost,
Work may be War-work, yet not kill,
Pray then that at my dingy post
My whoop may be a war-whoop still.

(ca. 1916)[1]

TO A TOLERANT MOTHER

The greatest saint of all is she
Who tolerant of each toy
Allows her little girls to play
With this extremely rude and rough
And most untidy boy.

TO CLARE NICHOLL

Clare was the friend of Francis
Who was kind to everything
(He *liked* the cats to howl at night
He *asked* the wasps to sting)

[1] Written when G. K. C. was recovering from whooping-cough.

To vulture, viper, slug and sloth,
To skunks with smelly hair,
And even to the wretch who lost
The manuscripts of Clare.

(1920s?)

TO DOROTHY COLLINS
FROM G. K. CHESTERTON

Here you watch the Bard's Career,
Month by month and year by year,
Writing, writing, writing verse,
Worse and worse and worse and worse.

(1927)[1]

TO DOROTHY—ON HER BIRTHDAY—WITH LOVE

"So careful of the Type she seems;"
She mends what Man so foully makes:
Searching for five minute misprints
In a forest of mistakes.

If I (in form) dictated this
You will agree, at any rate,
Some things are here which you believe
And I did not dictate.

As you were better than a friend
In more than friendship we agree—
Friendship at best may be a bond:
And Truth has made us free.

---

[1] Inscribed in a copy of his *Collected Poems*.

Who enters by that Door alone,
However, dubious or afraid
For that one hour is that one Mind
For which the world was made . . .

. . . So let them blare . . . creed, rack and rod,
Torture and Torquemada's chain . . .
. . . That was the hour when souls were free
That now are friends again.

(1932)

TO E. H. AND G. M.

(With thanks for a picture of the Three Kings)

Three Kings brought gifts to Him for whom
Was found within the Inn no room
You, the two Queens, more liberal
Give us back Kings and gifts and all.

He too receives more royal things
From the two Queens than the Three Kings
In many children more, for whom
You built the Inn and found the Room.

(Christmas, 1926)[1]

---

[1] Sent to Miss Hennell and Miss Meetes, of the Childrens' Convalescent Home, in Beaconsfield.

TO EDMUND CLERIHEW BENTLEY
The dedication of *The Man Who Was Thursday*

A cloud was on the mind of men, and wailing went the weather,
Yea, a sick cloud upon the soul when we were boys together.
Science announced nonentity and art admired decay;
The world was old and ended: but you and I were gay.
Round us in antic order their crippled vices came —
Lust that had lost its laughter, fear that had lost its shame.
Like the white lock of Whistler, that lit our aimless gloom,
Men showed their own white feather as proudly as a plume.
Life was a fly that faded, and death a drone that stung;
The world was very old indeed when you and I were young.
They twisted even decent sin to shapes not to be named:
Men were ashamed of honour; but we were not ashamed.

Weak if we were and foolish, not thus we failed, not thus;
When that black Baal blocked the heavens he had no hymns from us.
Children we were — our forts of sand were even as weak as we,
High as they went we piled them up to break that bitter sea.
Fools as we were in motley, all jangling and absurd,
When all church bells were silent our cap and bells were heard.

Not all unhelped we held the fort, our tiny flags unfurled;
Some giants laboured in that cloud to lift it from the world.
I find again the book we found, I feel the hour that flings
Far out of fish-shaped Paumanok some cry of cleaner things;
And the Green Carnation withered, as in forest fires that pass,
Roared in the wind of all the world ten million leaves of grass;
Or sane and sweet and sudden as a bird sings in the rain —
Truth out of Tusitala spoke and pleasure out of pain.

Yea, cool and clear and sudden as a bird sings in the grey,
Dunedin to Samoa spoke, and darkness unto day.
But we were young; we lived to see God break their bitter
    charms,
God and the good Republic come riding back in arms:

We have seen the city of Mansoul, even as it rocked, relieved—
Blessed are they who did not see, but being blind, believed.

This is a tale of those old fears, even of those emptied hells,
And none but you shall understand the true thing that it tells—
Of what colossal gods of shame could cow men and yet crash,
Of what huge devils hid the stars, yet fell at a pistol flash.
The doubts that were so plain to chase, so dreadful to with-
stand—
Oh, who shall understand but you; yea, who shall understand?
The doubts that drove us through the night as we two talked
amain,
And day had broken on the streets e'er it broke upon the brain.
Between us, by the peace of God, such truth can now be told;
Yea, there is strength in striking root, and good in growing old.
We have found common things at last, and marriage and a
creed,
And I may safely write it now, and you may safely read.

(1908)

TO ENID THE HUNTRESS

For you, who whirled with horse and hound,
    Have left the Cat so far behind,
Would I could wind great Nimrod's horn
    Which giants burst themselves to wind.

Would I could sing, as when of old,
    High riders heard the Hunting-Song,
My tones would be sublime and swift,
    My terms would be entirely wrong.

Mine were a most misleading map
    To trace the Run o'er slope and valley
Measured by Meets that will not meet,
    And Tally-ho's that do not tally.

But if old hunting-tales be true
   And Reynard bore the name of Puss,
Turn at that word a backward glance,
   And throw a kindly thought to us.

Who sit beside an ancient fire
   And watch grey ghosts of pussies pass,
Whom fortune beckons far afield,
   But not to Beaconsfield alas . . .

With one old dog who hunts for Cats,
   As all your dogs can hunt for foxes. . . .
Stoop from the saddle—take this old
   Most infantile of Christmas Boxes.

                      (1927–30)

TO ENID, WHO ACTED THE CAT
IN PRIVATE PANTOMIME

Though cats and birds be hardly friends,
   We doubt the Maeterlinckian word
That must dishonour the White Cat,
   Even to honour the Blue Bird.

And if once more in later days
   His baseless charge the Belgian brings,
Great ghosts shall rise to vindicate
   The right of cats to look at kings.

The Lord of Carabas shall come
   In gold and ermine, silk and furs,
To tell of that immortal cat
   That wore its boots and won its spurs.

Great Whittington shall show again
   The state that London lends her Lord,
Where the great golden griffins bear
   The blazon of the cross and sword.

And hear the ancient bells anew,
    And talk and not ignobly brag
What glorious fortunes followed when
    He let the cat out of the bag.

And Gray shall leave the graves of Stoke
    To weep over a gold-fish bowl—
Cowper, who, beaming at his cat,
    Forgot the shadow on his soul.

Then shall I rise and name aloud
    The nicest cat I ever knew,
And make the fairy fancies pale
    With half a hundred tales of you:

Till Pasht upon his granite throne
    Glare with green eyes to hear the news,
Jealous; and even Puss in Boots
    Will wish that he were in your shoes.

When I shall pledge in saucers full
    Of milk, on which the kitten thrives,
Feline felicities to you
    And nine extremely prosperous lives.
                    (ca. 1925)

TO FATHER O'CONNOR

Inscribed in a copy of *The Ball and the Cross*
Published in 1910

This is a book I do not like,
Take it away to Heckmondwike,
A lurid exile, lost and sad
To punish it for being bad.
You need not take it from the shelf
(I tried to read it once myself:

The speeches jerk, the chapters sprawl,
The story makes no sense at all)
Hide it your Yorkshire moors among
Where no man speaks the English tongue.

Hail Heckmondwike! Successful spot!
Saved from the Latin's festering lot,
Where Horton and where Hocking see
The grace of Heaven, Prosperity.
Above the chimneys, hung and bowed
A pillar of most solid cloud;
To starved oppressed Italian eyes,
The place would seem a Paradise,
And many a man from Como Lake,
And many a Tyrolese would take
(If priests allowed them what they like)
Their holidays in Heckmondwike.

The Belgian with his bankrupt woes,
Who through deserted Brussels goes,
The hind that threads those ruins bare
Where Munich and where Milan were —
Hears owls and wolves howl like Gehenna
In the best quarters of Vienna,
Murmurs in tears, "Ah, how unlike
The happiness of Heckmondwike!"

In Spain the sad guitar they strike,
And, yearning, sing of Heckmondwike;
The Papal Guard leans on his pike
And dreams he is in Heckmondwike.
Peru's proud horsemen long to bike
But for one hour in Heckmondwike;
Offered a Land Bill, Pat and Mike
Cry: "Give us stones — in Heckmondwike!"
Bavarian Bier is good, belike:
But try the gin of Heckmondwike.

The Flamands drown in ditch and dyke
Their itch to be in Heckmondwike:
Rise, Freedom, with the sword to strike!
And turn the world to Heckmondwike.

Take then this book I do not like—
It may improve in Heckmondwike.

(1910)

TO FREDA SPENCER

Whither is fled the Secretary Bird?
The woods bewail her; nor on echoing trees
Like the woodpecker's tapping traceries,
The tapping of her typewriter is heard,
Spelling a doubtful word.

Haply away with some wild swain she spurs,
The gentle Palmer, he whose pen of fire
Puts to his F. E. Spencer no Esquire
As is the wont of colder publishers,
But is, tender tho' terse,
Faithfully hers.

(ca. 1916)

TO HILAIRE BELLOC

The Dedication of *The Napoleon of Notting Hill*

For every tiny town or place
God made the stars especially;
Babies look up with owlish face
And see them tangled in a tree:

You saw a moon from Sussex Downs,
  A Sussex moon, untravelled still,
I saw the moon that was the town's,
  The largest lamp on Campden Hill.

Yea, Heaven is everywhere at home,
  The big blue cap that always fits,
And so it is (be calm; they come
  To goal at last, my wandering wits),
So is it with the heroic thing;
  This shall not end for the world's end,
And though the sullen engines swing,
  Be you not much afraid, my friend.

This did not end by Nelson's urn
  Where an immortal England sits—
Nor where our tall young men in turn
  Drank death like wine at Austerlitz.
And when the pedants bade us mark
  What cold mechanic happenings
Must come; our souls said in the dark,
  "Belike; but there are likelier things."

Likelier across these flats afar,
  These sulky levels smooth and free,
The drums shall crash a waltz of war
  And Death shall dance with Liberty;
Likelier the barricades shall blare
  Slaughter below and smoke above,
And death and hate and hell declare
  That men have found a thing to love.

Far from your sunny uplands set
  I saw the dream; the streets I trod,
The lit straight streets shot out and met
  The starry streets that point to God;

The legend of an epic hour
  A child I dreamed, and dream it still,
Under the great grey water tower
  That strikes the stars on Campden Hill.
(1904)

TO J. L.

Sing a song of Ninepence
  A pocket full of air,
A conscience full of agony,
  A soul full of despair.

For a cause so clear and high
  Misers might fork out;
Only that I quite forgot
  What it was about.
Was it for a fire-engine?
  A church? A Cricket club?
A mission to the Sandwich Isles?
  A model pump—or pub?

Is there in some stately fane
  Earnest Christians build,
Yawning yet the horrid gap
  Ninepence might have filled?
Do the dusky heathen cry
  O'er the southern brine,
"Ninepence more and we are saved,
  "All the ninety-nine".

Ah, for all I know, it fed
  Newcastle's need of coal,
A wedding-present for the Pope,
  An ice-box for the Pole.

Only when your face I see
  Visions tower like fate,
Joan as stern as Joan of Arc,
  Love as dread as hate.

Soften that relentless brow
  Pitying this weak pen,
Smile again; and all will be
  As right as ninepence then.
                    (1920s?)

TO L. K. C.[1]

Xmas 1921

Some call Lloyd George the Prince of Welshmen; some
Call him the Prince of Welshers; some are dumb,
I, with those two high titles in the scales,
Most heartily prefer the Prince of Wales.
                              (1921)

TO L. K. C. FROM G. K. C.

She might have followed where our neighbours
  On some far Alpine Peak keep house
Where mountains tower, avoiding only
  The mountain that produced a mouse.

But the crabs called her, and she answered
  She called them by their Christian names;
She smelt them in the type-writ story —
  She even caught them in the Thames.

---

[1] L. K. C. is Kathleen Chesshire, who preceded Dorothy Collins as Chesterton's secretary for about four years in the early 1920s.

There finds she in her time of leisure,
    For her too short, for us too long,
Anemones that need no water,
    Urchins that know where they belong.

But stars are there as well as starfish,
    Will she not find remembrance there?
See Charles filling Charles's Wain,
    And Ursula the Little Bear.

                          (early 1920s)

TO M. E. W.[1]

Words, for alas my trade is words, a barren burst of rhymes,
    Rubbed by a hundred rhymesters, battered a thousand times,
Take them, you, that smile on strings, those nobler sounds than
mine,
    The words that never lie, or brag, or flatter, or malign.

I give a hand to my lady, another to my friend,
    To whom you too have given a hand; and so before the end
We four may pray, for all the years, whatever suns be set,
    The sole two prayers worth praying — to live and not forget.

The pale leaf falls in pallor, but the green leaf turns to gold;
    We that have found it good to be young shall find it good to
    be old;
Life that bringeth the marriage bell, the cradle and the grave,
    Life that is mean to the mean of heart, and only brave to the
    brave.

In the calm of the last white winter, when all the past is ours,
    Old tears are frozen as jewels, old storms frosted as flowers.
Dear Lady, may we meet again, stand up again, we four,
    Beneath the burden of the years, and praise the earth once more.

                          (early 1900s?)

---

[1] M. E. W. is almost certainly Mildred Wain, a close early friend who was to marry
G. K. C.'s friend Waldo d'Avigdor.

TO PATRICIA GILBERT
WHO ACTED

Oh Patsey dear and did you hear
The news that's going round?
That Marie Tempest's cut her throat,
And Sibyl Thorndike's drowned,
And Marie Lohr has hanged herself;
The ladies of the stage
Expire in envy and despair
Now you have come of age.

(ca. 1925–26)

TO PUNCH[1]

. . . Punch . . . Punch . . . as yet you hardly know
    How excellent your father is:
Hush . . . if your eye should ever choose
    An utterance that is of use
A single joke that does amuse
    Occurring in the Daily News
        . . . Believe me, it is His.

Ah, Happy child . . . you never read
    The Daily News at all . . . your wont
Is of the story simplier set
    O Punch! The Paradoxer's Pet!
You do not read the "News" as yet
    And when you do, you won't.

---

[1] It was Edmund Clerihew Bentley, G. K.'s friend from schooldays and throughout life (E. C. B. lived until 1956) who would "walk, a little pompously, down the street and suddenly scale a lamp-post like a monkey, with the alleged intention of lighting a cigarette, and then drop down and resume his walk with an unchanged expression of earnestness and serenity" *Autobiography of G. K. Chesterton* (San Francisco, Ignatius Press, 1988), p. 63.

Punch, do not try to get inside
  Of every gate that heaves in sight
I know that in an elder time
  I've seen your pa (a well of crime)
With similar abruptness, climb
  A lamp-post for a light.

But do not do it; your papa
  Professionally, is prone to rot.
Forgive him, he is free and bold
  He is not really very old:
Remember you are three years old.
  Remember he is not.

                              (ca. 1905?)

TO RHODA[1]

O Roneo, Roneo, wherefore art thou Roneo?
(See Juliet) in whose name machines were taken,
Not to one bottom trusted (see Antonio;
You know perhaps my appetite for Bacon)
My thoughts pursue you and your wild valises
Envying your Roneos when they did their bunks;
But me, alas, you could not take to pieces
Or pack me into half a hundred trunks.

A rose would smell as sweet (more Bacon, please)
Losing its name by the Lutetian flood
Your name that is the golden rose of Greece
And the dark rose of Ireland in your blood
And the sealed roses of this English garden
That knew you and remember; send you mirth
Who at the outpost where the high wills harden
An exile, wait the cleansing of the earth.

[1] To Rhoda Bastable.

No trumpet but the telephonic tinkle
Keeps us (or some of us) upon the run
Far flash the red artilleries — though Winkle
Seems to suppose he is a Maxim gun.
I, waiting too the trumpet of the advance,
Here where you sat beside a beechwood fire
For Ireland and for England and for France
Pledge you deliverance and the world's desire.

                    (1900 – 1910?)

TO RHODA, otherwise called Rohda

(Lines composed in contemplation of the statue of El Greco at Sitges)

Greek Rose, if he men called the Greek
    Had chanced to pass your way
When Greek meets Greek — then, as you know,
    The band begins to play.

He would have drawn you on the spot
    He liked them long and slim.
(How much more graceful I might seem
    If I had sat for him!)

He would have splashed that sacred scene
    Across resplendent spaces
In the Acts of the Apostles (all
    With elongated faces)

He over whom the Gates of Hell
    Shall tower but not prevail
Stood waiting at your Gate — and you
    (How like you!) did not fail.

How many doors you oped for us
  Quite different from Hell's
Castles in Spain, cafés in France,
  Cathedrals and hotels.

He would have limned you in a blaze
  Bursting those golden locks
Who know the keys of every door
  (If not of every box).

Whose Muse was Beauty in the Gate
  Had hailed you, not in vain
Queen of the Catalonian Port
  Dear Door-Keeper of Spain.

But what wild horror, what regret
  What fury and what shame
Had filled the Greek who found the race
  That could not spell your name!

(1926)[1]

---

[1] Written to Frances' cousin who was working in Barcelona during the time Gilbert and Frances visited Spain.

A HAPPY — — XMAS.

God rest you, merry gentlemen,
Let nothing you dismay —
I have become a Wandering Wait
That sings on Xmas Day.

It was the Carol of a friend
That roused you from your bed,
It was my voice that reached your ears,
Your boot that reached my head.

~~For this I stood outside the gate to sing~~
~~You did not condescend to~~

God rest you, merry gentlemen,
When thus I yelled and prayed
You rested not, & it was plain
That something you dismayed.

For shepherds watching flocks by night
You did not care a pin;
When good King Wenceslas looked out
He hadn't a look in.

So as you scorned my vocal powers
And all my Xmas capers
I sank to writing verse, like this,
And working for the papers.

V

POEMS OF LOVE

AN APOLOGY

Nameless and gay my days have been,
  Nameless and gay my life could pass
Finding no trumpet like the birds
  No laurel greener than the grass.

But if I look but once again
  Into that princely face and pale
I lose my oldest liberty
  The peerless liberty to fail.

                              (1901)[1]

BAY COMBE

With leaves below and leaves above,
And groping under tree and tree,
I found the home of my true love,
Who is a wandering home for me.

Who, lost in ruined worlds aloof,
Bore the dread dove wings like a roof;
Who, past the last lost stars of space,
Carried the fire-light on her face.

Who, passing as in idle hours,
Tamed the wild weeds to garden flowers;
Stroked the strange whirlwind's whirring wings,
And made the comets homely things.

[1] A few months before they were married, Frances was in Florence, and Gilbert sent her a poem of remarkable interest in relation to his efforts and desires. He heads it "An Apology". I have quoted two stanzas. — *Maisie Ward.*

Where she went by upon her way
The dark was dearer than the day;
Where she paused in heaven or hell,
The whole world's tale had ended well.

With leaves below and leaves above,
And groping under tree and tree,
I found the home of my true love,
Who is a wandering home for me.

Where she was flung, above, beneath,
By the rude dance of life and death,
Grow she at Gotham—die at Rome,
Between the pine trees is her home.

In some strange town, some silver morn,
She may have wandered to be born;
Stopped at some motley crowd impressed,
And called them kinsfolk for a jest.

If we again in goodness thrive,
And the dead saints become alive,
Then pedants bald and parchments brown
May claim her blood for London town.

But leaves below and leaves above,
And groping under tree and tree,
I found the home of my true love,
Who is a wandering home for me.

The great gravestone she may pass by,
And without noticing, may die;
The streets of silver Heaven may tread,
With her grey awful eyes unfed.

The city of great peace in pain
May pass, until she find again
This little house of holm and fir
God built before the stars for her.

Here in the fallen leaves is furled
Her secret centre of the world.
We sit and feel in dusk and dun
The stars swing round us like a sun.

For leaves below and leaves above,
And groping under tree and tree,
I found the home of my true love,
Who is a wandering home for me.

(ca. 1908–12)

BY THE SEA

The summer fields shone quiet: and I stood
  And cursed them: bloom of hedge and bud of tree
And bright and high behind the hunch-backed wood
  The thunder and the splendour of the sea.

Bring back the Babylon where I was born
  The wheels that grind bring back, the hands that grope
And noise and blood and suffocating scorn
  An eddy of fierce faces—and a hope

That 'mid those million heads one head find place
  With brown hair curled like breakers of a sea,
And two eyes set so strangely in the face
  That all things else are nothing suddenly.

(ca. 1898)

CHOSEN

I heard a song that the fairies sang
  The flowers are red and the field is green,
But the pale in the midst of green and red
  Is the man that knew the heart of the Queen.

He is marked from the scroll of time
  Never to snigger or sulk or tire.
You have been loved of the well-beloved
  Even desired of the world's desire.

They were many about her path
  They were many, but you were one,
Here if you will is a song that ends.
  Here if you will is a song begun.

Time to come has it plots in store—
  Time that is past can ne'er turn liar.
You have been loved of the well-beloved,
  Even desired of the world's desire.

Life in your eyes was pale and proud,
  Bleak winds battered you where you stood
Lonely—"O man", the prophet said,
  "Hath He not shown you that which is good?"

Count no crown too mighty for thee.
  Turn not back from a whole hell's fire.
You have been loved of the well-beloved,
  Even desired of the world's desire.

(1896–99)

CREATION DAY

Between the perfect marriage day
  And that fierce future proud, and furled,
I only stole six days—six days
  Enough for God to make the world.

For us is a creation made
  New moon by night, new sun by day,
That ancient elm that holds the heavens
  Sprang to its stature yesterday—

Dearest and first of all things free,
   Alone as bride and queen and friend,
Brute facts may come and bitter truths,
   But here all doubts shall have an end.

Never again with cloudy talk
   Shall life be tricked or faith undone,
The world is many and is made,
   But we are sane and we are one.
          (1901)

THE CRYSTAL

I saw it; low she lay as one in dreams,
   And round that holy hair, round and beyond
My Frances, my inviolable, screamed
   The scandal of the dead men's demi-monde.

Close to that face, a window into heaven,
   Close to the hair's brown surf of broken waves
I saw the idiot faces of the ghosts
   That are the fungus, not the flower, of graves.

You whom the pinewoods robed in sun and shade
   You who were sceptred with thistle's bloom,
God's thunder! What have you to do with these
   The lying crystal and the darkened room.

Leave the weird queens that find the sun too strong,
   To mope and cower beneath Druidic trees,
The still, sweet gardens of the dastard's dream.
   God's thunder! What have you to do with these?

Low fields and shining lie in crystal-land
   Peace and strange pleasure: wonder-lands untrod,
But not plain words, nor love of open things,
   Truth, nor strong laughter, nor the fear of God.

I will not look: I am a child of earth,
  I see the sun and wood, the sea, and grass.
I only saw one spirit. She is there
  Staring for spirits in a lump of glass.

                                    (late 1890s)

THE EARTH'S FESTIVAL

Let the wind be a whirl of trumpets
      A flying clarion cry
Let the bronze and gold of the woodland
      As banners flicker and fly
For a fruit to the fruits is gathered
      Worth all that the world is worth
To the suns and the seas and the meadows
      — A love is born on the earth.

Have the powers crept close to the grapple?
      Have the kings in the dawn grown pale?
Is there war or peace or destruction,
      Is there truce or treaty or sale?
Sing men of charges and watchwords,
      Of truths of times unfurled?
Sing men of crowds and a question;
      I sing of two and the world.

Let the wind be a whirl of trumpets
      A flying clarion cry,
Let the bronze and gold of the woodland
      As banners flicker and fly
For a fruit to the fruits is gathered,
      Worth all that the world is worth
Cry aloud, ye tongues of the forest
      A love is born on the earth
                              (early 1890s)

THE EARTH'S FESTIVAL

The walls and the dome of the evening
Are walls and a dome as of fire
The grasses are gold and the roses
Dark red as low fires on the brier,
Stir deep, as dim banners and broidered
Bronze forests below and above,
A day dieth happy and kingly,
  And two have known love.

Flame, walls of the world as a temple
Gleam fenland and field as a floor
For two have made way through a woodland
And two have ta'en hands at a door
The fields give them fierier petals
The woodlands deep shadows and strong
The world giveth bounty and welcome
  And I give a song

And here is a rift in the firwood
And there is a fold in the fell
A rift for two faces to pause in
A fold where two lovers might dwell
A hay-waste their feet would make golden
An orchard their brows would make fair
All houses God built for these wedded
  If these were but there.

Two have heard through the dusk of things doubtful
The lute of the spirit that sings
With his feet on the globe everlasting
The song of the meaning of things
Two have gathered what earth has of worthy
Two have spelled what the old stars can teach
Two have opened their eyes and seen all things
  Each looking on each.

To the host of the mystical victors,
Who alone have been quickened and are
To the martyrs of love through the ages
He has blazoned and burnt with his star
To the bands of the aureoled chosen
Who have known how to see and to give
To the numberless army of lovers
　　　Two are added and live.

In the girth of a room and a garden
In the space of a house and a street
The plan of the world has had meaning
The life of the heart has been sweet
Two lives to themselves been sufficient
Two lives found that life had a law
Let none say they slumbered and fancied
　　　Who wakened and saw.

Two have seen as God saw in the circles
Of the plumage of passionate wings
Ere he bound on the limbs of the spirit
The armour of bodily things
Two are seen as the soul was seen; risen
Before God in the dome of the morn
Archetypal, primeval and perfect
　　　— A spirit unborn.

No eulogies starry and frantic
No loves that are trackless and vast,
No ruinous trust and delusion
No idols titanic of cast
Ever figured a man or a woman,
As they stand at the start or the goal
Ever climbed with long seasons of climbing,
　　　The height of a soul.

Once more are a man and a woman
Once again are a man and a wife

Girt round with the newest of Edens
By the tree of the shadow of Life
In the signs of their limbs and their spirits
Fresh secrets and futures unfurled
New children, new chances, new races
    To people a world.

This only is change and is triumph
This alone is a movement of things
More deep than the ruin of races
More high than the daydreams of Kings
For a stone to the house has been added
That is deeper than flood-time that mars
For a flower to the flowers has been gathered.
    A star to the stars
        (unfinished, mid to late 1890s)

EPITHALAMIUM ARGENTUM

(To Frances, for their Silver Wedding anniversary)

I need not say I love you yet
You know how doth my heart oppress
The intolerable tenderness
That broke my body when we met.
I need not say I love you yet.

But let me say I fear you yet
You the long years not vulgarise,
You open your immortal eyes
And we for the first time have met.
Cover your face; I fear you yet.

FRANCES[1]

Dearest, whatever others see
Herein, it is no mystery
That I find all the world is good
Since you are all the world to me

You will not blame my boastful hours
It is not of such souls as yours
To spew the wrath of sorrow out
Upon the harmless grass and flowers

Do you fight on for all the press
Wise as you are you cannot guess
How I shall flaunt before God's Knights
The triumph of my own princess

Almost this day of the strange star
We know the bonfire old and far
Whence all the stars as sparks are blown
Piled up to warm us after war

There, where we spread our hands like wings
And tell good tales of conquered things
The tale that I will tell of you
Shall dash the cup of all the Kings

I swear it shall be mine alone
To tell your tale before the throne
To tell your tale beside the fire
Eternal, Here I tell my own.

(1901)

---

[1] Written to Frances, his wife, for the first Christmas after their marriage — written on the fly-leaf of *The Wild Knight*.

FRANCES

God made thee mightily, my love,
He stretched His hands out of His rest
And lit the star of east and west
Brooding o'er darkness like a dove
God made thee mightily, my love.

God made thee patiently, my sweet,
Out of all stars He chose a star,
He made it red with sunset bar
And green with greeting for thy feet.
God made thee mightily, my sweet.

(ca. 1899)

FRANCES

(A Fragment)

'Twixt Bedford Park and Westminster
    Oft would a lady hurry,
Inside she was divine and deep
    And outside green and furry.

The golden armoury of God
    In truth was round her buckled.
—The son of man that is a worm
    He blew his nose and chuckled.

For weary weeks and maddening months
    In sunny days and shady
That amateurish Satan bored
    That green and brown young lady.

And he would slay the cynic thought
    That whispered "Ver non semper
Viret"—The spring will lose its crown
    And she will lose her temper.

. . . .

Over a thousand labours, low and high
He saw her face, lovely and grave and good,
Sleeping and waking, all her womanhood
Gilded the unsleeping watch of deity.

(late 1890s)

THE GARDEN OF THE VIRGIN[1]

I know you would have known the names
    Of all the flowers that fire the moor
Names that seem coloured from your soul
    So elvish and perverse and pure.

Names that you might have made yourself,
    As quaint as clouds, as kind as showers,
If Adam named the brutes and birds
    I know 'twas Eve that named the flowers

The dog rose bends, a stricken saint,
    Its fiery aureole rent and riven
The larkspur spurns the earth and climbs
    Until it catch the tints of heaven.

The goatsbeard gilds the gloaming meads;
    The foxglove—bells and steeple bent—
O'er this still chapel of the fields
    Shakes out, instead of music, scent.

---

[1] "'I advise the omission of the poem,' writes Edward Watkin, with the just indignation of a nature-lover. 'The larkspur, a rare casual occurring near cornfields, and a small plant, becomes a tall moorland plant that "spurns the earth and climbs". The goatsbeard said to "gild the *gloaming* meads" is popularly called "go-to-bed at noon" because no blossom is open after noon. The foxglove is not a sweet-scented flower.'" — Ward, *Return to Chesterton*, p. III.

But you—in you are all the flowers
  Not only in your body rare—
Those blue and starry flowers, your eyes,
  That brown and fragrant flower, your hair.
        (1919–20?)

IN THE BALANCE

A poet scrawled upon a page of verse
Wherein a priest and king battled: whose bones
Are grown to grass for eight dead centuries
The words that through the dark and through the day
Rang in my ears.

            Even as Becket, graced
By perilous pleasure of the Angevin—
Cried out "Am I the man for cross of Christ?"
In the vast fane filled with one presence dark
That spoke and shook the stars . . . "Thou art the Man."
So do I stand.

            A mitre and a cross!
God's blood! A cross is but a pair of sticks,
A mitre is a fool's cap out of school,
Candles are fireworks—fling them in the street—
Why should he fear to fill so poor a place?
When I stand up 'neath seven staring heavens,
Naked and arrogant and insolent
And ask for the crown jewels of the Lord

Lord I have been a Waster of the sun
A sleeper on the highways of the world
A garnerer of thistles and of weeds
A hewer of waste wood that no man buys
A lover of things violent, things perverse,
Grotesque and grinning and inscrutable

A savage and a clown — and there she stands
Straight as the living lily of the Lord.
O thy world-wisdom speak — am I the man?

Lo: I am man, even the son of man
Thou knowest these things: in my blood's heritage
Is every sin that shrieked in Babylon,
All tales untold and lost that reddened Heaven
In falling fire above the monstrous domes
Of cities damned and done with . . . there she goes
White in the living sunlight on the lawn,
Alive and bearing flowers . . . My God . . . my God,
Am I the man?

       Strong keeper of the world,
O King thou knowest man of woman born,
How weak as water and how strong as fire,
Judge Thou O Lord for I am sick of love
And may not judge. . . .

(ca. 1898–99)[1]

---

[1] Written a little time before G. K. C. proposed to Frances Blogg, his future wife.

JOSEPH

If the stars fell; night's nameless dreams
  Of bliss and blasphemy came true,
If skies were green and snow were gold,
  And you loved me as I love you;

O long light hands and curled brown hair,
  And eyes where sits a naked soul;
Dare I even then draw near and burn
  My fingers in the aureole?

Yes, in the one wise foolish hour
  God gives this strange strength to a man.
He can demand, though not deserve,
  Where ask he cannot, seize he can.

But once the blood's wild wedding o'er,
  Were not dread his, half dark desire,
To see the Christ-child in the cot,
  The Virgin Mary by the fire?
                    (mid 1890s)[1]

THE LAST MASQUERADE

A wan new garment of young green,
  Touched, as you turned your soft brown hair;
  And in me surged the strangest prayer
Ever in lover's heart hath been.

That I who saw your youth's bright page,
  A rainbow change from robe to robe,
  Might see you on this earthly globe,
Crowned with the silver crown of age.

[1] An earlier version has minor differences in punctuation and for the third line has "If fishes flew and forests walked".

Your dear hair powdered in strange guise,
  Your dear face touched with colours pale,
  And gazing through the mask and veil
The mirth of your immortal eyes.

                                        (late 1890s)

THE LEGEND OF GOOD WOMEN

(A fragment)

  I did not see thy shadow fall
  Through gap of hedge or chink of wall;
  God gave His whole wide world to me
  Before I gave myself to thee.

  I came not from the heartless fête
  From loves more low than any hate
  To smirch you with my drear defence
  And my polluting penitence,

  Nor ever failed I to believe
  The honour of the house of Eve.

                                        (ca. 1898)

A LITTLE LITANY

When God turned back eternity and was young,
  Ancient of Days, grown little for your mirth
(As under the low arch the land is bright)
  Peered through you, gate of heaven—and saw
                                the earth.

Or shutting out his shining skies awhile
  Built you about him for a house of gold
To see in pictured walls his storied world
  Return upon him as a tale is told.

Or found his mirror there; the only glass
  That would not break with that unbearable light
Till in a corner of the high dark house
  God looked on God, as ghosts meet in the night.

Star of his morning; that unfallen star
  In the strange starry overturn of space
When earth and sky changed places for an hour
  And heaven looked upwards in a human face.

Or young on your strong knees and lifted up
  Wisdom cried out, whose voice is in the street,
And more than twilight of twiformed cherubim
  Made of his throne indeed a mercy-seat.

Or risen from play at your pale raiment's hem
  God, grown adventurous from all time's repose,
Of your tall body climbed the ivory tower
  And kissed upon your mouth the mystic rose.

                    (ca. 1918–24)

LOVE, WE HAVE LOOKED ON MANY SHOWS

Love, we have looked on many shows
  As over lands from sea to sea
Man with his Guardian Angel goes
  His shining shadow more than he.

For us the Nile's first Kings lay covered
  Under a mountain made with hands;
Or red bud bloomed and red bird hovered
  Over the lost Red Indian lands.

Beside the sledge with fairy bells
   The snow slid by like seas of foam;
Mirrored in many marble wells,
   The sun sat regnant over Rome.

But not as distance, not as danger,
   Not chance, and hardly even change,
You found, not wholly as a stranger,
   The place too wondrous to be strange.

Great with a memory more than yearning,
   You travelled but you did not roam,
And went not wandering but returning
   As to some first forgotten home.

The mystic city, many-gated,
   Monstrously pillared, was your own;
Herodian stories gave words and waited
   Two thousand years to be your throne.

Strange blossoms burned as rich before you
   As that divine and beautiful blood;
The wild flowers were no wilder for you
   Than bluebells in an English wood.
                     (1926?)[1]

LOVE'S TRAPPIST

There is a place where lute and lyre are broken,
Where scrolls are torn and on a wild wind go,
Where tablets stand wiped naked for a token,
Where laurels wither and the daisies grow.

[1] Undated, but possibly written to celebrate the reception of Frances into the Catholic Church in 1926.

Lo: I too join the brotherhood of silence,
I am Love's trappist and you ask in vain,
For man through Love's gate, even as through Death's gate,
Goeth alone and comes not back again.

Yet here I pause, look back across the threshold,
Cry to my brethren, though the world be old,
Prophets and sages, questioners and doubters,
O world, old world, the best hath ne'er been told!

(early 1900s?)

A MARRIAGE SONG

Why should we reck of hours that rend
   While we two ride together?
The heavens rent from end to end
   Would be but windy weather,
The strong stars shaken down in spate
   Would be a shower of spring,
And we should list the trump of fate
   And hear a linnet sing.

We break the line with stroke and luck,
   The arrows run like rain,
If you be struck, or I be struck,
   There's one to strike again.
If you befriend, or I befriend,
   The strength is in us twain,
And good things end and bad things end,
   And you and I remain.

Why should we reck of ill or well
   While we two ride together?
The fires that over Sodom fell
   Would be but sultry weather.

Beyond all ends to all men given
   Our race is far and fell,
We shall but wash our feet in heaven,
   And warm our hands in hell.

Battles unborn and vast shall view
   Our faltered standards stream,
New friends shall come and frenzies new,
   New troubles toil and teem;
New friends shall pass and still renew
   One truth that does not seem,
That I am I, and you are you,
   And Death a morning dream.

Why should we reck of scorn or praise
   While we two ride together?
The icy air of godless days
   Shall be but wintry weather.
If hell were highest, if the heaven
   Were blue with devils blue,
I should have guessed that all was even,
   If I had dreamed of you.

Little I reck of empty prides,
   Of creeds more cold than clay;
To nobler ends and longer rides,
   My lady rides to-day.
To swing our swords and take our sides
   In that all-ending fray
When stars fall down and darkness hides,
   When God shall turn to bay.

Why should we reck of grin and groan
   While we two ride together?
The triple thunders of the throne
   Would be but stormy weather.

For us the last great fight shall roar,
   Upon the ultimate plains,
And we shall turn and tell once more
   Our love in English lanes.

           (ca. 1902)

MIRTH

Take this from one who, though his worth
Be spent on gloomier verse and prose
Knows well from what deep bed upgrows
The noble mystery of mirth:

Who gives this mark of love to thee
Scarce more for all thy graver phase
The deeper love, the keener gaze
Than none have ever known but he.

Scarce more for all the weightier lore
Than for that ever-generous cheer,
That gives to Fordham's jest a peer
And meets the shriek of d'Avigdor.

Revered, beloved, O you that hold
A nobler office in the club,
Than votes and titles and hubbub,
Gave Lucian or myself of old.

Too deep to show the inner scenes,
Like those whose thinking is their curse,
Exploit your mortal faith in verse,
And print your doubts in magazines.

Content to give the fancies vent,
And to our pleasure give your power,
And sway through many an honest hour,
The notes of laughter and content.

The words of feeling scarce are free
But some a feeling can recall
Turned from some constitutional brawl,
To brighten at a word from thee.

(late 1890s)

MUSIC

Sounding brass and tinkling cymbal,
   He that made me sealed my ears,
And the pomp of gorgeous noises,
   Waves of triumphs, waves of tears,

Thundered empty round and past me,
   Shattered, lost for evermore,
Ancient gold of pride and passion,
   Wrecked like treasure on a shore.

But I saw her cheek and forehead
   Change as at a spoken word,
And I saw her head uplifted
   Like a lily to the Lord.

Nought is lost, but all transmuted,
   Ears are sealed, yet eyes have seen:
Saw her smiles (O soul be worthy!),
   Saw her tears (O heart be clean!).

(1905–15)

ON BEING THANKED FOR A FAVOR

Tempt not with cheap words chivalrously given
Hope's secret blasphemy to half rebel
Like a lost soul that trespasses in heaven
Where the still glories scorch him more than hell

You have no right with generous jesting terms
To make your poor friend drunken as with wine,
No right to tell one of God's honest worms
That he has helped the noonday sun to shine.
(notebooks, mid 1890s)

ON THE DOWNS

When you came over the top of the world
In the great day on the Downs,
The air was crisp and the clouds were curled,
When you came over the top of the world,
And under your feet were spire and street
And seven English towns.

And I could not think that the pride was perished
As you came over the down;
Liberty, chivalry, all we cherished,
Lost in a rattle of pelf and perished;
Or the land we love that you walked above
Withering town by town.

For you came out on the dome of the earth
Like a vision of victory,
Out on the great green dome of the earth
As the great blue dome of the sky for girth,
And under your feet the shires could meet
And your eyes went out to sea.

Under your feet the towns were seven,
Alive and alone on high,
Your back to the broad white wall of heaven;
You were one and the towns were seven,
Single and one as the soaring sun
And your head upheld the sky.

And I thought of a thundering flag unfurled
And the roar of the burghers' bell:
Beacons crackled and bolts were hurled
As you came over the top of the world;
And under your feet were chance and cheat
And the slime of the slopes of hell.

It has not been as the great wind spoke
On the great green down that day:
We have seen, wherever the wide wind spoke,
Slavery slaying the English folk:
The robbers of land we have seen command;
The rulers of land obey.

We have seen the gigantic golden worms
In the garden of paradise:
We have seen the great and the wise make terms
With the peace of snakes and the pride of worms,
And them that plant make covenant
With the locust and the lice.

And the wind blows and the world goes on
And the world can say that we,
Who stood on the cliffs where the quarries shone,
Stood upon clouds that the sun shone on:
And the clouds dissunder and drown in thunder
The news that will never be.

Lady of all that have loved the people,
Light over roads astray,
Maze of steading and street and steeple,

Great as a heart that has loved the people:
Stand on the crown of the soaring down,
Lift up your arms and pray.

Only you I have not forgotten
For wreck of the world's renown,
Rending and ending of things gone rotten,
Only the face of you unforgotten:
And your head upthrown in the skies alone
As you came over the down.

(1916–21)

A PORTRAIT

Fair faces crowd on Christmas night
   Like seven suns a-row,
But all beyond is the wolfish wind
   And the crafty feet of the snow.

But through the rout one figure goes
   With quick and quiet tread;
Her robe is plain, her form is frail—
   Wait if she turn her head.

I say no word of line or hue,
   But if that face you see,
Your soul shall know the smile of faith's
   Awful frivolity.

Know that in this grotesque old masque
   Too loud we cannot sing,
Or dance too wild, or speak too wide
   To praise a hidden thing.

That though the jest be old as night,
   Still shaketh sun and sphere
An everlasting laughter
   Too loud for us to hear.

(late 1890s)

A PORTRAIT

Her hair is as a floating fire,
   The glory of the world's desire

Her visage sweet yet gaunt and free
   Elvish and broken startlingly

Her garb is green and climbs and clings
   Her arm is weighted of strange rings.

Her eyes are brown and dreamy, mild
   Making the elfin to a child.

Childish she is, and quick and hot
   Her heart is sealed: we know her not.
              (1892–94)

THE SONG OF SONGS

In the beginning was Love
   A field from the grey unscaled
   A garden out of the field
And out of the garden, Love.

Like to a hind is Love
   He ribs the wolds with a share
   Earth's gold to the garner to bear
To thresh from the garner, Love.

Like to a builder is Love
   He rends the floors of the earth
   To light, like a meteor's birth
— A perilous pinnacle, Love.

Day with its sweats is Love,
   Love with its dews is sleep,
   Love is the nights that creep
And the sun that awakes is Love.

Before labour is Love,
   Love is the labour's plan
   Love is the task of a man
The reward thereof is Love.

Chaos was earth by Love
   That after the aeons old
   Through secrets garnered and told
The earth might attain to — Love.
      (late 1880s)

SORROW

(From the French of Charles Guérin)

At last, at even, to my hearth I hark,
   Still faithful to my sorrow. And inside
   Even I and all my old magnanimous pride
Are broken down before her in the dark.

Sorrow's bare arm about my neck doth strain,
   Sorrow doth lift me to her living mouth
   And whispers, fierce and loving like the South,
Saying, "Dear Pilgrim, have you come again?

"Whether you walked by wastes of upland green,
   Whether you walked by wastes of ocean blue,
   Have you not felt me step by step with you,
A thing that was both certain and unseen?

"Or haply is it ended? haply you,
   Conquering and wholly cured of loving me,
   Are but a wavering lover who would be
Off with the old love ere he take the new?"

But, seeing my head did but in silence sink
   Before her ruthless irony and strong.
She gave me then that dreadful kiss to drink
   That is the bitter spring of art and song.

Then with strange gentleness she said, "I choose
    To be thine only, thine in all ways; yes,
Thy daughter and thy sister and thy muse,
    Thy wife and thine immortal ancestress.

"Feed not thy hate against my rule and rod,
    For I am very clean, my son, and sane,
Because I bring all brave hearts back to God,
    In my embraces being born again."

Thus spoke she low and rocked me like a child,
    And as I stared at her, as stunned awhile,
On her stern face there fell more slow and mild
    The splendour of a supernatural smile.

                        (1908)

A SPRING SONG

Lady, look up and laugh, at least
That we no vigil keep—
With pedants pure enough to curse
And wise enough to weep.

I know that fair before your feet
The dandelion flamed—
When heavens fall and stars are rent
You shall not be ashamed.

When you shall stand beneath the skies
With God's own garments blue
One ragged, reckless, shameless soul
Shall stand and speak with you.

Then shall he stand and speak a Word
Yea, one great Word I ween
"To us at least the rose was red
To us the grass was green."

                    (mid 1890s)

THE STRANGE MUSIC

Other loves may sink and settle, other loves may loose and slack,
But I wander like a minstrel with a harp upon his back,
Though the harp be on my bosom, though I finger and I fret,
Still, my hope is all before me: for I cannot play it yet.

In your strings is hid a music that no hand hath e'er let fall,
In your soul is sealed a pleasure that you have not known at all;
Pleasure subtle as your spirit, strange and slender as your frame,
Fiercer than the pain that folds you, softer than your sorrow's
    name.

Not as mine, my soul's anointed, not as mine the rude and light
Easy mirth of many faces, swaggering pride of song and fight;
Something stranger, something sweeter, something waiting you
    afar,
Secret as your stricken senses, magic as your sorrows are.

But on this, God's harp supernal, stretched but to be stricken
    once,
Hoary time is a beginner, Life a bungler, Death a dunce,
But I will not fear to match them — no, by God, I will not fear,
I will learn you, I will play you and the stars stand still to hear.

(1905–14)

THE THREE REALITIES

We tattered rhymers of the trade
Work with weak symbols for great power;
We paint a flower and call it Spring,
But Spring is more than any flower.

But 'mid the feeble names of things
The pallid types of tree and star,
God made three symbols on the earth
That truly mean the thing they are.

The first the circle — endlessness,
God's compass traced in sun and flower;
The next the cross, the eternal twain
Cross-purposes that make a power.

The third — your face — that single face,
Had I but seen it pictured well
On frescoes older than the gods,
It might have saved my soul from hell.

God made three signs that mean and are
Alone in all the world, these three;
God made two signs that make the world
And one that makes the world to me.

                              (late 1890s)

TO A LADY

Light of the young, before you have grown old
The world will have grown weary of its youth
All its cheap charity and loose-lipped truth
And passion that goes naked — and grows cold.

Tire of a pity so akin to hate
Turn on a truth that is so near to treason,
When Time, the god of traitors, in their season
Marks down for dated all the up-to-date.

Then shall men know by the great grace you are
How something better than blind fear or blunder
Bade us stand back, where we could watch with wonder
Ladies like landscapes, very fair and far.

A crowd shall call your high estrangéd face
A mask of blind reaction and resistance,
Because you have made large the world with distance
As God made large the universe with space.

Yet beautiful your feet upon the mountains
Moving in soundless music shall return,
And they that look into your eyes shall learn—
Having forced up the secret sea in fountains.

And having vulgarised infinity
And splashed their brains against the starry steeps.
In what unfathomable inward deeps
Dwells the last mystery men call Liberty.

When they shall say we scorned and held in thrall
Spirits like yours; the mother of the tribe
Slandered, a slave, a butt for slur and gibe,
You shall confound the one great slur of all.

The one great slander answered long ago
By Her that hid all things within her heart,
One speaking when the veil was rent apart
"Women alone can keep a secret so."

(1925)

TO FRANCES

Cast her in outer darkness old,
   And she shall laugh at fire and scars
Though meteors whizz and comets crash
   In the blind tourney of the stars.

Damn her in Dante's deepest floor
   Choked in the traitors' ice to be
The glory of that heart of flame
   Shall melt it to a summer sea.

(ca. 1900)

TO HIS WIFE, IN HER ILLNESS

I do not bring you health, or cold
  Coarse pity as the Gentiles do:
Though swathed in sickness sevenfold,
  The world shall come for health to you.

The hair on your unconquered head
  Shall freshen wanderers like a field
The very healers round your bed
  Shall touch your garment and be healed.

I weep not: there is naught in you
  Of darkened windows or of dread:
Your soul is blue as skies are blue
  And red as battlefields are red.

You burn all blood-red through the grey
  (O hands and eyes of my desire!)
You burn the sundering walls away
  You set the sundering Thames on fire.

You flush the river, reddening past,
  Round the tall house your flames are curled,
You will burn up the world at last,
  You are too healthy for the world.

                    (1902–4)

TO MY LADY

God made you very carefully,
He set a star apart for it,
He stained it green and gold with fields
And aureoled it with sunshine;

He peopled it with kings, peoples, republics,
And so made you, very carefully.
All nature is God's book, filled with His rough sketches
    for you.

               (ca. 1897–99)

TOGETHER

Under how many suns have we embraced
    In what long fields of flowers and steets of stone
In the strong light of summer, interlaced
    And made, like God, a darkness of our own.

Oh when the bitter wind of longing blows
    And all between us seems an aching space
Think that we hold each other close, so close;
    We cannot even see each other's face.

               (1906)

TRANSLATION FROM DU BELLAY

Happy, who like Ulysses or that lord
    Who raped the fleece, returning full and sage,
With usage and the world's wide reason stored,
    With his own kin can taste the end of age.
When shall I see, when shall I see, God knows!
    My little village smoke; or pass the door,
The old dear door of that unhappy house
    Which is to me a kingdom and much more?
Mightier to me the house my fathers made
    Than your audacious heads, O Halls of Rome!
More than immortal marbles undecayed,
    The thin sad slates that cover up my home;

More than your Tiber is my Loire to me,
  Than Palatine my little Lyré there;
And more than all the winds of all the sea
  The quiet kindness of the Angevin air.

(1904)

TRUE LOVERS

Shade of high shame and honourable blindness
When youth in storm of dizzy and distant things
Finds the wild windfall of a little kindness
And shakes to think that all the world has wings
The little smile that stirred the stars to laughter
The living hand that came from far away
God be their guard before their going and after
The little words that shall not pass away.

Make not this sex, this other side of things
A thing less distant than the world's desire
What colour to the edge of evening clings
And what far cry of frontiers and what fire
Fallen too far beyond the seas for seeking
Let it be with us when we closest come
And a wild signal in our secret speaking
To hang the proud horizon in our home.

Seal us for names and not for numbers, Master
Make us a home and not a herd, O God.
True lovers whom division no disaster
Brings by two ways to a trysting place untrod.[1]

---

[1] This poem is an earlier version of "A wedding in War-Time".

THE TWO WOMEN

Lo! very fair is she who knows the ways
   Of joy: in pleasure's mocking wisdom old,
The eyes that might be cold to flattery, kind;
   The hair that might be grey with knowledge, gold.

But thou art more than these things, O my queen,
   For thou art clad in ancient wars and tears.
And looking forth, framed in the crown of thorns,
   I saw the youngest face in all the spheres.
                       (late 1890s)

THE UNPARDONABLE SIN

I do not cry, beloved, neither curse.
   Silence and strength, these two at least are good.
   He gave me sun and stars and aught He could,
But not a woman's love; for that is hers.

He sealed her heart from sage and questioner—
   Yea, with seven seals, as he has sealed the grave.
   And if she give it to a drunken slave,
The Day of Judgment shall not challenge her.

Only this much: if one, deserving well,
   Touching your thin young hands and making suit,
   Feel not himself a crawling thing, a brute,
Buried and bricked in a forgotten hell.

Prophet and poet be he over sod,
   Prince among angels in the highest place,
   God help me, I will smite him on the face,
Before the glory of the face of God.
                       (late 1890s)

VANITY

A wan sky greener than the lawn,
   A wan lawn paler than the sky.
She gave a flower into my hand,
   And all the hours of eve went by.

Who knows what round the corner waits
   To smite? If shipwreck, snare, or slur
Shall leave me with a head to lift,
   Worthy of him that spoke with her.

A wan sky greener than the lawn,
   A wan lawn paler than the sky.
She gave a flower into my hand,
   And all the days of life went by.

Live ill or well, this thing is mine,
   From all I guard it, ill or well.
One tawdry, tattered, faded flower
   To show the jealous kings in hell.
               (late 1890s)

A WEDDING IN WAR-TIME

Our God who made two lovers in a garden,
And smote them separate and set them free,
Their four eyes wild for wonder and wrath and pardon
And their kiss thunder as lips of land and sea:
Each rapt unendingly beyond the other,
Two starry worlds of unknown gods at war,
Wife and not mate, a man and not a brother,
We thank thee thou hast made us what we are.

Make not the grey slime of infinity
To swamp these flowers thou madest one by one;

Let not the light that was thine enemy
Mix a mad twilight of the moon and sun;
Waken again to thunderclap and clamour
The wonder of our sundering and the song,
Or break our hearts with thine hell-shattering hammer
But leave a shade between us all day long.

Shade of high shame and honourable blindness
When youth, in storm of dizzy and distant things,
Finds the wild windfall of a little kindness
And shakes to think that all the world has wings.
When the one head that turns the heavens in turning
Moves yet as lightly as a lingering bird,
And red and random, blown astray but burning,
Like a lost spark goes by the glorious word.

Make not this sex, this other side of things,
A thing less distant than the world's desire;
What colour to the end of evening clings
And what far cry of frontiers and what fire
Fallen too far beyond the sun for seeking,
Let it divide us though our kingdom come;
With a far signal in our secret speaking
To hang the proud horizon in our home.

Once we were one, a shapeless cloud that lingers
Loading the seas and shutting out the skies,
One with the woods, a monster of myriad fingers,
You laid on me no finger of surprise.
One with the stars, a god with myriad eyes,
I saw you nowhere and was blind for scorn:
One till the world was riven and the rise
Of the white days when you and I were born.

Darkens the world: the world-old fetters rattle;
And these that have no hope behind the sun

May feed like bondmen and may breed like cattle,
One in the darkness as the dead are one;
Us if the rended grave give up its glory
Trumpets shall summon asunder and face to face:
We will be strangers in so strange a story
And wonder, meeting in so wild a place.

Ah, not in vain or utterly for loss
Come even the black flag and the battle-hordes,
If these grey devils flee the sign of the cross
Even in the symbol of the crossing swords.
Nor shall death doubt Who made our souls alive
Swords meeting and not stakes set side by side,
Bade us in the sunburst and the thunder thrive
Earthquake and Dawn; the bridegroom and the bride.

Death and not dreams or doubt of things undying,
Of whose the holy hearth or whose the sword;
Though sacred spirits dissever in strong crying
Into Thy hands, but Thy two hands, O Lord,
Though not in Earth as once in Eden standing,
So plain again we see Thee what thou art,
As in this blaze, the blasting and the branding
Of this wild wedding where we meet and part.

(1918–19)[1]

---

[1] See earlier version, "True Lovers", on page 374.

WHEN YOU ARE OLD

When you are old, when candle and evening cloud
Decay beside you spinning in your chair,
Then sing this song and marvel and cry aloud
Great Ronsard praised me in the days when I was fair.
There shall no maiden spin with you or sing
But shall say "Ronsard" and the name shall ring
And sound your name with everlasting praise.
I shall lie buried and a boneless shade
By the pale myrtles pluck my last repose;
You will be sitting where the embers fade
Nodding and gazing as the last ash glows
An old grey woman in grey garments furled.
You shall regret my love and your disdain.
Oh do not linger, Oh, before all is vain,
Gather, Oh gather the roses of the World.

(ca. 1900)[1]

[1] A translation of Ronsard's *Quand Vous Serez Bien Vielle*, probably ca. 1900. (Translations of this lyric have also been made by Charles Williams and W. B. Yeats.)

VI

SOCIETY AND POLITICS

AFRICA

A sleepy people, without priests or kings,
Dreamed here, men say, to drive us to the sea:
   O let us drive ourselves! For it is free
And smells of honour and of English things.
How came we brawling by these bitter springs,
   We of the North? — two kindly nations — we?
Though the dice rattles and the clear coin rings,
   Here is no place for living men to be.
Leave them the gold that worked and whined for it,
   Let them that have no nation anywhere
Be native here, and fat and full of bread;
But we, whose sins were human, we will quit
   The land of blood, and leave these vultures there,
Noiselessly happy, feeding on the dead.

                           (1904)

"THE APPEAL OF THE PEERS"

(On their rejection of Mr. Lloyd George's land budget of 1909)

Would you call upon the people; in what ear shall it be told?
Call on God, whose name is pity, though our sins be very old.
Will you call on street and township? Who but you have made the
   smoke
Something heavier than a vapour? Something sharper than a joke?
Who but you have taxed the townsmen of their tired and ugly tilth?
Who but you have made men forfeit for their right to live in filth?

Will you call on croft and village? On what village will you call
That four centuries of your lordship have not left a tithe too small?
Hamlets breaking, homesteads drifting, peasants tramping, towns
    erased;
Lo, my lords, we gave you England, and you gave us back a waste.
Yea, a desert labelled England, where you know (and well you know)
That the village Hampdens wither and the village idiots grow;
That the pride of grass grows mighty and the hope of men grows small.
Will you call on croft and village? Let the rabbits hear your call.

Will you call on crest and scutcheon? We might heed you, if we knew
Even one gutter-thief whose millions could not cut his way to you.
If there lived on earth one upstart from whose filthy face you shrank,
We would hear, my lords, more gravely of the grace and scorn of rank.
Now, if in your mob of merchants, usurers, idlers, cads, you keep
One that did have Norman fathers, let your Norman fathers sleep.
Let God's good grass grow above them, where their
    pointed pennons blew;
They were thieves and thugs and smiters; they were better men than
    you!

Will you call on cross and altar? And in God's name where were you
When the crashing walls of convents let the Tudor axes through?
Tell us of your deeds, Crusaders. Waken Ariosto's muse;
How you stood the church's champion, when the church
    had land to lose—
You, the Russells, with the ashes of a hundred altars shod,
You, the Howards, with your wallets bursting with the gold of God.
Will you call on cross and altar? Will you name the holy name?
No, by Heaven, you shall not name it. Smite your very mouths for
    shame!
Would you call upon the people? Would you waken these things then?
Call on God, whose name is Pity—Do not ask too much of men!

                                  (1940)[1]

---

[1] From *Forever Freedom*, ed. Josiah C. Wedgwood and Allan Nevins (London, 1940), pp.
195–97.

THE BURIED CITY

You that go forth upon the buried cities
Whose witchcraft holds the withered kings together
Seals up the very air of ancient seasons,
Like secret skies walled up from the world's weather
You that dig up dead towns—arise and strive:
Strike through the slums and save the towns alive!

Dig London out of London; pierce the cavern
Where Manchester lies lost in Manchester
You that re-chart the choked-up squares and markets
Retrace the plan our blindness made a blur:
Until a name no more, but wide and tall,
Arise and shine the shield of London Wall.

Strike you the stones of these most desert places
Huge warehouses the lonely watchmen tread
Where ringed in noise the hollow heart of London
Lies all night long a city of the dead.
Or does One watch high o'er this maze that sprawls,
High on the vanished spire of Old St. Pauls?

Lift up your heads, ye gates of our remembrance,
Be lifted up, ye everlasting walls,
The gates revolve upon their giant hinges
The guilds return unto their ancient halls
Tell Bishopsgate a Bishop rides to town
Not only come to pull the churches down.

You that let light into the sunken cities,
Let life into the void where light is vain
Ere vandals wreck the temples, porch and pillar,
Bring back the people to the porch again,
Who find in tombs strange flowers, flattened and dried,
Quicken the incredible seed of London Pride.

If our vain haste has smothered home in houses
As our vain creeds have smothered man in men,

Though in that rock tomb sleeps the King less deeply
Than in this brick tomb sleeps the Citizen,
What will not God achieve if Man awake
Since a rock-tomb was rended for our sake?

(ca. 1925)

BY A REACTIONARY

Smoke rolls in stinking, suffocating wrack
On Shakespeare's land, turning the green one black;
The crowds that once to harvest home would come
Hope for no harvest and possess no home,
While poor old tramps that liked a little ale,
In natural procession pass to gaol;
Because the world must, like the tramp, move on,
There does not seem much else that can be done.
As Lord Vangelt said in the House of Peers:
"None of us want Reaction." (Tory cheers.)

So doubtful doctors punch and prod and prick
A man thought dead; and when there's not a kick
Left in the corpse, no twitch or faint contraction,
The doctors say: "See . . . there is no Reaction."

(1925)

COMFORT FOR COMMUNISTS

"In January of last year Bezboznik complained that anti-religious
societies had been disbanded in seventy districts, while it had been
thought that in the region of Kovrov there was a whole system of atheist
cells, the President of that region wrote, . . . that neither in the town
nor in the region were there any cells left—in fact, 'in the entire district
there is now only one organised atheist—myself.' "

—From an article by Father C. C. Martindale, S.J., in the
Catholic Herald, May 11, 1935

"I'm all alone; I can't organise anyone,
There's nobody left to organise me,
And still I'm the only organised atheist
In all the province of Skunktz (E. C.).

Sometimes disgusting disorganised atheists
Orphan the stars without permit from me,
Unmake their Maker without their ticket
Or their copy of Form X. 793.

The Blasphemy Drill's getting slacker and slacker
Free Thought is becoming alarmingly free,
And I'll be the only organised atheist
Between the Bug and the big Black Sea."

Ours, ours is the key O desolate crier,
The golden key to what ills distress you
Left without ever a God to judge you,
Lost without even a Man to oppress you.

Look west, look west, to the Land of Profits,
To the old gold marts, and confess it then
How greatly your great propaganda prospers
When left to the methods of Business Men.

Ah, Mammon is mightier than Marx in making
A goose-step order for godless geese,
And snobs know better than mobs to measure
Where God shall flourish and God shall cease.

Lift up your heart in the wastes Slavonian,
Let no Red Sun on your wrath go down;
There are millions of very much organised atheists
In the Outer Circle of London town.

(1935)

AN ELECTION ECHO
1900

This is their triumph, ripe and rounded
They have burnt the wheat and gathered the chaff:
And we who have watched them, we who have fought them
Have we at least not cause to laugh?

Never so low at least we stumbled
Dead we have been, but not so dead,
As these that live on the life they squandered
As these that drink of the blood they shed.

We never boasted the thing we blundered,
We never flaunted the thing that fails,
We never quailed from the living laughter,
To howl to the dead who tell no tales.

'Twas another finger at least that pointed
Our wasted men or our emptied bags,
It was not we that sounded the trumpet
In front of the triumph of wrecks and rags.

Fear not these, they have made their bargain,
They have counted the cost of the last of raids,
They have staked their lives on the things that live not,
They have burnt their house for a fire that fades.

Five years ago and we might have feared them,
Been drubbed by the coward and taught by the dunce;
Truth may endure and be told and re-echoed,
But a lie can never be young but once.

Five years ago and we might have feared them;
Now, when they lift the laurelled brow,
There shall naught go up from our hosts assembled
But a laugh like thunder. We know them now.

(*The Speaker*, Oct. 20, 1900)[1]

ELEGY IN A COUNTRY CHURCHYARD

The men that worked for England
They have their graves at home:
And bees and birds of England
About the cross can roam.

But they that fought for England,
Following a falling star,
Alas, alas for England
They have their graves afar.

And they that rule in England,
In stately conclave met,
Alas, alas for England
They have no graves as yet.

(ca. 1920)

THE ESCAPE

We watched you building, stone by stone,
    The well-washed cells and well-washed graves
We shall inhabit but not own
    When Britons ever shall be slaves;

---

[1] The version in *Collected Poems* has two misprints, "trumpet" for "triumph" in the first line, and dates it 1906. It appeared in *The Speaker* on October 20, 1900.

The water's waiting in the trough,
  The tame oats sown are portioned free,
There is Enough, and just Enough,
    and all is ready now but we.
        But you have not caught us yet, my lords,
        You have us still to get.
        A sorry army you'd have got,
        Its flags are rags that float and rot,
        Its drums are empty pan and pot,
        Its baggage is — an empty cot;
        But you have not caught us yet.

A little; and we might have slipped —
  When came your rumours and your sales
And the foiled rich men, feeble-lipped,
  Said and unsaid their sorry tales;
Great God! It needs a bolder brow
  To keep ten sheep inside a pen,
And we are sheep no longer now;
    You are but Masters. We are Men.
        We give you all good thanks, my lords,
        We buy at easy price;
        Thanks for the thousands that you stole,
        The bribes by wire, the bets on coal,
        The knowledge of that naked whole
        That hath delivered our flesh and soul
        Out of your Paradise.

We had held safe your parks; but when
  Men taunted you with bribe and fee,
We only saw the Lord of Men
  Grin like an Ape and climb a tree;
And humbly had we stood without
  Your princely barns; did we not see
In pointed faces peering out
  What Rats now own the granary.

It is too late, too late, my lords,
We give you back your grace:
You cannot with all cajoling
Make the wet ditch, or winds that sting,
Lost pride, or the pawned wedding rings,
Or drink or Death a blacker thing
Than a smile upon your face.

(ca. 1913)

FOR A WAR MEMORIAL

(Suggested Inscription Probably not Selected by the Committee)

The hucksters haggle in the mart
The cars and carts go by;
Senates and schools go droning on;
For dead things cannot die.

A storm stooped on the place of tombs
With bolts to blast and rive;
But these be names of many men
The lightning found alive.

If usurers rule and rights decay
And visions view once more
Great Carthage like a golden shell
Gape hollow on the shore,

Still to the last of crumbling time
Upon this stone be read
How many men of England died
To prove they were not dead.

(1918–20)

FREE LOVE: A SONNET

Name the thing knowledge—name it liberty—
To me this laughter and light sundering seems
Dark with the dismal anarchy of dreams
Where everything is false and therefore free:
The ringing bird-bolt shot with certainty
Shrieks past exultant as a sea-bird screams;
The thistledown, on every air that streams,
Floats ever in a sad frivolity.

You too that toy with treacheries, you too,
You (if the perfect one should come in power),
Having the terrible human heart within,
The trumpet of the valorous voice in you,
Shall sell your days like dung for the great hour
Where liberty shall end and life begin.

(ca. 1905)

GENTLEMEN PREFER BLONDES

"My leader wishes me to marry. I shall therefore seek a Protestant, pure Aryan girl, blonde, slim and possessed of private means."

— Quoted in *Hail Hitler*

Not the wild Walkyr maid alone
In her tremendous teens
Drags men with ropes of golden hair
And also private means.

For us that second golden string
Is known behind the scenes;
We too rejoice in public men
Who know what "private" means.

Still the poor German has the worst
When Nazi might unscreens
Such rather private matters on
The way to private means.

And if he seeks the Dark Lady
Judith or Sheba's Queens
The public power may shoot him dead
By very private means.

(1934)

GLADSTONE

The fresh hair flickered at her brows
   The fur and frill against her throat
She turned her face, and all my Soul
   God with a living splendour smote.

She said "In that grey hall at rest
   Dead lies the Councilor and sage"
She shook the ruffles of her wrist
   And laid her fingers on a page.

And all day long the human flood,
   Rolled through the Red King's echoing hall
But thus, and thus, between her brows,
   I had not seen the shadows fall;

You never willed a nation's will
   Or towered and thundered with the news
Yet one Man, very mean and poor
   Thanks God who gave him eyes to choose.

Lifts to the stars his head to think
   He did not lose, though one of ten,
One moment of your face to see
   The mightiest of the sons of men.

(ca. 1897–98)

HUMAN NATURE: OR MARCONI MEMORIES

(From our "Simplified Psychology for Statesmen" series)

Human nature is a bird
Whose complaint is often heard,
And will make demands of any legislature;
And you need not claim to be
Giving seven pence for three;
It exceeds the wildest hopes of Human Nature.

Human Nature is a thing
It is difficult to sing,
And very much more difficult to deal with:
But you need not call it "function" —
You can own without compunction
That your brother is a man you take a meal with.

Human Nature it prefers
To be told of what occurs
Without suppressing any vital feature;
And when statesmen hold their peace
Until searched by the police,
It rasps the finer edge of Human Nature.

Human Nature, it is said,
Thinks investment should be made
By someone who has cash enough to pay it;
And that one who pouched the pay,
And had nothing more to say.
Need not go to South America to say it.

Human Nature is not keen
On the words "corrupt" or "clean"
Or any other shades of nomenclature;
But, when what the Party cost
Is discovered when it's lost,
A shade of doubt is merely Human Nature.

Human Nature it is prone
To be soft about the Throne,
And even make the Peerage paramounter;
But it startles it to drop
Into Mr. Pearson's shop,
And find a Scottish Lord behind the counter.

So till all men learn the truth
(And not only Handel Booth)
And the Gospel has been preached to every creature,
Even rotten things may fail,
Even thieves may go to gaol,
And all through not observing Human Nature.

(1913)

THE JUDGMENT OF ENGLAND

"Ill fares the land, to hastening ills of prey
Where Wealth accumulates and Men decay."
So rang of old the noble voice in vain
O'er the Last Peasants wandering on the plain,
Doom has reversed the riddle and the rhyme,
While sinks the commerce reared upon that crime,
The thriftless towns litter with lives undone,
To whom our madness left no joy but one;
And irony that glares like Judgment Day
Sees Men accumulate and Wealth decay.

(1925)

THE LIBERAL PARTY[1]

Before the beginning of lords and kings,
Before the beginning of thrones,
Did we not bargain for better things,
And pay a price for the stones?

False we grew in the house of peace,
Small in the days of pride;
Only never of war we cease,
Never of death we died.

Stones that shatter and blades that shine
And hate of man made mad,
These were ever our meat and wine—
Let us eat and drink and be glad.

Though we fought from a broken wreck,
Though they were banded thus,
He that trod on Napoleon's neck
Could not tread upon us.

What if again be dark and drouth?
What if the dogs have bayed?
We that laugh in the lions mouth—
Why should we be afraid?

Before the beginning of lords and kings,
Before the beginning of thrones,

---

[1] This version appeared in *The Speaker*, August 18, 1900. An earlier draft has "lands" for "lords" in the first line, and several minor variants. The fifth verse reads:

> You, that trample the giant folk
> Scattered the Kings as chaff.
> Look on the foes they send you now,
> Look upon these and laugh!

The draft version (ca. 1898) is written in pencil in a copy of Carlyle's *Sartor Resartus*, now in the possession of the G. K. Chesterton Study Centre, Bedford, England. *The Speaker* printed verses 1 and 6 in capitals, but they are not so in the holograph version.

Did we not bargain for better things,
And pay a price for the stones?

The old wounds burn. Hail! To the hour!
Hail to the feast of Cain!
When they have the thrones and rods and power
And we our youth again.

(*The Speaker*, Aug. 18, 1900)

LINES TO AN OLD PRO-BOER WHO ASKED FOR
A CONTRIBUTION TO A PEACE PERIODICAL

You cannot think my heart so tough
To shrieks that ring or shards that rend;
You cannot think me bad enough
Nor good enough for tortures, friend.

Nor do I lightly talk of tears
Through some vague pageant of the past;
The shriek of shafts, the shock of spears,
The bursting of the arbelast.

Do you recall in that base fight,
When men were crushed with clubs of gold,
The meek and murderous flag of white
Of which our English lies were told,

Till white had washed away the red
And a calmed country found release?
Look forth to-day, and count the dead
Under your leprous flag of peace.

Rather than peace's pearl to pray,
When cast before us by such swine,
I would again your friends and mine
Were riding to Pretoria.

(1914)

LINES TO THE STATUE OF FERDINAND FOCH

Opposite Victoria Station

We should not carve in stone. If putty fails
Or soap or sand or muddy-melting snow,
Did not some great Colonial artist show
A bust in butter of the Prince of Wales?
Something whose stuff is mutable as our own
Panic in puffs and shame a passing shower,
But not the memory of our generous hour
Throned like a judge. We should not work in stone.

Before his face whose ever-lifted head
Looks to Our Lady of All The Victories,
The yellow sheets spatter his land with lies
And of his land and ours defile the dead.
Our perishing people, without wall or barn,
Raves by in rout; and over its loud retreat
Forward and foe-ward, against the streaming street,
Rides head to wind the Horseman of the Marne.

(1932)[1]

---

[1] This peom was the conclusion of an article written for Armistice Day 1932 for *G. K.'s Weekly*. In it Chesterton meditated on the recrudescence of Prussian militarism, and the remark by a gossip-writer that "After all, so long as England can impress a film-producer, she is still herself", which led G. K. C. to the thought that perhaps the film rather than architecture or sculpture might best express our shifting and dissolving politics; "Our national policy may best be described as a Fade-Out. . . . [A]s I looked out of a window near Victoria Station and saw a certain equestrian statue being set up . . . something moved me to set down the following lines; and I think I will formally emplace them here, like my epitaph, or a belated contribution to Armistice Day" (Nov. 26, 1932).

LOST

So you have gained the golden crowns, so you have piled together
  The laurels and the jewels, the pearls out of the blue,
But I will beat the bounding drum and I will fly the feather
  For all the glory I have lost, the good I never knew.

I saw the light of morning pale on princely human faces,
  In tales irrevocably gone, in final night enfurled,
I saw the tail of flying fights, a glimpse of burning blisses,
  And laughed to think what I had lost — the wealth of all
    the world.

Yea, ruined in a royal game I was before my cradle;
  Was ever gambler hurling gold who lost such things as I?
The purple moth that died an hour ere I was born of woman,
  The great green sunset God shall make three days after
    I die.

When all the lights are lost and done, when all the skies are
    broken,
  Above the ruin of the stars my soul shall sit in state,
With a brain made rich, with the irrevocable sunsets.
  And a closed heart happy in the fulness of a fate.

So you have gained the golden crowns and grasped the golden
    weather,
  The kingdoms and the hemispheres that all men buy and
    sell,
But I will lash the leaping drum and swing the flaring feather,
  For the light of seven heavens that are lost to me like hell.
               (*The Speaker*, Sept. 1901)

MEN LIKE GODS

Workers fly back and forth like piston-rods
And clerks like clocks strike eight or nine or ten:
Say, you who know when men will be like gods,
In what wild future men will be like men.

(1920s)

THE MODERN MANICHEE

He sayeth there is no sin, and all his sin
Swells round him into a world made merciless;
The midnight of his universe of shame
Is the vast shadow of his shamelessness
He blames all that begat him, gods or brutes,
And sires not sons he chides as with a rod.
The sins of the children visited on the fathers
Through all generations, back to a jealous God.

The fields that heal the humble, the happy forests
That sing to men confessed and men consoled,
To him are jungles only, greedy and groping,
Heartlessly new, unvenerably old.
Beyond the pride of his own cold compassion
Is only cruelty and imputed pain:
Matched with that mood, a boy's sport in the forest
Makes comrades of the slayer and the slain.

The innocent lust of the unfallen creatures
Moves him to hidden horror but no mirth;
Misplaced morality rots in the roots unconscious,
His stifled conscience stinks through the green earth.
The green things thrust like horrible huge snails,
Horns green and gross, each lifting a leering eye
He scarce can call a flower; it lolls obscene,
Its organs gaping to the sneering sky.

Dark with that dusk the old red god of gardens,
Still pagan but not merry any more,
Stirs up the dull adulteries of the dust,
Blind, frustrate, hopeless, hollow at the core;
The plants are brutes tied with green rope and roaring
Their terrible dark loves from tree to tree:
He shrinks as from a shaft, if by him singing,
A gilded pimp and pandar, goes the bee.

He sayeth, "I have no sin; I cast the stone,"
And throws his little pebble at the shrine,
Casts sin and stone away against the house
Whose health has turned earth's waters into wine.
The venom of that repudiated guilt
Poisons the sea and every natural flood
As once a wavering tyrant washed his hands,
And touching, turned the water black with blood.

(1920s)

THE OLD SONG

(On the Embankment in stormy weather)

A livid sky on London
And like the iron steeds that rear
A shock of engines halted,
And I knew the end was near:
And something said that far away, over the hills and far away,
There came a crawling thunder and the end of all things here.
For London Bridge is broken down, broken down, broken
    down,
As digging lets the daylight on the sunken streets of yore,
The lightning looked on London town, the broken bridge of
    London town,
The ending of a broken road where men shall go no more.

I saw the kings of London town,
The kings that buy and sell,
That built it up with penny loaves
And penny lies as well:

And where the streets were paved with gold the shrivelled
    paper shone for gold,
The scorching light of promises that pave the streets of hell.
For penny loaves will melt away, melt away, melt away,
Mock the mean that haggled in the grain they did not grow;
With hungry faces in the gate, a hundred thousand in the
    gate,
A thunder-flash on London and the finding of the foe.

I heard the hundred pin-makers
Slow down their racking din,
Till in the stillness men could hear
The dropping of the pin:

And somewhere men without the wall, beneath the wood,
    without the wall,
Had found the place where London ends and England can
    begin.
For pins and needles bend and break, bend and break, bend
    and break,
Faster than the breaking spears or the bending of the bow,
Of pageants pale in thunder-light, 'twixt thunder-load and
    thunder-light,
The Hundreds marching on the hills in the wars of long ago.

I saw great Cobbett riding,
The horseman of the shires;
And his face was red with judgement
And a light of Luddite fires:
And south to Sussex and the sea the lights leapt up for
    liberty,
The trumpet of the yeomanry, the hammer of the squires;
For bars of iron rust away, rust away, rust away,
Rend before the hammer and the horseman riding in,

Crying that all men at the last, and at the worst and at the
    last,
Have found the place where England ends and England can
    begin.

His horse-hoofs go before you,
Far beyond your bursting tyres;
And time is bridged behind him
And our sons are with our sires.

A trailing meteor on the Downs he rides above the rotting
    towns,
The Horseman of Apocalypse, the Rider of the Shires.
For London Bridge is broken down, broken down, broken
    down;
Blow the horn of Huntingdon from Scotland to the sea—
. . . Only a flash of thunder-light, a flying dream of thunderlight,
Had shown under the shattered sky a people that were free.

                      (1916–21)

OUTLINE OF HISTORY

A fishbone pattern of flint arrows flattened
    A fossil vision of the Age of Stone—
And sages in war-weary empires quarrel
    With those quaint quarrels and forget their own.
What riddle is of the elf-darts or the elves
But the strange stony riddle of ourselves?

As by long worms the hills are pierced with holes,
    Where long day's journeyings without light of day
Lead to a painted cave, a buried sky,
    Whose clouds are creatures sprawling in coloured clay;
And men ask how and why such things were done
Darkly, with dyes that never saw the sun.

I have seen a statue in a London square.
  One whose long-winded lies are long forgot
Gleams with the rain above the twinkling bushes,
  And birds perch on him in that unroofed plot.
Unriddle that dark image; and I will show
The secret of your pictured rocks below.

As green volcanic skies bury dark sunsets,
  Green rust like snakes crawled, and their work concealed
The men who were red shadows in copper mirrors,
  When groaned the golden and the brazen shield.
And the slaves worked the copper for their lords,
Stiff swarthy kings holding their yellow swords.

We have written the names of hucksters on the heavens
  And tied our pigmy slaves to giant tools,
And chosen our nobles from the mart; and never
  Stank to the sky the praise of prouder fools.
And 'mid the blare, the doctors and the dons,
In the Age of Brass brood on the Age of Bronze.

We clothe the dead in their theatric raiment
  To hide their nakedness of normality;
Disguise by gilded mask or horned mitre
  The accusing faces of such men as we:
Till the last brotherhood of men brings down
Us with the troglodytes in their twilight town.

                       (1920s)

PARAGUAY

So down the years the song of the Singing Republic
Strikes and resounds and is fainter and fades away;
High on the hills the march of the Singing Republic;
High in the heavens undarkened and dies into day.

So down the days the Song of the Singing Republic
Cries upon God, Alosa ka, the deathless song;
Of the good that even the good and the wise destroyed not
Of a realm where even the righteous have done no wrong.

Falling from heaven and afar, as a faint voice calling
"Woe to the hypocrites, Woe; to the wise and few;
Woe to the Chosen, who chose not but only rejected;
And in Adam the Red Man have crucified Christ anew."

Fainter and fainter the Song of the Singing Republic;
Song unto song and music in music is furled,
And lost are the heroes in heaven and the saints return not;
Rolls on over the ruin of races the wheel of the world.

(ca. 1900)[1]

PERFECTION

Of all the heroes whom the poets sing
The one I like is General Goering:
A man of iron, cold and stern, it seems,
Ask him the simplest question and he screams,
If any other witness moves or speaks
The Court-House rings with long protracted shrieks;
These sounds, mysterious to the racial stranger,
Impress an Aryan people with the danger
Of interrupting strong and silent men
Just at the psychologic moment when
They are, for Reich, Race, Goering and Gore,
Having hysterics on the Court-House floor:
Howl at us, black and purple in the face,
To note the calm of the Germanic race.

---

[1] This appears to be a tribute to the pioneering work of the Jesuit missionaries in the second half of the 16th century. Chesterton regarded their "Reductions", self-governing Christian co-operatives, as an early form of Distributism. See the *Chesterton Review*, August 1987.

Not oft to any council, crowd or king,
Comes the high windfall of the Perfect Thing.
Those that dwell nearest Music's mightiest chords
Think the best German Songs are Without Words
Or, studying Heine's soul, may ponder long
How such a sneer became a Perfect Song:
Hitlerites may explain how Race can teach
Imperfect wits to make a Perfect Speech,
But all who know what crowns our mortal dream
Will own that Goering is a Perfect Scream.

(1933)

POLAND

Augurs that watched archaic birds
Such plumèd prodigies might read,
The eagles that were double-faced,
The eagle that was black indeed;
And when the battle-birds went down
And in their track the vultures come,
We know what pardon and what peace
Will keep our little masters dumb.

The men that sell what others make,
As vultures eat what others slay,
Will prove in matching plume with plume
That naught is black and all is grey;
Grey as those dingy doves that once,
By money-changers palmed and priced,
Amid the crash of tables flapped
And huddled from the wrath of Christ.

But raised for ever for a sign
Since God made anger glorious,
Where eagles black and vultures grey
Flocked back about the heroic house,

Where war is holier than peace,
Where hate is holier than love,
Shone terrible as the Holy Ghost
An eagle whiter than a dove.

(ca. 1920)

THE PORT OF LONDON AUTHORITY

Mr. Ben Tillett is reported to have once prayed in public
for the death of Lord Devonport — daily paper

We whom great mercy holds in fear,
    Boast not the claim to cry,
Stricken of any mortal wrong,
    "Lord, let this live man die!"

But not incuriously we ask,
    Pondering on life and death,
What name befits that round of years,
    What name that span of breath.

That perfect dullness counting hands
    That have no man or woman,
That fullness of the commonplace
    That can despise the common.

That startling smallness that can stop
    The breath like an abyss,
As staring at rows of noughts, we cry,
    "And men grow old for this!"

The thing that sniggers when it sneers,
    That never can forget,
The billycock outshines the cap,
    And then—the coronet!

O mighty to arise and smite,
    O mightier to forgive,
Sunburst that blasted Lazarus,
    Lord, let this dead man live!
                        (1920s)

THE REAL ANTHEM

From every folly vain
From every pride insane
    God save the King.

From every lawless claim
From every tyrant aim
From the oppressor's shame
    God save the King.

From the red stains of blood
From foul corruption's mud
    God save the King.

Our father strong to be
Our elect ruler free
Our nation's liberty
    God save the King.

THE SECRET PEOPLE

Smile at us, pay us, pass us; but do not quite forget.
For we are the people of England, that never have spoken
        yet.
There is many a fat farmer that drinks less cheerfully,
There is many a free French peasant who is richer and sadder
        than we.

There are no folk in the whole world so helpless or so wise.
There is hunger in our bellies, there is laughter in our eyes;
You laugh at us and love us, both mugs and eyes are wet:
Only you do not know us. For we have not spoken yet.

The fine French kings came over in a flutter of flags and
dames.
We liked their smiles and battles, but we never could say
their names.
The blood ran red to Bosworth and the high French lords
went down;
There was naught but a naked people under a naked crown.
And the eyes of the King's Servants turned terribly every way
And the gold of the King's Servants rose higher every day.
They burnt the homes of the shaven men, that had been quaint
and kind,
Till there was no bed in a monk's house, nor food that man
could find.
The inns of God where no man paid, that were the wall of
the weak,
The King's Servants ate them all. And still we did not speak.

And the face of the King's Servants grew greater than the
King:
He tricked them, and they trapped him, and stood round
him in a ring.
The new grave lords closed round him, that had eaten the
abbey's fruits,
And the men of the new religion, with their Bibles in their
boots,
We saw their shoulders moving, to menace or discuss,
And some were pure and some were vile; but none took heed
of us.
We saw the King as they killed him, and his face was proud
and pale;
And a few men talked of freedom, while England talked of
ale.

A war that we understood not came over the world and woke
Americans, Frenchmen, Irish; but we knew not the things
      they spoke.
They talked about rights and nature and peace and the people's
      reign:
And the squires, our masters, bade us fight; and scorned us
      never again.
Weak if we be for ever, could none condemn us then;
Men called us serfs and drudges; men knew that we were
      men.
In foam and flame at Trafalgar, on Albuera plains,
We did and died like lions, to keep ourselves in chains
We lay in living ruins; firing and fearing not
The strange fierce face of the Frenchmen who knew for what
      they fought,
And the man who seemed to be more than man we strained
      against and broke;
And we broke our own rights with him. And still we never
      spoke.

Our patch of glory ended; we never heard guns again.
But the squire seemed struck in the saddle; he was foolish,
      as if in pain.
He leaned on a staggering lawyer, he clutched a cringing
      Jew,
He was stricken; it may be, after all, he was stricken at
      Waterloo.
Or perhaps the shades of the shaven men, whose spoil is in
      his house,
Come back in shining shapes at last to spoil his last carouse:
We only know the last sad squires ride slowly towards the
      sea,
And a new people takes the land: and still it is not we.

They have given us into the hand of new unhappy lords,
Lords without anger and honour, who dare not carry their
      swords.

They fight by shuffling papers; they have bright dead alien
    eyes;
They look at our labour and laughter as a tired man looks at
    flies.
And the load of their loveless pity is worse than the ancient
    wrongs,
Their doors are shut in the evening; and they know no songs.

We hear men speaking for us of new laws strong and sweet,
Yet is there no man speaketh as we speak in the street.
It may be we shall rise the last as Frenchmen rose the first,
Our wrath come after Russia's wrath and our wrath be the
    worst.
It may be we are meant to mark with our riot and our rest
God's scorn for all men governing. It may be beer is best.
But we are the people of England; and we have not spoken
    yet.
Smile at us, pay us, pass us. But do not quite forget.

(1907)

A SONG OF COSMOPOLITAN COURAGE

I am so swift to seize affronts,
    My spirit is so high,
Whoever has insulted me
    Some foreigner must die.

I brought a libel action,
    For *The Times* had called me "thief",
Against a paper in Bordeaux,
    A paper called *Le Juif*.

The *Nation* called me "cannibal"
    I could not let it pass—
I got a retraction
    From a journal in Alsace.

And when *The Morning Post* raked up
  Some murders I'd devised,
A Polish organ of finance
  At once apologised.

I know the charges varied much;
  At times, I am afraid
The *Frankfurt Frank* withdrew a charge
  The *Outlook* had not made.

And what the true injustice
  Of the *Standard's* words had been,
Was not correctly altered
  In the *Young Turk's Magazine*.

I know it sounds confusing —
  But as Mr. Lammle said,
The anger of a gentleman
  Is boiling in my head.

(1913)

THE SONG OF LABOUR

A light, a glimmer outlines the crest of the mountain walls,
Starlike it broadens and brightens, and day o'er the valley fails;
It waketh the prince to praise, and it waketh the fool to mirth,
And it waketh a man to his toil and his place on the ordered earth.

There are uplands cloudlet-shadowed and mountains thunder-browed,
There are wastes of wood untravelled, and leagues of land unploughed,
Swamp-worlds heavy with poison, worlds grey and chill,
And I go, a clearer and builder, the voice of the human will.
God has struck all into chaos, princes and priests down-hurled,
But He leaves the place of the toiler, the old estate of the world.
In a season of doubt and of wrangle, in the thick of a world's uproar,
With the new life dark in wrestle, with the ghost of a life that is o'er,

When the old Priest fades to a phantom, when the old King nods
on his throne,
The old, old hand of Labour is mighty and holdeth its own.
Other leaders may rest upon words, wax proud, and neglect the hours,
But our work is real, and standeth, in leaf and in fruit and in flowers,
In roofs and farms and fences, in draining of mere and of fen,
In the endless going and coming in the homes of the children of men.
Through the blaze of the regal ages, through the wrack of the
feudal strife,
We toiled unseen for ever at the roots of the racial life.
The earth brought forth in abundance at the stroke of the hind
and the churl,
Till his roof was fired by the chieftain, his fields trodden down
by the earl.
Stand to it silently, brothers, and watch for the hour and the day.
We have tramped and toiled for the idle, we have sorrowed and
starved for the gay;
We have hewn out the road for the passers through thicket and
mountain high —
Stand to it bravely, brothers, for the day and the hour are nigh.
Sorry and weary it is, our terrible army of toil —
With swart limbs bent to the tool, and dark brows turned to the soil.
We look not to heaven, nor pray: we see not the stars overhead,
But we stamp our stern evangel on the face of the earth we tread.
Sorry and weary it is, our army of labour and pain —
Its words are vague and frantic, its hopes are dark and vain;
Yet laugh not aloud, ye mighty, nor triumph, nor pass ye on,
For the High God heareth for ever the voice of the work we have done;
He knows who have striven with Nature, and claimed and
conquered the earth,
He knows who have stood to a manhood where work is the title of
worth,
He knows who are feeding the nations, are working at eve and at morn.
And He knows who have sneered and been idle, and struck them, and
laughed them to scorn.

The poet may look into Nature for mirrors of passion and pain,
For the breadth of an isolation, the nurse of a black disdain;
The painter may look into Nature for shaping of sky and of land,
For blending of glorious hues and visions of fairyland;
But we who are dwelling with her can bend to her breast and hear
The roar of the endless purpose that grappleth sphere to sphere.
Therefore I go at the dawn to my work with a mighty mirth,
For the law of the earth is labour and man is the dust of the earth.

(The Speaker, Dec. 17, 1892)[1]

A SONG OF SWORDS

"A drove of cattle came into a village called Swords, and
was stopped by the rioters." — daily paper

In the place called Swords on the Irish road
It is told for a new renown
How we held the horns of the cattle, and how
We will hold the horns of the devil now
Ere the lord of hell, with the horn on his brow,
    Is crowned in Dublin town

Light in the East and light in the West,
And light on the cruel lords,
On the souls that suddenly all men knew,
And the green flag flew and the red flag flew,
And many a wheel of the world stopped too,
    When the cattle were stopped at Swords.

Be they sinners or less than saints
That smite in the street for rage,
We know where the shame shines bright; we know
You that they smite at, you their foe,
Lords of the lawless wage and low,
    This is your lawful wage.

[1] This was Chesterton's first appearance in the national press.

You pinched a child to a torture price
That you dared not name in words;
So black a jest was the silver bit
That your own speech shook for the shame of it,
And the coward was plain as a cow they hit
    When the cattle have strayed at Swords.

The wheel of the torment of wives went round
To break men's brotherhood;
You gave the good Irish blood to grease
The clubs of your country's enemies;
You saw the brave men beat to the knees:
    And you saw that it was good.

The rope of the rich is long and long—
The longest of hangmen's cords;
But the kings and crowds are holding their breath,
In a giant shadow o'er all beneath
Where God stands holding the scales of Death
    Between the cattle and Swords.

Haply the lords that hire and lend,
The lowest of all men's lords,
Who sell their kind like kine at a fair,
Will find no head of their cattle there;
But faces of men where cattle were:
    Faces of men—and Swords.

And the name shining and terrible,
The sternest of all man's words,
Still mark that place to seek or shun,
In streets where the struggling cattle run—
Grass and a silence of judgement done
    In the place that is called Swords.

$$(1913)^1$$

---

[1] In this poem G. K. C. took the place-name at its face value in English, but the Irish name is Sórd Colaim Chille, from a pure well said to have been blessed by St. Columcille. The occasion was the seizure, by locked-out and starving Dublin workers, of a herd of cattle—a swordlike stroke for liberty.

THE SONG OF THE WHEELS

Written during a Friday and Saturday in August, 1911

King Dives he was walking in his garden all alone,
Where his flowers are made of iron and his trees are made of
    stone,
And his hives are full of thunder and the lightning leaps
    and kills,
For the mills of God grind slowly; and he works with other
    mills.
Dives found a mighty silence; and he missed the throb and
    leap,
The noise of all the sleepless creatures singing him to sleep.
And he said: "A screw has fallen—or a bolt has slipped aside—
Some little thing has shifted": and the little things replied:

"Call upon the wheels, master, call upon the wheels;
We are taking rest, master, finding how it feels,
Strict the law of thine and mine: theft we ever shun—
All the wheels are thine, master—tell the wheels to run!
Yea, the Wheels are mighty gods—set them going then!
We are only men, master, have you heard of men?

"O, they live on earth like fishes, and a gasp is all their
    breath.
God for empty honours only gave them death and scorn of
    death,
And you walk the worms for carpet and you tread a stone
    that squeals
Only, God that made them worms did not make them wheels.
Man shall shut his heart against you and you shall not find
    the spring.
Man who wills the thing he wants not, the intolerable thing—
Once he likes his empty belly better than your empty head
Earth and heaven are dumb before him: he is stronger than
    the dead.

"Call upon the wheels, master, call upon the wheels,
Steel is beneath your hand, stone beneath your heels,
Steel will never laugh aloud, hearing what we heard,
Stone will never break its heart, mad with hope deferred—
Men of tact that arbitrate, slow reform that heals—
Save the stinking grease, master, save it for the wheels.

"King Dives in the garden, we have naught to give or hold—
(Even while the baby came alive the rotten sticks were sold.)
The savage knows a cavern and the peasants keep a plot,
Of all the things that men have had—lo! we have them
      not.
Not a scrap of earth where ants could lay their eggs—
Only this poor lump of earth that walks about on legs—
Only this poor wandering mansion, only these two walking
      trees,
Only hands and hearts and stomachs—what have you to do
      with these?
You have engines big and burnished, tall beyond our fathers'
      ken,
Why should you make peace and traffic with such feeble folk
      as men?

"Call upon the wheels, master, call upon the wheels,
They are deaf to demagogues, deaf to crude appeals;
Are our hands our own, master?—how the doctors doubt!
Are our legs our own, master? wheels can run without—
Prove the points are delicate—they will understand.
All the wheels are loyal; see how still they stand!"

King Dives he was walking in his garden in the sun,
He shook his hand at heaven, and he called the wheels to
      run,
And the eyes of him were hateful eyes, the lips of him were
      curled,
And he called upon his father that is lord below the world,

Sitting in the Gate of Treason, in the gate of broken seals,
"Bend and bind them, bend and bind them, bend and bind
    them into wheels,
Then once more in all my garden there may swing and sound
    and sweep—
The noise of all the sleepless things that sing the soul to sleep."

Call upon the wheels, master, call upon the wheels,
Weary grow the holidays when you miss the meals,
Through the Gate of Treason, through the gate within,
Cometh fear and greed of fame, cometh deadly sin;
If a man grow faint, master, take him ere he kneels,
Take him, break him, rend him, end him, roll him, crush him
    with the wheels.

(1911)

SONNET

On hearing a landlord accused (falsely, for all the Bard
can say) of neglecting one of the numerous white
horses that were or were not connected with
Alfred the Great

If you have picked your lawn of leaves and snails,
If you have told your valet, even with oaths,
Once a week or so, to brush your clothes,
If you have dared to clean your teeth, or nails,
While the Horse upon the holy mountain fails—
Then God that Alfred to his earth betrothes
Send on you screaming all that honour loathes,
Horsewhipping, Houndsditch, debts and *Daily Mails*.

Can you not even conserve? For if indeed
The White Horse fades; then closer creeps the fight
When we shall scour the face of England white,
Plucking such men as you up like a weed,
And fling them far beyond a shaft shot right
When Wessex went to battle for the Creed.

(1912)

SONNET WITH THE COMPLIMENTS OF THE
SEASON

*To a popular leader much to be congratulated on the
avoidance of a strike at Christmas*

I know you. You will hail the huge release,
Saying the sheathing of a thousand swords,
In silence and injustice, well accords
With Christmas bells. And you will gild with grease
The papers, the employers, the police,
And vomit up the void your windy words
To your New Christ; who bears no whip of cords
For them that traffic in the doves of peace.

The feast of friends, the candle-fruited tree,
I have not failed to honour. And I say
It would be better for such men as we,
And we be nearer Bethlehem, if we lay
Shot dead on scarlet snows for liberty,
Dead in the daylight upon Christmas Day.

(1911)

TO A CERTAIN NATION

We will not let thee be, for thou art ours.
   We thank thee still, though thou forget these things,
For that hour's sake when thou didst wake all powers
   With a great cry that God was sick of kings.

Leave thee there grovelling at their rusted greaves,
   These hulking cowards on a painted stage,
Who, with imperial pomp and laurel leaves,
   Show their Marengo—one man in a cage.

These, for whom stands no type or title given
    In all the squalid tales of gore and pelf;
Though cowed by crashing thunders from all heaven,
    Cain never said, 'My brother slew himself.'

Tear you the truth out of your drivelling spy,
    The maniac whom you set to swing death's scythe.
Nay; torture not the torturer—let him lie:
    What need of racks to teach a worm to writhe?

Bear with us, O our sister, not in pride,
    Nor any scorn we see thee spoiled of knaves,
But only shame to hear, where Danton died,
    Thy foul dead kings all laughing in their graves.

Thou has a right to rule thyself; to be
    The thing thou wilt; to grin, to fawn, to creep;
To crown these clumsy liars; ay, and we
    Who knew thee once, we have a right to weep.
                                                (1898)

TO THEM THAT MOURN

(W. E. G., 1898)[1]

Lift up your heads: in life, in death,
    God knoweth his head was high.
Quit we the coward's broken breath
    Who watched a strong man die.

If we must say, 'No more his peer
    Cometh; the flag is furled.'
Stand not too near him, lest he hear
    That slander on the world.

[1] William Ewart Gladstone, 1809-98.

The good green earth he loved and trod
   Is still, with many a scar,
Writ in the chronicles of God,
   A giant-bearing star.

He fell: but Britain's banner swings
   Above his sunken crown.
Black death shall have his toll of kings
   Before that cross goes down.

Once more shall move with mighty things
   His house of ancient tale,
Where kings whose hands were kissed of kings
   Went in: and came out pale.

O young ones of a darker day,
   In art's wan colours clad,
Whose very love and hate are grey—
   Whose very sin is sad,

Pass on: one agony long-drawn
   Was merrier than your mirth,
When hand-in-hand came death and dawn,
   And spring was on the earth.

               (1898)

A VERDICT

Mercy there is to ask: but not of these,
That count the stripes upon a coat and see
How they may judge. Enough—they judged themselves
And spoke: and hanged their soul upon a tree.

Mercy there is to seek: nor yet of these
His hungry foes, by fear made light and lithe:
Nay, judge not, torture not, the twisted souls—
What need of racks to teach a worm to writhe?

We wait for mercy in a narrower court:
Dreaming if pardon or black judgement brews
Beneath one brow: bound with such crown of thorns
As old-world warriors bound upon a Jew.

Mother of Arts, behold thy son! Away!
Of old long loves still this much left have we
As for some screaming harlot, still to pray
That in this hour he is not judging thee.

(The Speaker, Sept. 16, 1899)

WHO GOES HOME?

In the city set upon slime and loam
They cry in their parliament 'Who goes home?'
And there comes no answer in arch or dome,
For none in the city of graves goes home.
Yet these shall perish and understand,
For God has pity on this great land.

Men that are men again; who goes home?
Tocsin and trumpeter! Who goes home?
For there's blood on the field and blood on the foam
And blood on the body when Man goes home.
And a voice valedictory. . . . Who is for Victory?
Who is for Liberty? Who goes home?

(ca. 1913)

VII

LIGHT VERSE,
NONSENSE VERSE

It is requested that all communications be addressed to the Firm.

Telegraphic Address—"CENTURY, LONDON."

...SHER UNWIN,
PUBLISHER.

Office of
COSMOPOLIS.'
CENTURY DICTIONARY.
STORY OF THE NATIONS.
PSEUDONYM LIBRARY.
AUTONYM LIBRARY.
CENTURY LIBRARY.
ADVENTURE SERIES.
CHILDREN'S LIBRARY.
REFORMER'S BOOKSHELF.
CAMEO SERIES.
NEW IRISH LIBRARY.
MERMAID SERIES.
INDEPENDENT NOVEL SERIES.
LIVES WORTH LIVING SERIES.
CLIMBER'S GUIDES.
REVUE BLEUE.
REVUE SCIENTIFIQUE.
BUILDERS OF GREAT BRITAIN.
MASTERS OF MEDICINE.
LITERARY HISTORY SERIES.

11, Paternoster Buildings.
London;
E.C.

___ _____18

The Joys of Science. —

I took her & I flattened her
  Respectfully, I hope
I pasted her upon a slip
  Under the Microscope
With six-power lense - I saw her
Ah, I shall ne'er forget-
While hearts can break & flowers can blow
  That hour when first we met— .

Ah, with what prayer & fasting
Shall mortal man deserve
To see that glimpse of heaven
  Her os motor vagus nerve.
Gaze not, ye too inflammable
Beneath that harmless hair
The Convolutions of her brain
  Are perilously fair —

AN APOLOGY FOR CLOWNS

From the sermons in stone and the cymbals,
From the songs that are older than books,
That the fool of Shakespearean fancy
Is not such a fool as he looks;

That the changes hang heavy with question
In the land where our fathers were free,
That took from us flagons and fairies
And gave us tobacco and tea.

(1920s)

THE ARISTOCRAT

The Devil is a gentleman, and asks you down to stay
At his little place at What'sitsname (it isn't far away).
They say the sport is splendid; there is always something new,
And fairy scenes, and fearful feats that none but he can do;
He can shoot the feathered cherubs if they fly on the estate,
Or fish for Father Neptune with the mermaids for a bait;
He scaled amid the staggering stars that precipice, the sky,
And blew his trumpet above heaven, and got by mastery
The starry crown of God Himself, and shoved it on the shelf;
But the Devil is a gentleman, and doesn't brag himself.

O blind your eyes and break your heart and hack your hand
    away,
And lose your love and shave your head; but do not go to stay
At the little place in What'sitsname where folks are rich and
    clever;
The golden and the goodly house, where things grow worse
    for ever;

There are things you need not know of, though you live and
    die in vain,
There are souls more sick of pleasure than you are sick of pain;
There is a game of April Fool that's played behind its door,
Where the fool remains for ever and the April comes no more,

Where the splendour of the daylight grows drearier than the
    dark,
And life droops like a vulture that once was such a lark:
And that is the Blue Devil that once was the Blue Bird;
For the Devil is a gentleman, and doesn't keep his word.

                         (1912)

A BALLAD OF ABBREVIATIONS

The American's a hustler, for he says so,
    And surely the American must know.
He will prove to you with figures why it pays so
    Beginning with his boyhood long ago.
When the slow-maturing anecdote is ripest,
    He'll dictate it like a Board of Trade Report,
And because he has no time to call a typist,
    He calls her a Stenographer for short.

He is never known to loiter or malinger,
    He rushes, for he knows he has "a date";
He is always on the spot and full of ginger,
    Which is why he is invariably late.
When he guesses that it's getting even later,
    His vocabulary's vehement and swift,
And he yells for what he calls the Elevator,
    A slang abbreviation for a lift.

Then nothing can be nattier or nicer
    For those who like a light and rapid style,
Than to trifle with a work of Mr. Dreiser
    As it comes along in waggons by the mile.

He has taught us what a swift selective art meant
   By description of his dinners and all that,
And his dwelling, which he says is an Apartment,
   Because he cannot stop to say a flat.

We may whisper of his wild precipitation,
   That its speed is rather longer than a span,
But there really is a definite occasion
   When he does not use the longest word he can.
When he substitutes, I freely make admission,
   One shorter and much easier to spell;
If you ask him what he thinks of Prohibition
   He may tell you quite succinctly it is Hell.

                         (ca. 1920s)

A BROAD MINDED BISHOP REBUKES THE VERMINOUS ST. FRANCIS

If Brother Francis pardoned Brother Flea,
There still seems need of such strange charity,
Seeing he is, for all his gay goodwill,
Bitten by funny little creatures still.
            (G. K.'s Weekly, Oct. 16, 1926)

THE CHRISTIAN SOCIAL UNION, NOTTINGHAM

The Christian Social Union here
Was very much annoyed;
It seems there is some duty
Which we never should avoid,
And so they sang a lot of hymns
To help the Unemployed.

Upon a platform at the end
The speakers were displayed
And Bishop Hoskins stood in front
And hit a bell and said
That Mr Carter was to pray,
And Mr Carter prayed.

Then Bishop Gore of Birmingham
He stood upon one leg
And said he would be happier
If beggars didn't beg,
And that if they pinched his palace
It would take him down a peg.

He said that Unemployment
Was a horror and a blight,
He said that charities produced
Servility and spite,
And stood upon the other leg
And said it wasn't right.

And then a man named Chesterton
Got up and played with water,
He seemed to say that principles
Were nice and led to slaughter
And how we always compromised
And how we didn't orter.

Then Canon Holland fired ahead
Like fifty cannons firing,
We tried to find out what he meant
With infinite enquiring,
But the way he made the windows jump
We couldn't help admiring.

I understood him to remark
(It seemed a little odd)
That half a dozen of his friends

Had never been in quod.
He said he was a Socialist
Himself, and so was God.

He said the human soul should be
Ashamed of every sham,
He said a man should constantly
Ejaculate "I am"
When he had done, I went outside
And got into a tram.

(ca. 1906)[1]

COMMERCIAL CANDOUR

(On the outside of a sensational novel is printed the statement: The back of the cover will tell you the plot.)

Our fathers to creed and tradition were tied,
They opened a book to see what was inside,
And of various methods they deemed not the worst
Was to find the first chapter and look at it first.
And so from the first to the second they passed,
Till in servile routine they arrived at the last.
But a literate age, unbenighted by creed,
Can find on two boards all it wishes to read;
For the front of the cover shows somebody shot
And the back of the cover will tell you the plot.

Between, that the book may be handily padded,
Some pages of mere printed matter are added,
Expanding the theme, which in case of great need
The curious reader might very well read
With the zest that is lent to a game worth the winning,
By knowing the end when you start the beginning;

---

[1] The penultimate verse was omitted by G. K. C. from his *Autobiography*. It was given, slightly wrongly, in John O'Connor's *Father Brown on Chesterton*.

While our barbarous sires, who would read every word
With a morbid desire to find out what occurred,
Went drearily drudging through Dickens and Scott.
But the back of the cover will tell you the plot.

The wild village folk in earth's earliest prime
Could often sit still for an hour at a time
And hear a blind beggar, nor did the tale pall
Because Hector must fight before Hector could fall:
Nor was Scheherazade required, at the worst,
To tell her tales backwards and finish them first;
And the minstrels who sang about battle and banners

Found the rude camp-fire crowd had some notion of manners.
Till Forster (who pelted the people like crooks,
The Irish with buckshot, the English with books),
Established the great educational scheme
Of compulsory schooling, that glorious theme.
Some learnt how to read, and the others forgot,
And the back of the cover will tell you the plot.

O Genius of Business! O marvellous brain,
Come in place of the priests and the warriors to reign!
O Will to Get On that makes everything go—
O Hustle! O Pep! O Publicity! O!
Shall I spend three-and-sixpence to purchase the book,
Which we all can pick up on the bookstall and look?
Well, it may appear strange, but I think I shall not,
For the back of the cover will tell you the plot.

THE CROONER

No more the thunderous trumpets tell
To hold life light when life runs high:
A coon will croon to beat the Band
And those that hear and understand

Will only be too glad to die.
Men have forgotten how to whisper:
Men have forgotten how to shout:
They mumble into some machine
And through ten gadgets in between
An artificial yell comes out.
The hero's harp, the lover's lute[1]
Were low or loud as feelings flow:
Science has given the modern crowd
Something unquestionably loud
And still unquestionably low.

(late 1920s)

CYRANO

Cyrano, allez aux chiens
    Héro de l'art, l'amour, la guerre
Son nez à elle est moins que sien
    Mais c'est pour moi plus grande affaire
Ah! c'est facheuse, cette manière
    Je m'ennuie de ces [becs] si courts
Elle n'est poète, cette Boore la mère
    Qu'elle est heureuse, cette Madame Boore.

Princesse la vie, la vie coûte cher
    Tout Roi tombe, chacun son tour
Il n'y a qu'une belle chose sous l'éclair,
    Qu'elle est heureuse cette Madame Boore.

(late 1890s)[2]

---

[1] For this line I am indebted to the late Lord Byron. — G. K. C.

[2] Seemingly, this is the third (final) stanza and the *envoi* of a ballade written in French.

DARWINIANS AT PLAY

A voice from Leeds will rouse amain
Each pre-historic pre-historian
To fight his battles o'er again
Very Victorious — and Victorian
The day when Darwin's rule began.
And all his pupils' reading ended
In learning The Descent of Man
And not how far it has descended.

Each grey-haired sage will grin and gape
At Samson in the antique pass
Wielding the thigh-bone of an age
And not the jaw-bone of an ass
And stir the joke that's just as old
And dusty as the dear old dunce
For us, who need not to be told
He often uses both at once.

Pert youth may mock at Samson's fury
May snigger when the storm has burst
May hint that foremen of a jury
Sometimes consult the jury first.
But when Darwinians, roused and hot
Spring to their feet by slow degree
Who says Sir Arthur Keith is not
Discovering antiquities.

                              (mid 1920s)

ECONOMICS

On an undiscovered island
Lives an economical Man
And liking his bit of the dry land,
He keeps as dry as he can:
There never was wine or weeper
There never was blood or beer
Where he makes cheap comfort cheaper
And dear what a man holds dear.

On the sand where the sea-wave ripples
He proved a number of things
The folly of sticks for cripples
The folly of swords for kings;
And how a man's next-door neighbour
Should be suffered to starve in Hove
Because his particular labour
Is wanted in Ladbroke Grove.

But the Statesmen, true and tireless,
Got wind of his words one day,
Tapped by Marconi wireless,
In a very Marconi way:
And wherever there's public friction
Or the crowd is beginning to groan,
His views come through in a diction
Remarkably like their own.

We don't understand precisely
We almost think from the text,
If you export imports nicely
You can import exports next
It's explained at the next Election
To the finest logical shade:
And when you have freed Protection
Why then you protect Free Trade.

It's not very clear as stated
It might be a yes or a no
But whatever it is, it's fated,
And whatever it says, it's so
Till the whole bally lot go bumping
Where the bad and the good niggers went,
Where they don't care a dump for dumping
Or a cent for eighty per cent.

(1920s?)

EHEU FUGACES

Eheu fugaces, Postume
(An old quotation out of mode)
My coat of dreams is stolen away
My youth is passing down the road

The wealth of Youth, we spent it well
And decently, as very few can:
And is it lost? I cannot tell
And what is more, I doubt if you can:

The question's very much too wide
And much too deep and much too hollow,
And learned men on either side
Use arguments I cannot follow.

They say that in that better place
Where all things distant are made near,
We meet our morning face to face
And feel again our twentieth year.

Whose face was bent to the furrow,
Who ate not the fruit as it hung,
On the Twilight Tree, and did not know
The best or the worst too young

This is the worker's blessing
The world's first viols played
A flutter of robes and faces,
A heaven and earth new made.

I will sing of the great archangels,
And the dead Christ hung on Tree:
But the great strange song of the Second Youth
Is a song too high for me.

(mid 1890s)

THE ENGLISHMAN

St. George he was for England,
And before he killed the dragon
He drank a pint of English ale
Out of an English flagon.
For though he fast right readily
In hair-shirt or in mail,
It isn't safe to give him cakes
Unless you give him ale.

St. George he was for England,
And right gallantly set free
The lady left for dragon's meat
And tied up to a tree;
But since he stood for England
And knew what England means,
Unless you give him bacon
You mustn't give him beans.

St. George he is for England,
And shall wear the shield he wore
When we go out in armour
With the battle-cross before.

But though he is jolly company
And very pleased to dine,
It isn't safe to give him nuts
Unless you give him wine.

(1912)

ESKIMO SONG

"So that the audience in Chicago will have the advantage of hearing
Eskimos singing" (or words to that effect) — wireless programme

Oh who would not want such a wonderful thing
As the pleasure of hearing the Eskimos sing?
I wish I had Eskimos out on the lawn,
Or perched on the window to wake me at dawn:
With Eskimos singing in every tree
Oh that would be glory, be glory for me!

Oh list to the song that the Eskimos sing,
When the penguin would be, if he could, on the wing,
Would soar to the sun if he could, like the lark,
But for most of the time it is totally dark.

Or hark to the bacchanal songs that resound
When they're making a night of it half the year round,
And carousing for months till the morning is pale,
Go home with the milk of the walrus and whale.

Oh list to the sweet serenades that are hers,
Who expensively gowned in most elegant furs,
Leans forth from the lattice delighted to know
That her heart is like ice and her hand is like snow.

God bless all the dear little people who roam
And hail in the icebergs the hills of their home;
For I might not object to be listening in
If I hadn't to hear the whole programme begin.

And hear the President preach international peace,
And Parricide show an alarming increase,
And a Justice at Bootle excuse the police,
And how to clean trousers when spotted with grease,
And a pianist biting his wife from caprice,
And an eminent Baptist's arrival at Nice,
And a banker's regrettably painless decease,
And the new quarantine for the plucking of geese,
And a mad millionaire's unobtrusive release,
And a marquis divorced by a usurer's niece —
If all of these items could suddenly cease
And leave me with one satisfactory thing
I really should like to hear Eskimos sing.

EVOLUTION

(Being a substantial summary and digest of the mental substance of
about fifteen books on that subject, sent for review.)

My name is John Majuba-Jink,
I live down Tooting way;
My house is of a quiet pink,
Except on Empire Day.

My cousin Sarah seeks the Lord,
And likes to save a sinner:
We have her, and are rather bored,
On Boxing Day to dinner.

I keep a wife in tisty style
Also a motor-cycle
And I have read the Dily Mile
On J. McCybe on Hickel.

Also "The Martyrdom of Man"
By Mr Winwood Reade;
So cannot bow, like Sarah can,
My 'ead to any creed.

But in the works of daring thought
Of which I read reviews
I learn how Evolution wrought
All varied things to use.

How systems rugged and unripe,
And saints insane but fervent,
Produced at last the highest type;
Your most obedient servant.

In horns and talons, fins and wings,
In monsters of the sea
In shaggy shapeless forest things,
Were lovely hints of me.

St John that saw heaven's curtain-hems,
Like an old garment riven;
Saw Upper Tooting, bright with gems
Descending out of heaven.

And warring Alfred paused to drink
One wine-cup in his dearth;
And muttered "John Majuba Jink
Shall yet appear on earth."

And Aristotle's gleams of thought,
And Homer's hints of song,
Have found the goal they blindly sought
And now we shan't be long.

(1902–6)

THE EVOLUTIONIST TO HIS LADY

Why should I vaunt as stars that flame
    Thine eyes that see
God made a million stars that same
    Ere he made thee.

Aeon on aeon, great and small
   They thronged the skies
He fused the secrets of them all
   Into thine eyes.

Why should I laud as flowers that flush
   Thy cheeks that flame
Long meadows came to blanche and blush
   Ere thy face came,
The Eternal Gardener tireless went
   Through field and wood
And all their fiery changes blent
   Into thy blood.

Why should I praise as shells that dream
   Thine ears that hear
God heaped the sands with shells that gleam
   Ere thou wert near
All Elfin shapes through sands untrod
   Worlds green and blue
Rough sketches through the book of God
   To fashion you.

               (late 1890s)

GIRL GUIDES

When Cleopatra was made a Guide,
She let her militant duties slide,
And when her prattle had lost the battle
Tactfully tickled a snake and died.

When Boadicea was made a Guide,
Her visage the vividest blue was dyed;
So the coat was made of a similar shade
And she travelled on wheels with the spokes outside.

When Lady Godiva was made a Guide,
The uniform had to be simplified,
But the rates were high, and she was not shy,
And they say it was only the horse that shied.

When Bloody Mary was made a Guide,
She told the people that when she died
Topographical notes on her views and her votes
If they took her to bits would be found inside.

When Queen Victoria was made a Guide,
She never excelled on the giant stride,
Or won a place in the obstacle race,
And historians doubt if she even tried.

When Messalina was made a Guide . . .
. . . But the trouble is that the form I've tried,
Though far from clever, might last for ever,
With hundreds and hundreds of names beside.

(1920s?)

HENRY CHARD

I knew a youth named Henry Chard,
  Whose grandpa was deceased;
His grandma lived by selling lard,
His mother worked extremely hard,
His uncle was a railway guard,
  His father was a beast.

When Christmas came with green and red,
  And everything it means,
His grandpa went on being dead,
His grandma gave him rolls of thread,
His uncle, soldiers made of lead,
His mother even gave him bread,
  His father gave him beans.

A certain day, when Henry Chard
 Was standing on his head,
And turning cartwheels very hard,
The King came by with all his Guard;
With officers all plumed and starred,
And said, "I wish, oh Master Chard,
 I could do that instead."

He tried in vain: then, with a sigh,
 Our Henry he did choose
And made him Duke and C. S. I.
And Z. P. C. and K. X. Y.,
And he was everything that's high,
Till he at last was mentioned by
 The current "Daily News".

When Henry Chard heard this, his gay
 Indifference was shocking;
He said, "I won't be A. Q. K.,
Or X. Y. L. or P. D. A.
Your friends are Dukes, I guess, and they
Seem to be anything but gay,
And all I want on Christmas Day
 Is something in my stocking."

The King he swore a mighty vow,
 And did not seek to hide it:
"By Heaven and this Imperial brow,
There's something in your stocking now
That Heaven has put there, Heaven knows how,
 Though you have never spied it:
A wonderful thing with ears and eyes,
And cartwheels turned, and wonderful cries,
Oh! the self is sad and the soul is gone,
For all the kings that the sun shone on;
But well for you, when all is done,

If you can pull your stocking on
And find yourself inside it."

(1904)[1]

THE JAZZ

A Study of Modern Dancing, in the manner of Modern Poetry

TLANNGERSHSHSH!
Thrills of vibrant discord,
Like the shivering of glass;
Some people dislike it; but I do not dislike it.
I think it is fun,
Approximating to the fun
Of merely smashing a window;
But I am told that it proceeds
From a musical instrument,
Or at any rate
From an instrument.

Black flashes . . .
. . . Flashes of intermittent darkness;
Somebody seems to be playing with the electric light;
Some may possibly believe that modern dancing
Looks best in the dark.

I do not agree with them.
I have heard that modern dancing is barbaric,
Pagan, shameless, shocking, abominable.
No such luck—I mean no such thing.
The dancers are singularly respectable

[1] This poem was specially written for a party held in Rotherhithe, a poor district in East London, and organised by the *Daily News* Christmas Slum Fund. The poem was published as part of a report on the party, in the *Daily News*, December 15, 1904.

If I were writing an essay
—And you can put chunks of any number of essays
   Into this sort of poem—
I should say there was a slight disproportion
   Between the music and the dancing;
For only the musician dances
   With excitement,
While the dancers remain cold
   And relatively motionless
(Orpheus of the Lyre of Life
   Leading the forests in fantastic capers;
Here is your Art eclipsed and reversed,
   For I see men as trees walking.)

   If Mr. King stood on his head,
Or Mr. Simon butted Mr. Gray
   In the waistcoat,
Or the two Burnett-Browns
Strangled each other in their coat-tails,
   There would then be a serene harmony,
      A calm unity and oneness
   In the two arts.
   But Mr. King remains on his feet,
And the coat-tails of Mr. Burnett-Brown
   Continue in their customary position.

And something else was running in my head—
—Songs I had heard earlier in the evening;
   Songs of true lovers and tavern friends,
      Decent drunkenness with a chorus,

   And the laughter of men who could riot.
And something stirred in me;
   A tradition
Strayed from an older time,
   And from the freedom of my fathers:
That when there is banging, yelling and smashing to be done,

I like to do it myself,
  And not delegate it to a slave,
    However accomplished.
And that I should sympathise,
  As with a revolt of human dignity,
If the musician had suddenly stopped playing,
And had merely quoted the last line
Of a song sung by Mrs. Harcourt Williams:
  "If you want any more, you must sing it yourselves."

                       (ca. 1922)

THE JOYS OF SCIENCE

I took her and I flattened her
  Respectfully, I hope
I pasted her upon a slip
  Under the microscope
With six-power-lens—I saw her
  Ah, I shall ne'er forget
While hearts can beat and flowers can blow
    That hour when first we met.

Ah, with what prayer and fasting
  Shall mortal man deserve
To see that glimpse of heaven
  Her motor vagus nerve
Gaze not, ye too inflammable
  Beneath that harmless hair
  The convolutions of her brain
  Are perilously fair.

I breathed into that microscope
  A vow of melting tone
I swore by men and angels
  The thunder and the throne

That ere one brave brown hair were touched
  On that triumphant head.
My serum's red corpuscula
  Should cheerfully be shed.

Spurn not the Men of Science
  They sob beneath your sneers
While with their large thermometers
  They test their burning tears.
They cleave the rock and rend the flower
  They find—is this their sin—
Nature, the Great King's daughter
  All glorious within.

(late 1890s)

LILIES OF THE VALLEY

(The Tragedy of an Idealist)

"Sic itur ad astra"

Lilies white in the valley lay
"Ladders to Heaven" the old wives say—
"I will go up to Heaven" the cricket said,
"Though I'm bound to admit that I am not dead."

The cricket's colours were bright and blent,
His legs were many and excellent;
The cricket was light of limb and wing,
But the cricket's soul was a serious thing.

He scaled the heights of the lily's crest,
And sat there silent and much impressed;
On the top of a full-grown stalk you are
Terribly near to the morning star.

He gave one chirp out of life and limb
To help the chaunt of the cherubim,

But a breeze blew sudden from Heaven knows where,
And the stalk that swung in the wind was bare.

The beetle and mole, in the twilight dim,
Found a moral at once for him,
"There are heights too sacred for foot to press,
Besides you die, and it makes a mess."

The cricket's head in a pool they found,
They collected his legs from the country round,
But One thing troubled the beetle and mole,
They never could find the cricket's soul.

(ca. 1898)[1]

LINES TO WATERLOO STATION

An overflowing of feeling

Come hither, Fisher Unwin,
   And leave your work awhile,
Uplooking in my face a span
   With bright adoring smile.
All happy leaping Publishers
   Round Paternoster Row,
Gay Simpkin, dreamy Marshall
   And simple Samson Low,
Come round, forgetting all your fears,
   Your hats and dinners too,
While I remark with studied calm,
   "Hurrah for Waterloo!"

Nay start not, fearful Putman,
   I sing no warrior's fall

[1] A holograph version was inscribed: Miss Mildred Wain, with profound respect, Gilbert K. Chesterton. "Yet ought you to suffer fools gladly" — St. Paul.

(Macmillan, smile again, and dry
   The tears of Kegan Paul)
But seldom on the spot I sing
   Is heard the peal of guns,
Men do not charge for batteries
   They only charge for buns,
No chief expires, no trumpet
   I blow, except my own,
But harmless season tickets
   Expire without a groan.

I've been in all the waiting-rooms,
   I never chanced to see
An army: but observant
   I never claimed to be—
If someone through my body drove
   A bayonet like a spit
I listened to Miss Frances Blogg
   And did not notice it.

Yet still thy Gladstone bags shall woo
   Thy labels bashful kiss
Geologists shall reconcile
   Thy cake with Genesis,
For out of thee the Sacred Seven
   Went forth to better spheres
And left the Bard upon the shore
   With chocolate and tears.

When dark and low the moon hath sunk
   The booking-Office shut,
When wolves howl in the waiting-rooms
   (Be still, O David Nutt!)
Under the sad and naked stars
   A figure walks alone.
His hair is white, and in his eyes
   A blessing wild as hate,

And in his feverish grasp for aye
  He clutches One-and-Eight.
He seeks not how to separate
  His neck-tie from his hair
He walks upon the railway-line,
  His soul is buried there.

(ca. 1898)[1]

LINES WRITTEN IN DEJECTION

When the white feet of afternoon
  Were on the shining meads
I wrote this nasty little book
  That no-one ever reads.

The humblest names have caused to flow
  The tears of sympathy
Men wept for James and Sarah Green
  But no-one weeps for me.

"Silent and damned" the cryptic line
  O'er which we pored and crammed
They may be silent if they like,
  I will be merely damned.

(ca. 1920?)[2]

---

[1] Maisie Ward, in *Return to Chesterton*, prints the poem as far as the fourth line of the fourth verse, then adds "Here the page ends—and with it all that can be found of the poem." The ending I found at Top Meadow Cottage in G. K. C.'s own handwriting, in 1989.

[2] Inscribed in a copy of *Robert Browning*, now in the possession of The Rt. Hon. Kenneth Baker, M.P.

"James" is almost certainly an error, and the reference is to a little-known poem by Wordsworth, "George and Sarah Green", of which the first stanza reads:

> Who weeps for strangers? Many wept
> For George and Sarah Green;
> Wept for that pair's unhappy fate,
> Whose grave may here be seen.

(See *Chesterton Review*, Feb and May 1983.)

LINES WRITTEN IN OXFORD

A seed is fallen among the clods
  Of creedless sense and senseless sin
In dons that waddle in the Quads
  Low gleams of mental life begin
  The Fabians in Clifford's Inn
Are growing human by degrees
I watch the slow light war and win
I wait the changing of the Cheese.

(ca. 1910)

THE LITERAL LAND

The heroine who is a Pearl-fisher dwelling on an islet off Fairyland is fished up on board. She explains to the people on the yacht the law of Fairyland, that everything is realised which anyone mentions or desires.

Through secret seas of blue and gold and skies of blood and fire
We sail with leaping canvas to the Land of Heart's Desire.
No wonder that its skies are queer, all red and green and grey
When the people there are wishing different weathers all the day.

But O my friends, of naughty names and similes beware;
When Uncle Brown is rude at tea don't call him "an old bear"
For you'll be even more disturbed when in a flash you see
A grizzly Bear as big as a house sit bolt upright to tea.

If you should call your children "pigs" because they bite their nails
The incautious word will fill the room with squeaks and curly tails.
A man once said "the lion's share" with metaphoric pride;
He was eaten by his metaphor—which is not dignified.

When merry friends around your board incline to sing and spout
Don't talk about your quarters as the place where you "hang out"
For it is really awkward from Society to swing—
And find yourself outside the window, flapping on a string.

But once my eyes beheld a sight that baffled blood and breath,
To paint it were a madman's dream to dream of it were death.
The screaming farmers reeled afar, the fowls of heaven fled off
For in the centre stood the horse who really ate his head off.

Through secret seas of green and gold and skies of blood and fire
We sail with leaping canvas to the Land of Heart's Desire.
We're near it now: I've warned you—I've told you all I've seen
If we make any muddles now we must be jolly green

(*screams*) Ah!

(*The whole group has gone green in a strong emerald light thrown on the stage. They all rise in tumult. The ship has crossed the boundary.*)

(late 1890s)

THE LOGIC OF PROGRESS

Can progress pause? We know from this prediction
Girls will be shaved like convicts from conviction
Or holy faith, when every happy hoyden
Shares a monastic tonsure with Miss Royden.

To rest even here were retrograde and dull:
Baldness will crawl over the female skull,
Till save for one faint streak the scalp is bare
And beauty draws us with a single hair.

(1925)

THE LOGICAL VEGETARIAN

"Why shouldn't I have a purely vegetarian drink? Why shouldn't I take
vegetables in their highest form, so to speak? The modest vegetarians
ought obviously to stick to wine or beer, plain vegetarian drinks, in-
stead of filling their goblets with the blood of bulls and elephants, as
all conventional meat-eaters do, I suppose" — Dalroy.

You will find me drinking rum,
Like a sailor in a slum,
You will find me drinking beer like a Bavarian.
You will find me drinking gin
In the lowest kind of inn,
Because I am a rigid Vegetarian.

So I cleared the inn of wine,
And I tried to climb the sign,
And I tried to hail the constable as "Marion."
But he said I couldn't speak,
And he bowled me to the Beak
Because I was a Happy Vegetarian.

Oh, I knew a Doctor Gluck,
And his nose it had a hook,
And his attitudes were anything but Aryan;
So I gave him all the pork
That I had, upon a fork
Because I am myself a Vegetarian.

I am silent in the Club,
I am silent in the pub.,
I am silent on a bally peak in Darien;
For I stuff away for life
Shoving peas in with a knife,
Because I am at heart a Vegetarian.

No more the milk of cows
Shall pollute my private house
Than the milk of the wild mares of the Barbarian;
I will stick to port and sherry,
For they are so very, very,
So very, very, very Vegetarian.

                                        (1913)

MACAROONS

I seek the place of Macaroons
And none can tell me where it lies
Not French or Flemings or Walloons
Dutchmen in opulent pantaloons
Or German bands with big bassoons
Or Yankees weeping for saloons
Or yellow Chinks or coal-black coons
Or Monds or Samuels or Sassoons
Or Indians making them pontoons
Or Bengal's natures or Rangoon's
Where Hilary her soul attunes

To Winters milder than our Junes
Agreeably varied by typhoons,
Or Malay pirates made maroons
Or Danes upon their sandy dunes
Or Highland lads or Lowland loons
Or bold Hibernian gossoons
Can find the land where Macaroons
Grow upon trees in Paradise.

(ca. 1930?)

MACAROONS: AN ODE

(To Miss Gladys Meates of the Convalescent Home)

A lady sent me Macaroons
Would I could send a song as sweet
For this, the best of earthly boons,
But as I turn my rhyming runes,
I find the rhymes to Macaroons
Are neither numerous nor neat.

Though I went wandering in balloons
Like Empire-builders from the East
Who paint the map and pinch the spoons
From Cairo to the Cameroons,
In my life-search for Macaroons
It would not help me in the least.

Where on South Seas the warm wind swoons
New Novels tell us all they do—
Their dwellings are by blue lagoons,
Their morals are like blue baboons,
Nor once or twice in bluer moons,
They paint their simple village blue.

(ca. 1930?)

ME HEART

I come from Castlepatrick, and me heart is on me sleeve,
And any sword or pistol boy can hit it with me leave,
It shines there for an epaulette, as golden as a flame,
And naked as me ancestors, as noble as me name.
For I come from Castlepatrick and me heart is on me sleeve,
But a lady stole it from me on St. Gallowglass's Eve.

The folk that live in Liverpool, their heart is in their boots;
They go to hell like lambs, they do, because the hooter hoots.
Where men may not be dancin', though the wheels may dance
    all day;
And men may not be smokin'; but only chimneys may.
But I come from Castlepatrick, and me heart is on me sleeve,
But a lady stole it from me on St. Poleander's Eve.

The folk that live in black Belfast, their heart is in their mouth,
They see us making murders in the meadows of the South;
They think a plough's a rack, they do, and cattle-calls are
    creeds,
And they think we're burnin' witches when we're only burnin'
    weeds;
But I come from Castlepatrick, and me heart is on me sleeve,
But a lady stole it from me on St. Barnabas's Eve.

(ca. 1913)

THE MERGER

St. Nicholas distributed as he list,
His gifts, and is a good Distributist:
The Heathens, on the other hand, are not:
He mixed two children: and
          they went to pot.
(1930)

MR. FORD

Though Mr. Ford can quite afford
To sell his motors cheap
I can't afford a Mr. Ford
He costs too much to keep,
He will not play with wooden toys
They must be made of steel,
I never knew him bowl a hoop
Unless it was a wheel.

Suppose the masses profit by
The Mass-production plan
I do not want to be a mass
I thought I was a man.
I can't afford a millionaire
However pure and new
I keep a wife, and I keep a house
I keep a temper too.

Though Mr. Ford can quite afford
To pay his workmen well
I can't afford a Mr. Ford
The price would be a sell,
I'd have to pawn the village pub
And scrap the village forge
And let the Peace Ship standardise
The standard of St. George.

I can't afford a Mr. Ford
My plot of peas and beans
Won't grow sufficient greenbacks
But just sufficient greens;
Nor would I lose it all to toil
In servitude and strain
Till I had made a plutocrat
To pay me back again.

(1920s)

MR LEONARD MAGNUS

Mr Leonard Magnus, being endowed for research
       with several large state bounties
Tried once to pronounce an old High German verb
       and was picked up in several counties
When family went out collecting his limbs
       their spirits were bluer than Reckitt's
And his death was observed an annual fast by the
       whole population of Beckett's.

MRS. BAINES

"We are not amused"
            — Queen Victoria

Puck and the woodland elves shall weep with me
For that lost joke I made in Ledborough Lane,
The joke that Mrs. Baines declined to see
Although I made it very loud and plain.
I made the joke again and yet again,
I analysed it, parsed it and explained:
I did my very best to entertain,
But Mrs. Baines would not be entertained.
            (ca. 1918?)

THE OLD GENTLEMAN IN THE PARK

Beyond the trees like iron trees,
    The painted lamp-posts stand.
The old red road runs like the rust
    Upon this iron land.

Cars flat as fish and fleet as birds,
  Low-bodied and high-speeded,
Go on their belly like the Snake,
  And eat the dust as he did.

But down the red dust never more
  Her happy horse-hoofs go.
O, what a road of rust indeed!
  O, what a Rotten Row!
          (1925)

ON BEING FORBIDDEN TO
FEED THE DOG

No more, no more, no more!
Such language holds the solemn sea,
The sands upon the shore shall bloom
The thunder-blasted tree
Or the stricken eagle soar
—No more, old man, no more.
          (ca. 1920s)

"ON HIMSELF"

Weicht zacht gemeine herren geuze zein
(I think it sums up all my views of life)
But what's my view?—that flowers are very fair
And figures in the ledger very dull
But figures somehow just as good as flowers
But somehow not so nice . . . and God made all . . .
And that's near all my mind is equal to
After a day of Parent's National.

This Chesterton—he wrote to me again,
Man (like a torture) long—and lingering—
A friend of ours at home—you know him too?
—O yes—there's good in everyone. No doubt.

                                        (ca. 1897)[1]

PIONEERS, O PIONEERS

Nebuchadnezzar the King of the Jews
Suffered from new and original views,
He crawled on his hands and knees, it's said,
With grass in his mouth and a crown on his head.
      With a wowtyiddly, etc.

Those in traditional paths that trod
Thought the thing was a curse from God,
But a Pioneer men always abuse
Like Nebuchadnezzar the King of the Jews.

Black Lord Foulon the Frenchmen slew
Thought it a Futurist thing to do.
He offered them grass instead of bread;
So they stuffed him with grass when they cut off his head.
      With a wowtyiddly, etc.

For the pride of his soul he perished then—
But of course it is always of Pride that men,
A Man in Advance of his Age accuse,
Like Nebuchadnezzar the King of the Jews.

Simeon Scudder of Styx, in Maine,
Thought of the thing and was at it again.

---

[1] The original is in holograph. The verse is written as though it were by Frances, who worked at the Parent's National Educational Union. I am told that the first line does not make sense, and it is neither German nor Dutch.

He gave good grass and water in pails
To a thousand Irishmen hammering rails.
    With a wowtyiddly, etc.

Appetites differ; and tied to a stake
He was tarred and feathered for Conscience' Sake.
But stoning the prophets is ancient news,
Like Nebuchadnezzar the King of the Jews.
               (1912–13)

PLAKKOPYTRIXOPHYLISPERAMBULANT—
IOBATRIX

A Twenty Minutes' Holiday from Writing Fiction?
12 p.m.

Fear not, fear not, my children,
  The last weird embers fade,
Blue corpses through the windows peer,
  But still you seem afraid,
Perhaps there's Something in the room,
  Whatever would you do
If I were not among you now
  To cheer and comfort you?

Heed not that pale thing in the door,
  It smiles so like a skull,
You hear hoarse spectres scream and clank,
  You find the evening dull?
Then let me tell a merry tale
  Of dear old days of yore,
About a dragon of the wastes
  That drank of human gore.

It dwelt among untrodden ways,
  And ate the plaintive dove;

A dragon there were few to praise
And very few to love.
(I use this piece of Wordsworth
To show how much I know)
Uproariously popular
It was, as dragons go.

If I could only paint the Thing!
Just imitate its wink,
All you five infants, one by one,
Would rise and take to drink:
Or roll in death-pangs on the floor,
And lie there choked and blue,
O how I wish I could describe
This animal to you.

Some swore its fur was bushy brown,
Some swore that it was green,
With savage eyes of bluish grey:
Some swore that they had seen
In coils upon a sofa wreathed,
It, writhing as in pangs,
And tearing Bovril chocolate
With huge, abhorrent fangs.

Some said that far to eastward
They saw It, garbed in grey,
Standing upon a platform
And bellowing all day.
Some said that far to northward,
Through all the white snow-wreath,
They saw it, white and wolfish,
With half-a-million teeth.

When skies were blue with summer
It glittered, bright and blue,
And once, the stricken wanderer
In screaming terror flew,

For on the shining tableland
White gauze did round it glance,
And with one rose to crown it
He saw the dragon dance.

The Witless Youth in wonder
Sat lank upon a stone,
His Hat was monumental
Its secret—all his own.
The Sage was mild and hoary
And skilled in Wisdom's page,
The Youth sat meek (as always)
And to him spoke the Sage.

"Go not to smite the Dragon
That wasteth field and fen,
Around her reeking cavern
Are strewn the hearts of men;
But youth is foolish: You, Sir,
Are singularly so—
So learn her horrid habits
At least, before you go.

"If you would raise her bristles up
And set her eye in flames,
Then seek the Hankin-Pankin
And read the Jenry-James;

Go with a train of spiders huge
With all their threads and thrums
From ledgers all declaiming
Interminable sums . . .

"But would you see the awful smile,
And soften down the Eye,
Then fetch the Stompy-Steinthal
And bring the Rompy-Rye;
And choirs of ladies tall and proud

With all one kind of nose,
And bucketsful of flowers,
And basketsful of clothes.'

(Unfinished, or if finished the last page has been lost.)
(ca. 1910)

POOR RELATIONS

Dean Inge says that Science has given us a new
conscience about "our cousins the animals".

"Brothers," St. Francis called the Brutes,
But in Dean Inge his sermon,
The blind Darwinian struggle gives
Us Cousins—very German.

(1927)

PROLOGUE TO THE OLD VIC PANTOMIME

Specially written for the purpose by G. K. Chesterton

Of old, when mummers mummed on Christmas Day,
Men did not fear to mix the grave and gay.
When pious tales were played for simple folk,
The Devil danced and Judas was a joke.
We do not dare, in days grown dull and mild,
To be so childish near the Holy Child—
Lest jokes that in the Age of Faith went down
Shock all the unbelievers in the town.
The Devil has too many friends to-day
For us to mock him in the ancient way:
Judas is barred; the Censorship's provisions
Forbid reflections upon politicians.
Should Herod rant, our jest might seem to strike—
—Well, anyone you like—or do not like;

Secular things have more solemnity
Than things held sacred in the days gone by:
And new scribes wait to watch the holiest die
Who cannot mock, but only crucify.

But pardon us if, joining faith and laughter,
We put the wisdom first, the folly after.
And taking hymn and dance one at a time,
Have first the play and then the pantomime.
You have seen how men, poor folk that march and fight,
Saw the desire of Nations in the night.
Peace of the fighters and of simple men.

But they too mocked and jested even then.
The more shame ours, if life call us in vain
To smile at pleasure as they smiled at pain:
And in the peace that should their dreams fulfil
Dullness destroys what danger could not kill;
Deep in the dug-outs, loud in doggerel rhyme,
The soul of our most ancient Pantomime.
Then smile and pardon me, if I appear
Between these two divided dramas here
To save your minds from too abrupt a jog,
At once a prologue and an epilogue—
To end the last and introduce the next—
Which has Jack Horner and a Pie for text.

Jack Horner was a worthy youth; for so
He himself stated and he ought to know.
If you think Jack, in the mere plum's removal
Had insufficient grounds for self-approval
Think you how many of the wise and great
Counted most worthy, pillars of the state
Have for all credit, claim and aim in sum
To make a corner and to take the plum—
Enough! Our theme has tumbled from the sky,
But let tumblers tumble. For the Pie

(And as Prince Hamlet said, the Pie's the thing)
Is open; and the birds begin to sing.

(1925)

THE RED SEA

Our souls shall be Leviathans
In purple seas of wine
When drunkenness is dead with death,
And drink is all divine;
Learning in those immortal vats
What mortal vineyards mean;
For only in heaven we shall know
How happy we have been.

Like clouds that wallow in the wind
Be free to drift and drink;
Tower without insolence when we rise,
Without surrender sink:
Dreams dizzy and crazy we shall know
And have no need to write
Our blameless blasphemies of praise,
Our nightmares of delight.

For so in such misshapen shape
The vision came to me,
Where such titanic dolphins dark
Roll in a sunset sea:
Dark with dense colours, strange and strong
As terrible true love,
Haloed like fish in phosphor light
The holy monsters move.

Measure is here and law, to learn,
When honour rules it so,
To lift the glass and lay it down
Or break the glass and go.

But when the world's New Deluge boils
From the New Noah's vine.
Our souls shall be Leviathans
In sanguine seas of wine.

(ca. 1918–21)

THE RIDDLE OF THE CONJURER

I have a hat, but not to wear;
I wear a sword, but not to slay,
And ever in my bag I bear
A pack of cards, but not to play.

(From the play, *Magic*, 1913)

THE ROAD TO ROUNDABOUT

Some say that Guy of Warwick,
The man that killed the Cow,
And brake the mighty Boar alive
Beyond the bridge at Slough;
Went up against a Loathly Worm
That wasted all the Downs,
And so the roads they twist and squirm
(If I may be allowed the term)
From the writhing of the stricken Worm
That died in seven towns.
  I see no scientific proof
  That this idea is sound,
  And I should say they wound about
  To find the town of Roundabout,
  The merry town of Roundabout,
  That makes the world go round.

Some say that Robin Goodfellow,
Whose lantern lights the meads
(To steal a phrase Sir Walter Scott
In heaven no longer needs),
Such dance around the trysting-place
The moonstruck lover leads;
Which superstition I should scout,
There is more faith in honest doubt
(As Tennyson has pointed out)
Than in those nasty creeds.
    But peace and righteousness (St. John)
    In Roundabout can kiss,
    And since that's all that's found about
    The pleasant town of Roundabout,
    The roads they simply bound about
    To find out where it is.

Some say that when Sir Lancelot
Went forth to find the Grail,
Grey Merlin wrinkled up the roads
For hope that he should fail;
All roads lead back to Lyonesse
And Camelot in the Vale,
I cannot yield assent to this
Extravagant hypothesis,
The plain, shrewd Briton will dismiss
Such rumours (*Daily Mail*).
    But in the streets of Roundabout
    Are no such factions found,
    Or theories to expound about,
    Or roll upon the ground about,
    In the happy town of Roundabout,
    That makes the world go round.
                (1913)

THE ROLLING ENGLISH ROAD

Before the Roman came to Rye or out to Severn strode,
The rolling English drunkard made the rolling English road.
A reeling road, a rolling road, that rambles round the shire,
And after him the parson ran, the sexton and the squire;
A merry road, a mazy road, and such as we did tread
The night we went to Birmingham by way of Beachy Head.

I knew no harm of Bonaparte and plenty of the Squire,
And for to fight the Frenchman I did not much desire;
But I did bash their baggonets because they came arrayed
To straighten out the crooked road an English drunkard made,
Where you and I went down the lane with ale-mugs in our
    hands,
The night we went to Glastonbury by way of Goodwin Sands.

His sins they were forgiven him; or why do flowers run
Behind him; and the hedges all strengthening in the sun?
The wild thing went from left to right and knew not which
    was which,
But the wild rose was above him when they found him in the
    ditch.
God pardon us, nor harden us; we did not see so clear
The night we went to Bannockburn by way of Brighton Pier.

My friends, we will not go again or ape an ancient rage,
Or stretch the folly of our youth to be the shame of age,
But walk with clearer eyes and ears this path that wandereth,
And see undrugged in evening light the decent inn of death;
For there is good news yet to hear and fine things to be seen,
Before we to go Paradise by way of Kensal Green.

                                              (1913)

"THE SARACEN'S HEAD"

"The Saracen's Head" looks down the lane,
Where we shall never drink wine again,
For the wicked old women who feel well-bred
Have turned to a tea-shop "The Saracen's Head."

"The Saracen's Head" out of Araby came,
King Richard riding in arms like flame,
And where he established his folks to be fed
He set up a spear — and the Saracen's Head.

.   .   .   .

But the "Saracen's Head" outlived the Kings,
It thought and it thought of most horrible things,
Of Health and of Soap and of Standard Bread,
And of Saracen drinks at the "Saracen's Head."

So the "Saracen's Head" fulfils its name,
They drink no wine — a ridiculous game —
And I shall wonder until I'm dead,
How it ever came into the Saracen's Head.

(1912 – 13)

SOCIOLOGICAL TRIOLETS

(Written on first looking into Mr. Bellamy's "Looking Backwards";
or "Much have I travelled in these Realms of Gold")

I

The Collectivist State
Is a prig and a bandit.
I despise and I hate
The Collectivist State;
It may be My Fate,
But I'm damned if I'll stand it!
The Collectivist State
Is a prig and a bandit.

II

The Capitalist State
Is a garden of roses:
It's been proved in debate
— The Capitalist State—
But, strange to relate,
We are holding our noses,
The Capitalist State
Is a Garden of Roses.

III

The Communist State
Is all mixed up together.
Where we participate
— The Communist State—
There can be no hate—
(But we all hate the weather)
The Communist State
Is all mixed up together.

IV

The Syndical State
Raises awful emotion
In the Wise and the Great,
"The Syndical State".
What the words indicate
They haven't a notion.
The Syndical State
Raises awful emotion.

V

The Anarchist State
Is a flat contradiction.
So let Tolstoy narrate
The Anarchist State—

His powers, which were great,
Were more suited to fiction;
The Anarchist State
Is a flat contradiction.

VI

The Servile (ow!) State
Is like this, only worse,
Degradation's its fate—
The Servile (oo!) State
It's debased, desecrate
—And it don't care a curse—
The Servile (ugh!) State
Is like this, only worse.

VII

The Distributive State
You'd like if you'd met it
But you buy at hard rate
The Distributive State.
It means Early and Late
—And don't you forget it—
The Distributive State
You'd like if you'd met it.
                         (1912)

THE SONG AGAINST GROCERS

God made the wicked Grocer
For a mystery and a sign,
That men might shun the awful shops
And go to inns to dine;
Where the bacon's on the rafter
And the wine is in the wood,

And God that made good laughter
Has seen that they are good.

The evil-hearted Grocer
Would call his mother 'Ma'am,'
And bow at her and bob at her,
Her aged soul to damn,
And rub his horrid hands and ask
What article was next,
Though *mortis in articulo*
Should be her proper text.

His props are not his children,
But pert lads underpaid,
Who call out 'Cash!' and bang about
To work his wicked trade;
He keeps a lady in a cage
Most cruelly all day,
And makes her count and calls her 'Miss'
Until she fades away.

The righteous minds of innkeepers
Induce them now and then
To crack a bottle with a friend
Or treat unmoneyed men,
But who hath seen the Grocer
Treat housemaids to his teas
Or crack a bottle of fish-sauce
Or stand a man a cheese?

He sells us sands of Araby
As sugar for cash down;
He sweeps his shop and sells the dust
The purest salt in town,
He crams with cans of poisoned meat
Poor subjects of the King,
And when they die by thousands
Why, he laughs like anything.

The wicked Grocer groces
In spirits and in wine,
Not frankly and in fellowship
As men in inns do dine;
But packed with soap and sardines
And carried off by grooms,
For to be snatched by Duchesses
And drunk in dressing-rooms.

The hell-instructed Grocer
Has a temple made of tin,
And the ruin of good innkeepers
Is loudly urged therein;
But now the sands are running out
From sugar of a sort,
The Grocer trembles; for his time,
Just like his weight, is short.

(1912)

THE GOOD GROCER

(An Apology)

Babes, when I too was young and always right
And tangled in that not unrighteous fight
Beneath the Wooden Flag, the Painted Sign,
We poured our blood — or anyhow our wine —
For feast of all our fathers, and liberties;
Not having Charity before my eyes
I cursed a Grocer . . . saying that he, by fault,
Put sand in sugar and no salt in salt,
Trapped men with stinking fish that leapt from tins;
And rising to the toppling top of sins
Discouraged Pubs and spoilt the English Inns.

The Heavens, I learn as still I linger and live,
Punish more generously than men forgive,
No grinning Grocer slew me with a sweet
I writhed across no tins of poisoned meat;
Only . . . where far in the warm western shires
Steep stooping woods are dipped in sunset fires
The children told me that, aloof, alone,
Dwelt the Good Grocer whom I had not known.

Ah not forgotten, the children that I knew,
Not if they died—not even if they grew—
How their locks flamed and limbs like arrows sped
And faces shone with the wild news they said,
The Fairy Grocer—his were magic sales
His books might have been filled with fairy tales
He might have tipped sardines back in the sea
Given all his goods away with a pound of tea;
Sanding no sugar, on the other hand,
Have spread his sugar o'er the shores for sand:
And there took hands—and handfuls in their hands
And mouthfuls in their mouths; stuffed more and more
Till they had made erosion of the shore,
Bit bays and inlets out of all the coast
Like giant bites out of titanic toast.

To you, dear children of old days I send
This apologia to your early friend,
You know, though I said salt was dust in mirth,
Our dust can still be salt, and salt of the earth;
A Wizard is an easier thing to be
Than being a Good Grocer, as is he.

(1920s or 1930s)

THE SONG AGAINST SONGS

The song of the sorrow of Melisande is a weary song and a dreary
    song,
The glory of Mariana's grange had got into great decay,
The song of the Raven Never More has never been called a cheery
    song,
And the brightest things in Baudelaire are anything else but gay.

But who will write us a riding song
Or a hunting song or a drinking song,
Fit for them that arose and rode
When day and the wine were red?
But bring me a quart of claret out,
And I will write you a clinking song,
A song of war and a song of wine
And a song to wake the dead.

The song of the fury of Fragolette is a florid song and a torrid song,
The song of the sorrow of Tara is sung to a harp unstrung,
The song of the cheerful Shropshire Lad I consider a perfectly
    horrid song,
And the song of the happy Futurist is a song that can't be sung.

But who will write us a riding song
Or a fighting song or a drinking song,
Fit for the fathers of you and me,
That know how to think and thrive?
But the song of Beauty and Art and Love
Is simply an utterly stinking song,
To double you up and drag you down
And damn your soul alive.

(1912)

THE SONG OF RIGHT AND WRONG

Feast on wine or fast on water
And your honour shall stand sure,
God Almighty's son and daughter
He the valiant, she the pure;
If an angel out of heaven
Brings you other things to drink,
Thank him for his kind attentions,
Go and pour them down the sink.

Tea is like the East he grows in,
A great yellow Mandarin
With urbanity of manner
And unconsciousness of sin;
All the women, like a harem,
At his pig-tail troop along;
And, like all the East he grows in,
He is Poison when he's strong.

Tea, although an Oriental,
Is a gentleman at least;
Cocoa is a cad and coward,
Cocoa is a vulgar beast,
Cocoa is a dull, disloyal,
Lying, crawling cad and clown,
And may very well be grateful
To the fool that takes him down.

As for all the windy waters,
They were rained like tempests down
When good drink had been dishonoured
By the tipplers of the town;
When red wine had brought red ruin
And the death-dance of our times,
Heaven sent us Soda Water
As a torment for our crimes.

(1913)

A SONG OF SELF-ESTEEM

The Simple Social Lifer is a harmless sort of elf,
He feeds a dog on mutton that he mustn't eat himself.
I tolerate his sandals and his tresses long and lank,
I reverence his madness but I deprecate his Swank.

O the Swank of the Crank in the future's foremost rank,
And the child of all the ages there was nobody to spank.
He has told us all he means by his water and his beans
In a style that might be pardoned on the theory that he
drank.

The Banker is an expert on economy and strikes,
He uses all your money to do anything he likes;
And the usurer who uses it you're called upon to thank.
I do not mind the swindle but I do not like the swank.

O the Swank of the Bank and the cheque you give it
For the cryptic explanations when the rate of wages sank.
But I hope to see the fun when a Frenchman with a gun
Shall ask him what the devil he is doing with the Franc.

The Yankee is a dab at electricity and crime,
He tells you how he hustles and it takes him quite a time,
I like his hospitality that's cordial and frank,
I do not mind his money but I do not like his swank.

O the Swank of the Yank on the Prohibition Plank,
O take the water-waggoner and drown him in the tank.
Since the Faith of Tennessee has wafted o'er the sea,
The odour of its sanctity — and Golly how it stank!

(mid 1920s)

THE SONG OF THE DOG QUOODLE

They haven't got no noses,
The fallen sons of Eve,
Even the smell of roses
Is not what they supposes,
But more than mind discloses,
And more than men believe.

They haven't got no noses,
They cannot even tell
When door and darkness closes
The park old Gluck encloses
Where even the Law of Moses
Will let you steal a smell.

The brilliant smell of water,
The brave smell of a stone,
The smell of dew and thunder,
The old bones buried under,
Are things in which they blunder
And err, if left alone.

The wind from winter forests,
The scent of scentless flowers,
The breath of brides' adorning,
The smell of snare and warning,
The smell of Sunday morning
God gave to us for ours.

* * *

And Quoodle here discloses
All things that Quoodle can,
They haven't got no noses,
They haven't got no noses,
And goodness only knowses
The Noselessness of Man.

(1913)

THE SONG OF THE GREAT SEA SERPENT
(From the note-book of Captain Dalroy of the Old Ship)

The stories of the Sea Serpent rest only on the evidence of sailors and
have little truly scientific support — *The Daily Press*

Has anybody seen the Great Sea Serpent?
                    Serpent of the Sea.
Is anybody friends with the Great Sea Serpent?
                    Nobody seems to be.
Nobody, for nobody can understand
Why the Great Sea Serpent isn't seen on land,
Hanging about Westminster or walking down the Strand,
                    Or dropping in to tea.

(Chorus): Has anybody seen, etc.

The people who have seen the Great Sea Serpent
                    Did extremely wrong:
For nobody must see the Great Sea Serpent
                    Nobody who hears this song.
Nobody, for nobody must trust his eyes
If he sees it swell to enormous size
Trailing through the hemisphere and towering to the skies
                    A thousand fathoms long.

The people who have seen the Great Sea Serpent
                    Were men of low degree,
For nobody has seen the Great Sea Serpent
                    But men that sail the sea;
And only because all of them are frauds and fakes,
Nelson and the Collingwoods and Drakes and Blakes,
Always putting rum away and always seeing snakes.
                    Britannia rules the sea.

(Chorus): Has anybody seen, etc.

$(1923)^1$

---

[1] Written for a Gift Book, 'The Book of the Balfour Hospital Bazaar', Orkney, Scotland,
August 1923.

THE SONG OF THE OAK

The Druids waved their golden knives
And danced around the Oak
When they had sacrificed a man;
But though the learned search and scan
No single modern person can
Entirely see the joke.
But though they cut the throats of men
They cut not down the tree,
And from the blood the saplings sprang
Of oak-woods yet to be.
  But Ivywood, Lord Ivywood,
  He rots the tree as ivy would,
  He clings and crawls as ivy would
  About the sacred tree.

King Charles he fled from Worcester fight
And hid him in the Oak;
In convent schools no man of tact
Would trace and praise his every act,
Or argue that he was in fact
A strict and sainted bloke.
But not by him the sacred woods
Have lost their fancies free,
And though he was extremely big
He did not break the tree.
  But Ivywood, Lord Ivywood,
  He breaks the tree as ivy would,
  And eats the woods as ivy would
  Between us and the sea.

Great Collingwood walked down the glade
And flung the acorns free.
That oaks might still be in the grove
As oaken as the beams above,
When the great Lover sailors love

Was kissed by Death at sea.
But though for him the oak-trees fell
To build the oaken ships,
The woodman worshipped what he smote
And honoured even the chips.
  But Ivywood, Lord Ivywood,
  He hates the tree as ivy would,
  As the dragon of the ivy would
  That has us in his grips.

(ca. 1913)

THE SONG OF THE SEA-WEALTH[1]

Down, down there in the great green sea—
  Oysters dwell in the dreaming deep
Oysters never can hear or see
  Never can love or laugh or weep
I could glitter with pearls, I wis
  If I were as dull as an oyster is.

Down, down there in the great green sea
  I have seen the wreck of the good ships lie
More of gold than you give to me
  Gold that none shall sell or buy.
I could be laden with gold may be
  If I were as cold as the heart of the sea.

I have seen the bony hands of the dead
  Grasping gold to a Kingdom's fee
Kings and merchants, mighty and dread
  Hear the lesson learnt in the sea
We could be all of us richer far
  If we were as dead as the dead men are.

(ca. 1898–1900)

---

[1] This song occurs in the first act, on board the ship, where Pearl, the diving-girl and hero-ine receives the adoration of the jewel-merchant, who urges against her sentiment the usual cynicism as to the wealth he has to offer. She leads him to the side of the ship and sings, sitting on the bulwark and looking or pointing down into the sea.

SONGS FOR THE CITY

"If reapers sing while reaping, why should not auditors sing while
auditing and bankers while banking?" — G. K. C., *Tremendous Trifles*

Up my lads, and lift the ledgers, sleep and ease are o'er.
Hear the Stars of Morning shouting: 'Two and Two are Four'.
Though the creeds and realms are reeling, though the sophists
                                                    roar,
Though we weep and pawn our watches, Two and Two are Four.

and . . . for times of financial crisis and courage —

> "There's a run upon the Bank —
>   Stand away!
> For the Manager's a crank and the Secretary drank,
>   and the Upper Tooting Bank
>   Turns to bay!
>
> Stand close: there is a run
>   On the Bank.
> Of our ship, our royal one, let the ringing
>   legend run,
>   that she fired with every gun
>   Ere she sank.

. . . the specimen verse of the Post-Office Hymn ran thus:

> "O'er London our letters are shaken like snow,
> Our wires o'er the world like the thunderbolts go,
> The news that may marry a maiden in Sark,
> Or kill an old lady in Finsbury Park."
> Chorus (with a swing of joy and energy):
> "Or kill an old lady in Finsbury Park."

(1907 – 8)

STILTON AND MILTON
Or Literature in the 17th and 20th Centuries

Pardon, dear Lady, if this Christmas time,
The Convalescent Bard in halting rhyme
Thanks you for that great thought that still entwines,
The Wicked Grocer with more wicked lines;
These straggling Crayon lines — who cares for these,
Who knows the difference between Chalk and Cheese.

Not wholly sound the saw, accounted sure,
That weak things perish and strong things endure:
Milton, six volumes on my groaning shelves,
May groan till Judgement Day and please themselves,
As, harsh with leaden type and leathery pride,
Puritan Bards must groan at Christmas tide:

My table groans with Stilton — for a while:
Paradise Found not Lost, in Milton's style
Green as his Eden; as his Michael strong:
But O, my friend, it will not groan there long.

                                        (1916)[1]

THOUGHT AND REFLECTIONS
(A cycle of eight triolets)

Thoughts on the Offer of Being a Fish

If I were a fish I should
Miss occasional luxury
Such as climbing in the wood
(If I were a fish I should)

---

[1] May be 1916, when G. K. C. was convalescent after mumps.

Church-going is also good
Mostly I should miss the sea
If I were a fish I should
Miss occasional luxury.

Singular Effects of Malediction

"He's a Critic—damn his eyes!"
And his eyes were damned at once
Green he saw the summer skies
(He's a critic, damn his eyes!)
All the rest of him was wise
But his eyes saw seven suns
He's a Critic. Damn his eyes
And his eyes were damned at once.

A Reflection on the Clerical Character

Jesus died upon the Cross
But He was not born on it.
Once he played at pitch and toss
(Jesus died upon the Cross)
When he lost he paid his loss
Priest are you a man of wit?
Jesus died upon the Cross
But he was not born on it.

Advice to a Young Man on Writing Verses

Ride upon the Nightmare, bard
Do not let it ride on you.
You shall break the devil-guard
Ride upon the Nightmare, bard
Hunt the comets, riding hard
Break heaven of devils blue.
Ride upon the Nightmare, bard
Do not let it ride on you.

A Comforting Reflection

You might not be in love with me
If I were better than I am.
I might have ten arms like a tree
(You might not be in love with me)
And have all colours like the sea.
Have wings, or horns just like a ram
You might not be in love with me
If I were better than I am.

Reflection of the Pious Farmer

Shall I fear a devil's horns
More than I should fear a cows?
If a spike his head adorns
Shall I fear a devil's horns?
Twenty spikes were on the thorns
Wreathed upon the Master's brows.
Shall I fear a devil's horns
More than I should fear a cows?

My Experiment in Greek Philosophy Recounted

When I tried to know myself
I discovered I was gone.
Loves and toils and books on shelf
When I tried to know myself
Hats and sticks and wood and delf
Were no longer I and one.
When I tried to know myself
I discovered I was gone.

My Discovery Touching an Ancient Legend

'Twas the man who burnt his ships,
Love, who set the Thames on fire
Joy can not be found in sips
('Twas the man who burnt his ships)

Break the goblet at your lips
For the wrath of your desire.
'Twas the man who burnt his ships,
Love, who set the Thames on fire.

(ca. 1905–10)

TO YOUNG PESSIMISTS

Some sneer; some snigger; some simper;
In the youth where we laughed, and sang.
And *they* may end with a whimper
But *we* will end with a bang.

(1927)[1]

TRIOLET

I wish I were a jelly fish
That cannot fall downstairs:
Of all the things I wish to wish
I wish I were a jelly fish
That hasn't any cares,
And doesn't even have to wish
"I wish I were a jelly fish
That cannot fall downstairs."

(1928)

---

[1] Inscribed in a copy of *The Secret of Father Brown* presented to Father O'Connor.

TRUE SYMPATHY
or
PREVENTION OF CRUELTY TO TEACHERS[1]

I was kind to all my masters
    And I never worked them hard
To goad them to exactitude
    Or speaking by the card.

If one of them should have the air
    Of talking through his hat
And call a curve isosceles
    I let it go at that.

The point was without magnitude;
    I knew without regret
Our minds were moving parallel
    Because they never met.

Because I could not bear to make
    An Algebraist cry
I gazed with interest at X
    And never thought of Why.

That he should think I thought he thought
    That X was A B C
Was far, far happier for him
    And possibly for me.

While other teachers raved and died
    In reason's wild career,
Men who had driven themselves mad
    By making themselves clear,

[1] From the *Catholic Herald*, December 15, 1939, where it appeared with the following editorial note: "G. K. Chesterton wrote this poem for a very young friend of his and now, after many years, the little friend, quite beyond the algebra stage, allows us to publish these verses for the first time."

My teachers laugh and sing and dance,
   Aged, but still alive;
Because I often let them say
   That two and two are five.

Angles obtuse appeared acute,
   Angles acute were quite
Obtuse; but I was more obtuse:
   Their angles were all right.

I wore my Soul's Awakening smile
   I felt it was my duty:
Lo! Logic works by Barbara
   And life is ruled by Beauty.

And Mathematics merged and met
   Its Higher Unity,
Where Five and Two and Twelve and Four
   They all were One to me.
                (late 1920s or early 1930s)[1]

WALTON-ON-THE NAZE

(The result of stopping two days at Walton with nothing
to read but the Bible in one's bedroom.)

Let Walton rejoice and be glad: it hath gained approval of Me.
And the Wise of the Earth are as naught and the judges vanity
There are rich romantic glimpses: there are bowers of bashful mud
(I know a railing down by the Pier, that simply stirs the blood)
O stately trees of Walton—(that is a tree, I think)
O mystical water of Walton, too holy for Man to drink;
The rich of the earth and the mighty, that sit on the golden throne,
That go upon Continental Tours with bicycles not their own
That wax proud with the grace of gold: that are filled of the soul's
   desire
That provide you with one and eightpence to send off a sixpenny wire

They mock: they shoot out the lip: they grin like a dog: or a pup
Like those of the Psalmist's enemies who hadn't been well brought up.

                              (ca. 1896–1900?)

WHAT IS A BUSLUS?

The best authorities are vague;
The learned Dr. Bock (of Prague)
Writes "Totally unlike a rat . . ."
I cannot argue much from that.

Pottiger says "Its Knobs are round:
See Beeswax". I have also found
This doubtful note of Dr. Moon,
"Delightful in the afternoon."

Count Posky writes (in joke, I hope)
"Coughs rather like an antelope."
And what can Jupp of Cambridge mean
By saying "Kindness turns it green"?

Some say a Buslus is a bird
And some a science: I have heard
It talked of as a club, a pigeon,
A tool, a fish and a religion.

For many an age, for many an hour,
I've sat and wondered in this tower.
O stars, O seas, O all that is,
I wonder what a Buslus is!

                              (1920s)

WHEN I CAME BACK TO FLEET STREET

When I came back to Fleet Street,
  Through a sunset nook at night,
And saw the old Green Dragon
  With the windows all alight,
And hailed the old Green Dragon
  And the Cock I used to know,
Where all good fellows were my friends
  A little while ago;

I had been long in meadows,
  And the trees took hold of me,
And the still towns in the beech-woods,
  Where men were meant to be.
But old things held; the laughter,
  The long unnatural night,
And all the truth they talk in hell,
  And all the lies they write.

For I came back to Fleet Street,
  And not in peace I came;
  Still drink in debt to-day;
Chained to the rich by ruin,
  Cheerful in chains, as then
When old unbroken Pickwick walked
  Among the broken men.

Still he that dreams and rambles
  Through his own elfin air,
Knows that the street's a prison,
  Knows that the gates are there:
Still he that scorns or struggles
  Sees, frightful and afar,
All that they leave of rebels
  Rot high on Temple Bar.

All that I loved and hated,
   All that I shunned and knew,
Clears in broad battle lightning,
   Where they, and I, and you,
Run high the barricade that breaks
   The barriers of the street,
And shout to them that shrink within,
   The Prisoners of the Fleet.

              (1913)

WINE AND WATER

Old Noah he had an ostrich farm and
   fowls on the largest scale,
He ate his egg with a ladle in an egg-cup
   big as a pail,
And the soup he took was Elephant Soup
   and the fish he took was Whale,
But they all were small to the cellar he
   took when he set out to sail
And Noah he often said to his wife when
   he sat down to dine,
"I don't care where the water goes if it
   doesn't get into the wine."

The cataract of the cliff of heaven fell
   blinding off the brink
As if it would wash the stars away as suds
   go down a sink,
The seven heavens came roaring down for
   the throats of hell to drink,
And Noah he cocked his eye and said,
   "It looks like rain, I think,

The water has drowned the Matterhorn
   as deep as a Mendip mine,
But I don't care where the water goes if it
   doesn't get into the wine."

But Noah he sinned, and we have sinned;
   on tipsy feet we trod,
Till a great big black teetotaller was sent
   to us for a rod,
And you can't get wine at a P.S.A., or
   chapel, or Eisteddfod,
For the Curse of Water has come again
   because of the wrath of God,
And water is on the Bishop's board and
   the Higher Thinker's shrine,
But I don't care where the water goes if
   it doesn't get into the wine.

                 (1913)

A WISH

I wish I were a Girl Guide,
And looked so bright and neat
And made my young subordinates
Salute me in the street.
But none have ever called me neat
And few have called me bright,
And the young who see me are amused
And double up at sight.

I wish I were a Girl Guide,
And wore so large a hat
Curled up abruptly at the side
With a nice cockade like that.

My hat is large but shabby
And without that cock or curl
Few would mistake me for a guide
Or even for a girl.

(1920s)

Walton-on-the-Naze

(The result of stopping two days at Walton with nothing to read but
the Bible in one's bedroom. —)

Yet Walton rejoice and be glad: it hath gained approval of ME.
And the wise of the Earth are as naught and the judge vanity
There are rich romantic glimpses: there are towns of bashful mud
(I know a railing down by the Pier, that simply stirs the blood)
O stately trees of Walton — (that is a tree, I think)
O mystical water of Walton, too holy for man to drink;
The rich of the Earth and the mighty, that sit on the golden throne,
That go upon Continental Tours with bicycles not their own
That wax proud with the grace of gods: that are filled of the soul's desire
That provide you with one and eightpence to send off a sixpenny wire
They mock: they shoot out the lip: they spin like a dog: or a pup
Like those of the Psalmist's enemies who had not been well brought up.

VIII

SATIRE AND CRITICISM

AFTER READING A BOOK OF MODERN VERSE

(Written for a private collection)

The poet, exquisite and pale
Weighed the seven heavens in a scale,
The streaming seraphs hooked and dived
And pinned their plumage side by side
Knocked down like toys the eternal towers,
And plucked the stars like pretty flowers
And cried, before the fearful Face,
"I fear you not; my mortal race
Begot you; and, a man like me,
You dreamed a dream in Galilee—
You that were God: What are you now?"
The insulted reared his thunderous brow
And said at last, "Thou sayest true,
I was a man. But what are you?"

(ca. 1897)

THE APOLOGY OF BOTTOM THE WEAVER

Once when an honest weaver slept,
  And Puck passed by, a kindly traitor,
And on his shoulders set the head
  Of a Shakespearean commentator,

The man had walked proverbial ways,
  Fair Science frowned not on his birth,
Nor lost in long and tangled dreams,
  The mother-wit of mother-earth.

Elaborate surgeons had not found
  The cobweb made the cure too brief,
Nor vegetarians taught the rule
  Of eating mustard without beef.

Only in that green night of growth
  Came to him, splendid, without scorn,
The lady of the dreams of men;
  The rival of all women born.

And he, for all his after weaving,
  Drew up from that abysmal dream
Immortal art, that proves by seeming
  All things more real than they seem.

The dancing moth was in his shuttle,
  The pea's pink blossom in his woof,
Your driving schools, your dying hamlets,
  Go through them all and find the proof—

That you, where'er the old crafts linger,
  Draw in their webs like nets of gold,
Hang up like banners for a pattern,
  The leavings of the looms of old.

And even as this home-made rhyme
  Drags but the speech of Shakespeare down,
These home-made patterns but repeat
  The traceries of an ancient clown.

And while the modern fashions fade,
  And while the ancient standards stream,
No psycho-analyst has knocked
  The bottom out of Bottom's dream.

                              (early to mid 1920s)

A CHRISTMAS CAROL

(The chief constable has issued a statement declaring that carol singing in
the streets by children is illegal, and morally and physically injurious. He
appeals to the public to discourage the practice. —daily paper)

God rest you merry gentlemen,
Let nothing you dismay;
The Herald Angels cannot sing,
The cops arrest them on the wing,
And warn them of the docketing
Of anything they say.

God rest you merry gentlemen,
May nothing you dismay:
On your reposeful cities lie
Deep silence, broken only by
The motor horn's melodious cry,
The hooter's happy bray.

So, when the song of children ceased
And Herod was obeyed,
In his high hall Corinthian
With purple and with peacock fan,
Rested that merry gentleman;
And nothing him dismayed.

(1921)

FRAGMENT IN CORRECTION OF D. H. LAWRENCE

(From the essay "On Free Verse", in *Avowals
and Denials*, Methuen 1934)

They are not dead! The sun like a golden lion
Goes down to that red desert where he dies;
The moon, that is bare of all but bodily beauty,
The moon, that is careless of all but bodily beauty,

Looks down on the dying lion where he lies;
Like a queen, from the steep skies.

(1930s)

THE GOOD RICH MAN

Mr. Mandragon the Millionaire, he wouldn't have wine or
    wife,
He couldn't endure complexity; he lived the simple life.
He ordered his lunch by megaphone in manly, simple tones,
And used all his motors for canvassing voters, and twenty
    telephones;
Besides a dandy little machine,
Cunning and neat as ever was seen
With a hundred pulleys and cranks between,
Made of metal and kept quite clean,
To hoist him out of his healthful bed on every day of his life,
And wash him and brush him, and shave him and dress him
    to live the Simple Life.

Mr. Mandragon was most refined and quietly, neatly dressed,
Say all the American newspapers that know refinement best;
Neat and quiet the hair and hat, and the coat quiet and neat.
A trouser worn upon either leg, while boots adorn the feet;
And not, as any one might expect,
A Tiger Skin, all striped and flecked,
And a Peacock Hat with the tail erect,
A scarlet tunic with sunflowers decked,
That might have had a more marked effect,
And pleased the pride of a weaker man that yearned for wine
    or wife;
But fame and the flagon, for Mr. Mandragon obscured the
    Simple Life.

Mr. Mandragon the Millionaire, I am happy to say, is dead;
He enjoyed a quiet funeral in a crematorium shed,
And he lies there fluffy and soft and grey, and certainly quite
refined,
When he might have rotted to flowers and fruit with Adam
and all mankind,
Or been eaten by wolves athirst for blood,
Or burnt on a big tall pyre of wood,
In a towering flame, as a heathen should,
Or even sat with us here at food,
Merrily taking twopenny ale and cheese with a pocket-knife;
But these were luxuries not for him who went for the Simple
Life.

(ca. 1912)

THE HIGHER UNITY

The Rev. Isaiah Bunter has disappeared into the interior of the Solomon
Islands, and it is feared that he may have been devoured by the natives,
as there has been a considerable revival of religious customs among the
Polynesians. — *A real paragraph from a real Paper; only the names altered.*

It was Isaiah Bunter
    Who sailed to the world's end,
And spread religion in a way
    That he did not intend.

He gave, if not the gospel-feast,
    At least a ritual meal;
And in a highly painful sense
    He was devoured with zeal.

And who are we (as Henson says)
    That we should close the door?
And should not Evangelicals
    All jump at shedding Gore?

And many a man will melt in man,
  Becoming one, not two,
When smacks across the startled earth
  The Kiss of Kikuyu.

When Man is the Turk, and the Atheist,
  Essene, Erastian[,] Whig,
And the Thug and the Druse and the Catholic
  And the crew of the Captains's gig.

(1914)

THE HORRIBLE HISTORY OF JONES

Jones had a dog; it had a chain;
Not often worn, not causing pain;
But, as the I.K.L. had passed
Their "Unleashed Cousins Act" at last,
Inspectors took the chain away;
Whereat the canine barked "hurray!"
At which, of course, the S.P.U.
(Whose Nervous Motorists' Bill was through)
Were forced to give the dog in charge
For being Audibly at Large.
None, you will say, were now annoyed,
Save haply Jones—the yard was void.
But something being in the lease
About "alarms to aid police,"
The U.S.U. annexed the yard
For having no sufficient guard;
Now if there's one condition
The C.C.P. are strong upon
It is that every house one buys
Must have a yard for exercise;
So Jones, as tenant, was unfit,
His state of health was proof of it.

Two doctors of the T.T.U.'s
Told him his legs, from long disuse,
Were atrophied; and saying "So
From step to higher step we go
Till everything is New and True,"
They cut his legs off and withdrew.
You know the E.T.S.T.'s views
Are stronger than the T.T.U.'s:
And soon (as one may say) took wing
The Arms, though not the Man, I sing.
To see him sitting limbless there
Was more than the K.K. could bear.
"In mercy silence with all speed
That mouth there are no hands to feed;
What cruel sentimentalist,
O Jones, would doom thee to exist—
Clinging to selfish Selfhood yet?
Weak one! Such reasoning might upset
The Pump Act, and the accumulation
Of all constructive legislation;
Let us construct you up a bit—"
The head fell off when it was hit:
Then words did rise and honest doubt,
And four Commissioners sat about
Whether the slash that left him dead
Cut off his body or his head.

An author in the Isle of Wight
Observed with unconcealed delight
A land of old and just renown
Where Freedom slowly broadened down
From Precedent to Precedent . . .
And this, I think, was what he meant.

(1905–14)

THE NEW FICTION

("Leave them alone", we seem to hear Mr. Galsworthy say
of his young people. From a Review by Mr. Bettany)

Little Blue-Fits has lost his wits,
    And doesn't know where to find them;
Leave them alone and they'll come home,
    And leave their tales behind them.

The remarkable tales, with remarkable sales,
    And Bonnets and Bees in disorder;
For the Bonnets we view are exceedingly Blue,
    And decidedly over the Border.

(1925)

THE NEW FREETHINKER

John Grubby, who was short and stout
And troubled with religious doubt,
Refused about the age of three
To sit upon the curate's knee;
(For so the eternal strife must rage
Between the spirit of the age
And Dogma, which, as is well known,
Does simply hate to be outgrown).
Grubby, the young idea that shoots,
Outgrew the ages like old boots;
While still, to all appearance, small,
Would have no Miracles at all;

And just before the age of ten
Firmly refused Free Will to men.
The altars reeled, the heavens shook,
Just as he read of in the book;

Flung from his house went forth the youth
Alone with tempests and the Truth,
Up to the distant city and dim
Where his papa had bought for him
A partnership in Chepe and Deer
Worth, say, twelve hundred pounds a year.
But he was resolute. Lord Brute
Had found him useful; and Lord Loot,
With whom few other men would act,
Valued his promptitude and tact;
Never did even philanthropy
Enrich a man more rapidly:
'Twas he that stopped the Strike in Coal,
For hungry children racked his soul;
To end their misery there and then
He filled the mines with Chinamen,
Sat in that House that broke the Kings,
And voted for all sorts of things—
And rose from Under-Sec. to Sec.
With scarce a murmur or a check.
Some grumbled. Growlers who gave less
Than generous worship to success,
The little printers in Dundee,
Who got ten years for blasphemy,
(Although he let them off with seven)
Respect him rather less than heaven.
No matter. This can still be said:
Never to supernatural dread,
Never to unseen deity,
Did Sir John Grubby bend the knee;

Never did dream of hell or wrath
Turn Viscount Grubby from his path;
Nor was he bribed by fabled bliss
To kneel to any world but this.

The curate lives in Camden Town,
His lap still empty of renown,
And still across the waste of years
John Grubby, in the House of Peers,
Faces that curate, proud and free,
And never sits upon his knee.

(1912)

THE NEW OMAR

A book of verses underneath the bough,
   Provided that the verses do not scan,
A loaf of bread a jug of wine and Thou,
   Short-haired, all angles, looking like a man.

But let the wine be unfermented, pale,
   Of chemicals compounded, God knows how —
This were indeed the Prophet's Paradise,
   O Paradise were Wilderness enow.

(1925)

NURSERY RHYMES NO. 1: PROPERTY

Little Bo-Peep has lost her Sheep
But hopes that mutton will soon be cheap
When so many cooks are nothing loth
For the task of spoiling the mutton-broth.
And the lords of the Meat Trust, she has been told,
Have cornered mutton and "got it cold"
Through experts, each guaranteed as fit
For the duty of making a hash of it,
In mutton cutlets and mutton pies
She endeavours in vain to recognise

The face of a single personal pet . . .
. . . But Woollen Goods Will Be Cheaper Yet
In shirts and shapes of every size
For pulling the wool over mortal eyes;
And Bradford mills are a lovely sight
Rows and rows of them, brisk and bright . . .
. . . But somehow or other they never recall
The days she walked on the mountain wall
Where the Shepherd Kings of an elder sky
Hoary as hills on the hills trailed by
And something went with her march along
Of David's valour and Virgil's song
When her voice was a clarion calling a clan
And her crook was a sceptre, the sceptre of man,
To gather her flock where the eagles fly
Or lay down her life when the wolf went by.

Little Bo-Peep is paid in full
Stuffed with mutton and choked in wool
But little Bo-Peep has lost her Sheep
And cannot do anything else but weep.
                    (*G. K.'s Weekly*, Nov. 19, 1927)

NURSERY RHYMES NO. 2: EDUCATION

Tom, Tom, the piper's son
Learned that pipers' days are done
Since oaten pipe and pastoral song
To rude and rural scenes belong
And all the tune that he could play
Was *Over the hills and far away*.

The schools receive him; and he reads
The round of all our real needs

The daylight hope of liberal days
One life to live, one world to praise,
The life that ends where it began
Here in the market-place of man,
They bid him trace in wheel and star
The God of all things as they are
They called the laurelled lords of fame
To put his petty pipe to shame
And rock-hewn Homer's hornèd lyre
And Maro's harp of heart's desire
Moaned with the tears of mortal things
And Shakespeare clashed his thousand strings
Crying and replying like a crowd
And Dante's iron lute was loud
With high unhuman love and hate —
— At the calm signal of the State
And just enactment of the School
They drowned the piping of the fool.

But all the tune that they could play
Was *Over the hills and far away*.
            (*G. K.'s Weekly*, Nov. 26, 1927)

NURSERY RHYMES NO. 3[1]

Little Jack Horner
Sat in a corner
Eating a Christmas pie;
He put in his thumb
And pulled out a plum,
And said: "My Lords — ha! and ah — gentlemen — hum!
The conclusion to which the Committee has come

---

[1] G. K. C. did not give this poem its own title, as he did with the other two.

On the sociological residuum
Of the weak, the unfit, and the blind and the dumb—
The (in short) economic excrescence which some
In less technical terms have described as the Slum
Discovers a Nervous Prostration made numb
By the use of beer, brandy, gin, whisky, and rum,
Affecting the sensitive sensorium
With a blasting effect as of bullets (dum-dum);
And making our workers so gloomy and glum
That they can't take delight in the landscape of Brum,
And will seldom leap up like a chivalrous chum
To make somebody else's big enterprise hum,
And receive in return, by a sound rule of thumb,
The more or less crumby proportion of crumb
Which falls from the table of Baron de Tum
Of Consolidate Glue and Incorporate Gum,
And the British Adventure in Bam-Buzalum.
The table all laden with Clicquot and Mumm
To which they might, too, have aspired, and become
Successful as we are: survived in the scrum
Of the fittest who fight for Honorarium,
And make in Imperio Imperium,
To the manifest gain of Lord Cockalorum;
And at last, to arrive at the Summum Bonum,
The Evolving Eden and Elysium,
The Pattern of Fate with its thread and its thrum,
The End of Existence when—er—that is, um
I appear; and the world has discarded its scrum
Of ignorance, dirt, and of mere tedium.
And the beer and the bloodshed in which it has swum,
And the dissolute cask and the bellicose drum,
And the world that revolves like a mad teetotum
Round Me"—(or, to state his oration in sum)
    He said: "What a good boy am I."
        (*G.K.'s Weekly*, May 19, 1927)

ON A PROHIBITIONIST POEM

Though Shakespeare's Mermaid, ocean's mightiest daughter,
With vintage could the seas incarnadine:
And Keats's name that was not writ in water
      Was often writ in wine.

Though wine that seeks the loftiest habitation
Went to the heads of Villon and Verlaine,
Yet Hiram Hopper needs no inspiration
      But water on the brain.

          (1925)

ON PROFESSOR FREUD

The ignorant pronounce it Frood,
To cavil or applaud.
The well-informed pronounce it Froyd,
But I pronounce it Fraud.
      (1925)

ON READING "GOD"

(Mr. Middleton Murry explains that his book with this title records
his farewell to God.)

Murry, on finding *le Bon Dieu*
Chose difficile à croire
Illogically said "Adieu"
But God said "Au revoir."
      (1932)

THE ORATOR OF THE OPPOSITION

Lord Lurch, C.B. (and now M.P.),
The Tory victor in Long Lea,
Displayed his own unfailing tact
Concerning the Insurance Act.
He said it was a dreadful thing
(His audience made the welkin ring).
He said it was a painful fact
(They cheered until the ceiling cracked).
A gross abuse of public powers
(His audience buried him in flowers).
While they applauded every word,
In such a way that none were heard,
He swiftly said he would amend,
As his right honourable friend,
The Leader of the Opposition,
Had truly said, that worst condition.
That second colon in Clause Three;
The real blot, the infamy
And shame of this accursed Act . . .
Leaving it otherwise intact.

Then stride about his social pen
And walk and jest with gentlemen,
And praise the Cecils in their pride
(Now the Sassoons are satisfied).
Be friends with Balfour; and not *quite*
So intimate with Otto Beit;
And watch benignant Hebrews bless
His hatred for its harmlessness;
And steal the plaudits of the poor
By cursing what he dare not cure;
And keep the favours of the rich
By scratching only when they itch,
And mocking only when they wink,
And still have all their fizz to drink,

And still have all their grouse to gorge;
By God! I'd sooner be Lloyd George.
(*The Eye Witness*, Oct. 17, 1912)[1]

A PARTY QUESTION

"You hear a great deal about His Mother, for Our Lady has become
the patron of a party, whereas Christ was never a party leader."
— Mr Arnold Lunn on "Roman Converts"

The golden roses of the glorious mysteries
      Grew wild as cowslips on the common land
Hers, who was more humanity's than history's,
      Until you banned them as a badge is banned.

The silver roses of the sorrow of Mary,
      And the red roses of her royal mirth,
Were free; till you, turned petulant and wary,
      Went weeding wild flowers from your mother-earth

Mother of Man; the Mother of the Maker;
      Silently speaking as the flowering trees,
What made of her a striker and a breaker
      Who spoke no scorn even of men like these?

She named no hypocrites a viper race,
      She nailed no tyrant for a vulpine cur,
She flogged no hucksters from the holy place;
      Why was your new wise world in dread of her?

Whom had she greeted and not graced in greeting,
      Whom did she touch and touch not his peace;
And what are you, that made of such a meeting
      Quarrels and quibbles and a taunt to tease?

---

[1] G. K. C. wrote only some of the series Rhymes for the Times. This is no. 18.

Who made that inn a fortress? What strange blindness
　　Beat on the open door of that great heart,
Stood on its guard against unguarded kindness
　　And made the sun a secret set apart?

By this we measure you upon your showing
　　So many shields to her who bore no sword,
All your unnatural nature and the flowing
　　Of sundering rivers now so hard to ford.

We know God's priests had drunken iniquity,
　　Through our sins too did such offences come,
Mad Martin's bell, the mouth of anarchy,
　　Knox and the horror of that hollow drum.

We know the tale; half truth and double treason,
　　Borgia and Torquemada in the throng,
Bad men who had no right to their right reason,
　　Good men who had good reason to be wrong.

But when that tangled war our fathers waged
　　Stirred against her—then could we hear right well,
Through roar of men not wrongfully enraged,
　　The little hiss that only comes from hell.

　　　　　　　　　　　　　　　(1924–25)

A PATRIOTIC SONG

　　The Golden Hind went bowling
　　Nor'westward of the Main,
　　And Drake drank deep of Spanish wine
　　And spat the lees at Spain.
　　Till northward on the colder coasts
　　The savages came out
　　To hail the ship with tossing spear
　　And tomahawk and shout:

For the red gods and the witch-doctors
Had cursed the golden grape
Bidding him yield up Malvoisie
And wine in every shape.

> And need I say that Drake complied
> And poured the wine over the side,
> Invited all the Reds inside
> And let them ransack far and wide
> The ship that was his sinful pride
> For anything his men might hide,
> That so he might escape.

The top-sails of the Victory
Turned westward on a day
Great Nelson saw his sunrise land
Like a sunset fade away.
And pledged immortal beauty
And the isle beyond the foam
In the dark wine of Oporto
That his father drank at home.
His hand and glass were lifted
When they reached the rebel shore
And Hiram Hugginburg came forth
And bade him drink no more.

> And naturally Nelson ran
> To do his bidding and began
> To empty every cup and can
> And snatch the rum from every man
> Who (ignorant of Hiram's ban)
> Had broken with him the battle-van
> From the Nile to Elsinore.

Lo, of that leaping pennant learn,
Of those world-wandering graves,
In what more modest modern style
Britannia rules the waves.

If, loyal to some foreign cause,
We still are careful, clause by clause,
Obeying other countries' laws.
We never shall be slaves.

(1926)

THE PEACE OF PETROL

(To be sung to the air of "Kabul River" on the conclusion
of an English peace brought about by American
intervention)

He has many a car and chuffer
  (Still the bugle, sheathe the sword),
So I left my mates to suffer
  All because of Mr. Ford.
Ford, Ford, Ford of many millions,
  Ford of many motors in the Park;
And our lord will laugh like thunder at the Good Cause going
    under
  When we stab it, to oblige him, in the dark.

We'll give up the blasted place
  (Drop the bugle, break the sword)
For one smile upon his face,
  O, the shiny face of Ford!
Ford, Ford, Ford; the French are falling,
  And the Serbians on the mountains lying stark,
All their eyes on us, disdaining, and it ain't no use explaining
  That a millionaire has bought us for a lark.

O the motors he can make!
  (Sell the bugle, pawn the sword)
We'll be humbled for his sake,
  Break our faith and keep our Ford.

Ford, Ford, Ford—till death remove him
   To a place on which it's needless to remark.
And the rich whose minds are muddy, who consider honour
      bloody,
   Go down to their damnation in the dark.

                                                    (1915)

THE PHILANTHROPIST

(With Apologies to a Beautiful Poem)

Abou Ben Adhem (may his tribe decrease
By cautious birth-control and die in peace)
Mellow with learning lightly took the word
That marked him not with them that love the Lord,
And told the angel of the book and pen
"Write me as one that loves his fellow-men:
For them alone I labour; to reclaim
The ragged roaming Bedouin and to tame
To ordered service; to uproot their vine
Who mock the Prophet, being mad with wine;
Let daylight through their tents and through their lives
Number their camels, even count their wives;
Plot out the desert into streets and squares,
And count it a more fruitful work than theirs
Who lift a vain and visionary love
To your vague Allah in the skies above."

Gently replied the angel of the pen:
"Labour in peace and love your fellow-men:
And love not God, since men alone are dear,
Only fear God; for you have cause to fear."

                                        (ca. 1918–21)

RACE-MEMORY

(by a dazed Darwinian)

I remember, I remember,
  Long before I was born,
The tree-tops where my racial self
  Went dancing round at morn.

Green wavering archipelagos,
  Great gusty bursts of blue,
In my race-memory I recall
  (Or I am told I do).

In that green-turreted Monkeyville
  (So I have often heard)
It seemed as if a Blue Baboon
  Might soar like a Blue Bird.

Low crawling Fundamentalists
  Glared up through the green mist,
I hung upon my tail in heaven
  A Firmamentalist.

* * *

I am too fat to climb a tree,
  There are no trees to climb;
Instead, the factory chimneys rise,
  Unscaleable, sublime.

The past was bestial ignorance:
  But I feel a little funky,
To think I'm further off from heaven
  Than when I was a monkey.

(1925)

REFUTATION

Refutation of the only too prevalent slander that parliamentary leaders are indifferent to the strict fulfilment of their promises and the preservation of their reputation for veracity.

> They said (when they had dined at Ciro's)
> The land would soon be fit for heroes;
> And now they've managed to ensure it,
> For only heroes could endure it.
>   (ca. 1920?)

THE REVOLUTIONIST:
OR LINES TO A STATESMAN

> "I was never standing by, while a revolution was going on."
>   — Speech by the Rt. Hon. Walter Long

> When Death was on thy drums, Democracy,
> And with one rush of slaves the world was free,
> In that high dawn that Kings shall not forget,
> A void there was and Walter was not yet.
> Through sacked Versailles, at Valmy in the fray,
> They did without him in some kind of way;
> Red Christendom all Walterless they cross,
> And in their fury hardly feel their loss. . . .
> Fades the Republic, faint as Roland's horn,
> Her trumpets taunt us with a sacred scorn. . . .
> Then silence fell: and Mr. Long was born.

> From his first hours in his expensive cot
> He never saw the tiniest viscount shot.
> In deference to his wealthy parents' whim
> The mildest massacres were kept from him.
> The wars that dyed Pall Mall and Brompton red
> Passed harmless o'er that one unconscious head:

For all that little Long could understand
The rich might still be rulers of the land.
Vain are the pious arts of parenthood,
Foiled Revolution bubbled in his blood;
Until one day (the babe unborn shall rue it)
The Constitution bored him and he slew it.

If I were wise and good and rich and strong—
Fond, impious thought, if I were Walter Long—
If I could water sell like molten gold,
And make grown people do as they were told,
If over private fields and wastes as wide
As a Greek city for which heroes died,
I owned the houses and the men inside—
If all this hung on one thin thread of habit
I would not revolutionize a rabbit.

I would sit tight with all my gifts and glories,
And even preach to unconverted Tories,
That the fixed system that our land inherits,
Viewed from a certain standpoint, has its merits.
I'd guard the laws like any Radical,
And keep each precedent, however small,
However subtle, misty, dusty, dreamy,
Lest man by chance should look at me and see me;
Lest men should ask what madman made me lord
Of English ploughshares and the English sword;
Lest men should mark how sleepy is the nod
That drills the dreadful images of God!

Walter, be wise! avoid the wild and new!
The Constitution is the game for you.
Walter, beware! scorn not the gathering throng,
It suffers, yet it may not suffer wrong,
It suffers, yet it cannot suffer Long.
And if you goad it these grey rules to break,
For a few pence, see that you do not wake

Death and the splendour of the scarlet cap,
Boston and Valmy, Yorktown and Jemmappes,
Freedom in arms, the riding and the routing,
The thunder of the captains and the shouting,
All that lost riot that you did not share—
And when that riot comes—you *will* be there.

(1909)

ROTARIANS

The Symbol

The speaking at the Rotary is Praise devoid of Proof
The talking at the Rotary turns mostly on the oof
But both require an Emblem; and a Wheel is just the thing
When you argue in a circle and do business in a Ring.

At a Rotarian Lunch

Broken on another wheel than Rotary
St. Catherine's body set her spirit free
Here rests the body that the soul may squirm
In all joints broken to a jointless worm.

A Declaration of Dependence

The Jeffersonian justice which
Degenerate hucksters quote
Republicans have had by right
Rotarians by rote.

(1927)

THE SHAKESPEARE MEMORIAL

Lord Lilac thought it rather rotten
That Shakespeare should be quite forgotten,
And therefore got on a Committee
With several chaps out of the City,
And Shorter and Sir Herbert Tree,
Lord Rothschild and Lord Rosebery,
And F. C. G. and Comyns Carr,
Two dukes and a dramatic star,
Also a clergyman now dead;
And while the vain world careless sped
Unheeding the heroic name —
The souls most fed with Shakespeare's flame
Still sat unconquered in a ring,
Remembering him like anything.

Lord Lilac did not long remain,
Lord Lilac did not come again.
He softly lit a cigarette
And sought some other social set
Where, in some other knots or rings,
People were doing cultured things,
— Miss Zwilt's Humane Vivarium
— The little men that paint on gum
— The exquisite Gorilla Girl. . . .
He sometimes, in this giddy whirl
(Not being really bad at heart),
Remembered Shakespeare with a start —
But not with that grand constancy
Of Clement Shorter, Herbert Tree,
Lord Rosebery and Comyns Carr
And all the other names there are;
Who stuck like limpets to the spot,
Lest they forgot, lest they forgot.

Lord Lilac was of slighter stuff;
Lord Lilac had had quite enough.

(1912)

SOME WISHES AT XMAS

Mince-pies grant Wishes: let each name his Prize,
But as for us, we wish for more Mince-pies.

Mr. Epstein

What wish has Epstein's art portrayed?
   Toward what does Rima rise?
Those little hands were never made
   To tear out eagles' eyes:
She for Green Mansions yearns; but not
So green a mansion as she got.

Dean Inge

What deep desires inspire the Gloomy Dean,
While Rima chants The Wearing of the Green?
Does he have childlike hopes at Christmas time
And sing a carol or a nursery rhyme?
Does he hang up a stocking—or a gaiter—
Or ask for gifts from any Alma Mater?
(Tell me, do Matthew, Mark, and Luke and John
Bless beds the Higher Critics lie upon?
Or if, while the Fourth Gospel is re-read,
"Synoptists" sleep on a three-cornered bed).
Or, like the Deutero-Job, who far away
On his interpolated ash-heap lay,
Damns he the day whereon his body and soul
Escaped the vigilance of Birth-Control?
Or, softened while the herald angel sings,
Does he more mildly wish for lesser things
That warning cracks, marking the house that falls,
Should decorate St. Peter's not St. Paul's;
Or wish in all good faith to friends held dear
A Gloomy Christmas and a Glum New Year?

A Merry Christmas to a Merrier Dean!
Whatever he may want, whatever mean,
He won't be happy till he gets it; when
He does, perhaps he won't be happy then.

A Lady M.P.

She wants a new England, more bright and more clean,
Where foul tap-room revelries never are seen.
And after the quarter-staff flies the quart-pot,
For she wants a new England where these things are not,
And our love of old England is vain in her sight,
As the noise of blind drunkards that strive in the night,
As if our old England like fable could fade,
And a Puritan purge through the ages had made
A Shaker of Shakespeare, a grave man of Gay,
And a Pussyfoot Johnson with Boswell to play.
For she wants a new England, where censors and prigs
Can browbeat our jokes and can bridle our jigs.
The title is apt, and the tale is soon told,
She wants a New England, three hundred years old.

The Communists

There are two normal nuisances
    That stir us late or soon:
One is the man who wants the earth,
    The other wants the moon.
Choosing between these last and Jix,
    We much prefer the lunatics.

Jix

Since Christmas time brings charity
    For Jix and for the Kaiser,
We wish that they were wise enough
    To wish that they were wiser.

Mr. H. G. Wells

Oh, how can we number
The wishes of Wells,
And the numerous heavens
He worked for like hells—
From World State to Samurai
Constantly ranging,
One long transformation scene
Endlessly changing—
But no wishes come true
Though the fairies have grace with him.
For his own Fairy Godmother
Cannot keep pace with him.

Mr. Winston Churchill

Everyone knows what Winston wants
And Baldwin best of all:
To do him justice, though he wants
To sound The Clarion Call,
He also wants to paint and write
And have a jolly time—
Though he has put his shirt on War
With Communistic Crime,
The shirt, with which we're all acquainted,
Is not so black as it is painted.

Pirandello

He wishes that his wishes
Were too real to be true,
And that black and white were altered
If we wish till all is blue:
And with causes causing something
Something else will then ensue,
Without knowing what precisely
Something else will turn into.

Till I doubt that I am I, and
I deny that you are you—
Subject always to his wishes,
Could we only find the clue
To what really are his wishes:
But he wishes that he knew.

(1925)

THE SONG OF THE STRANGE ASCETIC

If I had been a Heathen,
  I'd have praised the purple vine,
My slaves should dig the vineyards,
  And I would drink the wine.
But Higgins is a Heathen,
  And his slaves grow lean and grey,
That he may drink some tepid milk
  Exactly twice a day.

If I had been a Heathen,
  I'd have crowned Neæra's curls,
And filled my life with love affairs,
  My house with dancing girls;
But Higgins is a Heathen,
  And to lecture rooms is forced,
Where his aunts, who are not married,
  Demand to be divorced.

If I had been a Heathen,
  I'd have sent my armies forth,
And dragged behind my chariots
  The Chieftains of the North.
But Higgins is a Heathen,
  And he drives the dreary quill,
To lend the poor that funny cash
  That makes them poorer still.

If I had been a Heathen,
  I'd have piled my pyre on high,
And in a great red whirlwind
  Gone roaring to the sky;
But Higgins is a Heathen,
  And a richer man than I:
And they put him in an oven,
  Just as if he were a pie.

Now who that runs can read it,
  The riddle that I write,
Of why this poor old sinner,
  Should sin without delight—
But I, I cannot read it
  (Although I run and run),
Of them that do not have the faith,
  And will not have the fun.

                  (1913)

A SPEECH REPORTED

In Birmingham among my own
Dear people I appear,
For I was born at Camberwell,
Not very far from here.
And if you choose another man,
My public life is closed:
But you will find it difficult,
For I am unopposed.

Have we not armies at the front
Whom we can turn to mobs?
Who, for their love of Me, have shown
Some deference to Bobs.

They're sensitive; and if they knew
Their Joseph had been hissed,
They'd have no nerve to strike the foe
Who now does not exist.

Sir Robert Reid thinks men depraved
Who differ from him. I
Have no such thoughts—beyond distrust
Of their sincerity.
I seldom call them "traitors" even:
I turn, with grace sufficient,
The "other cheek"—a thing in which
I never was deficient.

I challenge them, as they've replied
I challenge them again
To name my words provocative,
For why should "Sponge" give pain?
"Sponge" is a cool and cleanly thing,
And serves our nation well,
And on my private slate I find
It is invaluable.

(1900)

TO A HOLY ROLLER

(The sect of the Holy Rollers demonstrated against evolution at Dayton)

"Roll on," said Gilbert to the earth:
    "Roll on," said Byron to the sea:
Accepting natural features thus,
    Freely I say "Roll on" to thee.

Time like an ever rolling stream
    Bears his most rolling sons away

Bryanite saint, Darwinian sage,
  And even Dayton has its day.

Earth changes; sings another bard,
  "There rolls the deep where grew the tree";
Convulsions viewed with equal calm
  By Tennyson and Tennessee.

But ere you roll down history's slope,
  A moment you may set us thinking
How Prohibition suits their mood,
  Who get so drunk by never drinking.

What rows of bottles, blends of liquor,
  We need to reach in one wild leap
Those reels and rolls you get for nothing,
  Great Bacchic Maenads on the cheap!

I blame you not that, writhing prone,
  You flout the grave Darwinian's view,
Of his extremely Missing Link,
  For he is quite amusing too.

Marking the human ape evolve
  (He puts his rolling into Latin),
Through epochs barely large enough
  To swing an old Egyptian cat in.

Since you believe Man truly tilled
  The Garden for the great Controller,
You back your Garden party up,
  Like a consistent Garden Roller.

We, too, may deem on Adam's birth
  Some more mysterious splendour shone,
Than prigs can pick off monkey's bones,
  Never you mind! Roll on! Roll on!

Grovel and gambol on all fours
  Till you have proved beyond dispute,
That human dignity is freed
  From all connection with the brute.
                    (1925)

TRUE SENSIBILITY

"A Russian woman would be quite offended
if a man opened a door for her."

The Bolshevist lady is no less refined
    Than Victorian misses, but more.
They shrank if a man might be under the bed;
    She shrieks if he opens the door.

Though shirt-sleeves might shock them, the Bolshevist maid
    Is far more fastidious than that.
They frowned at a man if he took off his coat;
    She faints when he takes off his hat.

She blushes at anything all day long,
    Which is why it is commonly said
That while other young ladies are normally pink,
    She is now irretrievably Red.

(1925)

VISION

"He was a man of vision; he foresaw London's
development and made a fortune out of building-land."

(Example of respect for the dead as conceived by the modern
capitalist journalist, on whom alone be all responsibility for the
comment.)

Where there is no Vision
The people perish
. . . Restrain your rude derision,
Where there is no Vision
When they state with such precision
The Hope they cherish.
Where there is no Vision
The people perish.

(1934)

THE WORLD STATE

Oh, how I love Humanity,
  With love so pure and pringlish,
And how I hate the horrid French,
  Who never will be English!

The International Idea,
  The largest and the clearest,
Is welding all the nations now,
  Except the one that's nearest.

This compromise has long been known,
  This scheme of partial pardons,
In ethical societies
  And small suburban gardens—

The villas and the chapels where
  I learned with little labour
The way to love my fellow-man
  And hate my next-door neighbour.
                    (1925)

IX

BATTLE, CHIVALRY AND HONOR

THE BALLAD OF KING ARTHUR[1]

King Arthur on Mount Badon
  Bore the Virgin on his back
When Britain trod the Roman way
  And the red gods went back.
Back to their desolate lands of dawn
  And peace to westward lay
About the crowned and carven thing
  He carried all the day.

The light on Badon battle
  Was dark with driving darts
And dark with rocking catapults
  Reared yet of Roman arts
And dark with Raven banners riven
  But not too dark to see
What shape it was above the shields
  In the sunburst of victory.

King Arthur on Mount Badon
  Bore Our Lady on his shield
High on that human altar held
  Above the howling field,
High on that living altar heaved
  As a giant heaves a tower
She saw all heathenry appalled
  And the turning of the hour.

The sun on Badon battle
  In sanguine seas went down
And night had hid the Roman wall
  That hid the Christian town

---

[1] There was an earlier draft, of three verses only, little different from verses 7, 8 and 9 as given above.

And dim it hung on camp and dyke
  But not too dim to show
What statue stood against the stars
  On Badon long ago.

Great tales are told of dead men gone
  And all men live by tales
And glory be to the endless tale
  Whose old news never fails.
Arthur is lost in Lyonesse
  Kings sought his grave in vain
And old men quote and question still
  If Arthur comes again.

The crawling dragon climbed his crest
  The heralds paint his shield,
The fairies stole the Roman sword
  Rusted on Badon field.
They mixed his name with dames of France
  And witches out of Wales:
Great tales are told of dead men gone,
  And dead men tell no tales.

The Queens that bore King Arthur's bier
  In many a pageant pass;
Strange ladies walking by still lakes
  Like shadows in a glass:
And well it were that on the world
  Such splendid shadows shone
Though round his throne a thousand queens
  Praised him like Solomon

The Queen that wronged King Arthur's house
  Had lovers in all lands
And many a poet praised her pride
  At many a queen's commands:
And the King shrank to a shadow
  Watching behind a screen
And the Queen walked with Lancelot
  And the world walked with the Queen

The presses throbbed, the books piled high,
    The chant grew rich and strong:
The Virgin Queen the courtiers knew
    Had much esteem for song.
The Faerie Queen the poets praised
    Heard every fairy tale
But many a song were broken short
    And many a voice would fail—

Stillness like lightning strike the street
    And doubt and deep amaze
And many a courtly bard be dumb
    Beside his butt and bays
And many a patron prince turned pale—
    If one such flash made plain
The Queen that stands at his right hand
    If Arthur comes again

                                (early 1920s?)

THE BALLAD OF THE BATTLE OF GIBEON

Five kings ruled o'er the Amorite,
Mighty as fear and old as night;
Swathed with unguent and gold and jewel,
Waxed they merry and fat and cruel.
Zedek of Salem, a terror and glory,
Whose face was hid while his robes were gory;
And Hoham of Hebron, whose loathly face is
Heavy and dark o'er the ruin of races;
And Piram of Jarmuth, drunk with strange wine,
Who dreamed he had fashioned all stars that shine;
And Debir of Eglon wild, without pity,
Who raged like a plague in the midst of his city;
And Japhia of Lachish, a fire that flameth,
Who did in the daylight what no man nameth.

These five kings said one to another,
'King unto king o'er the world is brother,
Seeing that now, for a sign and a wonder,
A red eclipse and a tongue of thunder,
A shape and a finger of desolation,
Is come against us a kingless nation.
Gibeon hath failed us; it were not good
That a man remember where Gibeon stood.'
Then Gibeon sent to our captain, crying,
'Son of Nun, let a shaft be flying,
For unclean birds are gathering greedily;
Slack not thy hand but come thou speedily.
Yea, we are lost save thou maintain'st us,
For the kings of the mountains are gathered against us.'

Then to our people spake the Deliverer,
'Gibeon is high, yet a host may shiver her;
"Gibeon hath sent to me crying for pity,
For the lords of the cities encompass the city
With chariot and banner and bowman and lancer,
And I swear by the living God I will answer.
Gird you, O Israel, quiver and javelin,
Shield and sword for the road we travel in;
Verily, as I have promised, pay I
Life unto Gibeon, death unto Ai."

Sudden and still as a bolt shot right
Up on the city we went by night.
Never a bird of the air could say,
"This was the children of Israel's way."
Only the hosts sprang up from sleeping,
Saw from the heights a dark stream sweeping;
Sprang up straight as a great shout stung them
And heard the Deliverer's war-cry among them,
Heard under cupola, turret, and steeple
The awful cry of the kingless people.
Started the weak of them, shouted the strong of them,

Crashed we a thunderbolt into the throng of them,
Blindly with heads bent and shields forced before us,
We heard the dense roar of the strife closing o'er us.
And drunk with the crash of the song that it sung them,
We drove the great spear-blade in God's name
      among them.

Redder and redder the sword-flash fell,
Our eyes and our nostrils were hotter than hell;
Till full all the crest of the spear-surge shocking us,
Hoham of Hebron cried out mocking us,
"Nay, what need of the war-sword's plying,
Out of the desert the dust comes flying.
A little red dust, if the wind be blowing—
Who shall reck of its coming or going?"
Back the Deliverer spake as a clarion,,
"Mock at thy slaves, thou cater of carrion!
Laughest thou at us, in thy kingly clowning,
We, that laughed upon Rameses frowning,
We that stood up, proud, unpardoned,
When his face was dark, and his heart was hardened?
Pharaoh we knew and his steeds, not faster
Than the word of the Lord in thine ear, O master."
Sheer through the turban his wantons wove him,
Clean to the skull the Deliverer clove him;
And the two hosts reeled at the sign appalling,
As the great king fell like a great house falling.

Loudly we shouted, and living, and dying,
Bore them all backward with strength and strong
      crying;
And Caleb struck Zedek hard at the throat,
And Japhia of Lachish Zebulon smote.
The war-swords and axes were clashing and groaning,
The fallen were fighting and foaming and moaning.
The war spears were breaking, the war-horns were
      braying,

Ere the hands of the slayers were sated with slaying.
And deep in the grasses grown gory and sodden,
The treaders of all men were trampled and trodden:
And over them, routed and reeled like cattle,
High over the turn of the tide of the battle,
High over noises that deafen and cover us,
Rang the Deliverer's voice out over us.

"Stand thou still, thou sun upon Gibeon,
Stand thou, moon, in the valley of Ajalon!
Shout thou, people, a cry like thunder,
For the kings of the earth are broken asunder.
Now we have said as the thunder says it,
Something is stronger than strength and slays it.
Now we have written for all time later,
Five kings are great, yet a law is greater.
Stare, O sun! in thine own great glory,
This is the turn of the whole world's story.
Stand thou still, thou sun upon Gibeon,
Stand thou, moon, in the valley of Ajalon!

"Smite! amid spear-blades blazing and breaking,
More than we know of is rising and making.
Stab with the javelin, crash with the car!
Cry! for we know not the thing that we are.
Stand, O sun! that in horrible patience
Smiled on the smoke and the slaughter of nations.
Thou shalt grow sad for a little crying,
Thou shalt be darkened for one man's dying—
Stand thou still, thou sun upon Gibeon,
Stand thou, moon, in the valley of Ajalon!"

After the battle was broken and spent
Up to the hill the Deliverer went,
Flung up his arms to the storm-clouds flying,
And cried unto Israel, mightily crying,
"Come up, O warriors! come up, O brothers!
Tribesmen and herdsmen, maidens and mothers;

The bondman's son and the bondman's daughter,
The hewer of wood and the drawer of water,
He that carries and he that brings,
And set your foot on the neck of kings."

This is the story of Gibeon fight —
Where we smote the lords of the Amorite;
Where the banners of princes with slaughter
     were sodden,
And the beards of seers in the rank grass trodden;
Where the trees were wrecked by the wreck of cars,
And the reek of the red field blotted the stars;
Where the dead heads dropped from the swords
     that sever,
Because His mercy endureth for ever.

                    (late 1870s)

BLESSED ARE THE PEACEMAKERS

Of old with a divided heart
   I saw my people's pride expand,
Since a man's soul is torn apart
By mother earth and fatherland.

I knew, through many a tangled tale,
   Glory and truth not one but two:
King, Constable, and Amirail
   Took me like trumpets: but I knew

A blacker thing than blood's own dye
   Weighed down great Hawkins on the sea;
And Nelson turned his blindest eye
   On Naples and on liberty.

Therefore to you my thanks, O throne,
   O thousandfold and frozen folk;
For whose cold frenzies all your own
   The Battle of the Rivers broke;

Who have no faith a man could mourn,
    Nor freedom any man desires;
But in a new clean light of scorn
    Close up my quarrel with my sires;

Who bring my English heart to me,
    Who mend me like a broken toy;
Till I can see you fight and flee,
    And laugh as if I were a boy.

(1914)

THE CRUSADER RETURNS FROM CAPTIVITY

I have come forth alive from the land of purple and poison and
    glamour,
Where the charm is strong as the torture, being chosen to
    change the mind;
Torture of wordless dance and wineless feast without clamour,
    Palace hidden in palace, garden with garden behind;
Women veiled in the sun, or bare as brass in the shadows,
    And the endless eyeless patterns where each thing seems an
    eye. . . .
And my stride is on Caesar's sand where it slides to the English
    meadows,
    To the last low woods of Sussex and the road that goes to
    Rye.

In the cool and careless woods the eyes of the eunuchs burned
    not,
    But the wild hawk went before me, being free to return or
    roam,
The hills had broad unconscious backs; and the tree-tops turned
    not,
    And the huts were heedless of me; and I knew I was at home.

And I saw my lady afar and her holy freedom upon her,
    A head, without veil, averted, and not to be turned with
    charms,

And I heard above bannerets blown the intolerant trumpets of
    honour,
  That usher with iron laughter the coming of Christian arms.

My shield hangs stainless still; but I shall not go where they
    praise it,
  A sword is still at my side, but I shall not ride with the King.
Only to walk and to walk and to stun my soul and amaze it,
  A day with the stone and the sparrow and every marvellous
    thing.

I have trod the curves of the Crescent, in the maze of them that
    adore it,
  Curved around doorless chambers and unbeholden abodes,
But I walk in the maze no more; on the sign of the cross I
    swore it,
  The wild white cross of freedom, the sign of the white cross-
    roads.

And the land shall leave me or take, and the Woman take me
    or leave me,
  There shall be no more night, or nightmares seen in a glass;
But Life shall hold me alive, and Death shall never deceive me
  As long as I walk in England in the lanes that let me pass.

                                (1913)

THE DEAD HERO

  We never saw you, like our sires,
    For whom your face was Freedom's face,
  Nor know what office-tapes and wires
    With such strong cords may interlace;
  We know not if the statesmen then
    Were fashioned as the sort we see,
  We know that not under your ken
    Did England laugh at Liberty.

Yea; this one thing is known of you,
　We know that not till you were dumb,
Not till your course was thundered through,
　Did Mammon see his kingdom come.
The songs of theft, the swords of hire,
　The clerks that raved, the troops that ran.
The empire of the world's desire,
　The dance of all the dirt began.

The happy jewelled alien men
　Worked then but as a little leaven;
From some more modest palace then
　The Soul of Dives stank to Heaven.
But when they planned with lisp and leer
　Their careful war upon the weak,
They smote your body on its bier,
　For surety that you could not speak.

A hero in the desert died;
　Men cried that saints should bury him,
And round the grave should guard and ride,
　A chivalry of Cherubim.
God said: "There is a better place,
　A nobler trophy and more tall;
The beasts that fled before his face
　Shall come to make his funeral.

"The mighty vermin of the void
　That hid them from his bended bow,
Shall crawl from caverns overjoyed,
　Jackal and snake and carrion crow.
And perched above the vulture's eggs,
　Reversed upon its hideous head,
A blue-faced ape shall wave its legs
　To tell the world that he is dead."

(1910–14)

THE ENGLISH GRAVES

Were I that wandering citizen whose city is the world,
I would not weep for all that fell before the flags were furled;
I would not let one murmur mar the trumpets volleying forth
How God grew weary of the kings, and the cold hell in the
    north.
But we whose hearts are homing birds have heavier thoughts
    of home,
Though the great eagles burn with gold on Paris or on Rome,
Who stand beside our dead and stare, like seers at an eclipse,
At the riddle of the island tale and the twilight of the ships.

For these were simple men that loved with hands and feet and
    eyes,
Whose souls were humbled to the hills and narrowed to the
    skies,
The hundred little lands within one little land that lie,
Where Severn seeks the sunset isles or Sussex scales the sky.

And what is theirs, though banners blow on Warsaw risen
    again,
Or ancient laughter walks in gold through the vineyards of
    Lorraine,
Their dead are marked on English stones, their loves on Eng-
    lish trees,
How little is the prize they win, how mean a coin for these—
How small a shrivelled laurel-leaf lies crumpled here and
    curled:
They died to save their country and they only saved the world.

(early 1920s)

THE GRAVE OF ARTHUR

Hic Jacet Arturus Rex Quondam Rexque Futurus

Down through the rocks where the dark roots dry,
The last long roots of the Glaston Thorn,
Dead is the King that never was born,
Dead is the King that never shall die.

They found him between the pyramids
In the subterranean land, men say,
And there was not rending nor rolling away
Of linen nor lifting of coffin-lids,

But the giant bones like the columns lie,
The far-flung towers of a flattened city
That is dead with a doom too old for pity
(Dead is the King who does not die).

Coiled on his left from neck to knee,
Huge and hollow the horn is curled,
White as the worm that devours the world,
Carved with the cold white snakes of the sea.

Flat on his right, in the dust grown grey,
Is patterned the vast cross-hilted sword
Graven with the Coming of Christ the Lord,
Gold with the trumpets of Judgment Day.

Between the first and the last he lies
And between the false and the true dreams he:
Born without birth of a fabled sea
Armoured in death till the dead shall rise.

And back and forth as a tolling bell
And forth and backward the Roman rhyme
Rolls in a ring that mocks at time
Tolling the truth that none can tell.

In the high still hollow where Time is not
Or all times turn and exchange and borrow
In the glass wherein God remembers to-morrow
And truth looks forward to times forgot.

Where God looks back on the days to be
And heaven is yet hoping for yesterday;
The light in which time shall be taken away
And the soul that faces all ways is free,

The rune shall be read though it twist and turn,
And the riddle be learnt that is past all learning,
Of the Man unborn who is ever returning
And ever delaying, till God return.

And for ever and ever till death discover
Why truth speaks double in dreams and day;
And the Myth and the Man that wandered away
Make tryst together as lover to lover,

A dream shall wail through the worm-shaped horn
'Dead is a King that never was born'
And a trumpet of truth from the Cross reply
'Dead is the King who shall not die'.

(ca. 1930)

IN MEMORIAM M. D.

If there had been but three of you,
We might have held the way:
While that foul thing could still devour
Which can but now decay:
The dogs who had their day—and now
Who have their judgement day.

If there had been but two of you—
She of your name, men say,

Who barred the door with broken bone
To bid the murderers stay—
If there had been but two of you
We might have barred the way.

The yellow liveries of gold
Were many and we were few:
Out of the gilded gutter gates;
Out of the sewers we knew,
Nothing so noble as Murder came
But all the thieves went through.

Not of this vain world, Margaret,
Not on this fallen star
The Heart that breaks the Fetter and Lock,
The arm that breaks the bar.
On the far side of Time's tapestry
Your towering triumphs are.

Bribery and slavery and sloth,
That had no part in you,
May tear or tame the trampled earth:
The tale will still be true
When we shall name to later lives
A lady that we knew.

                              (Sept. 1931)[1]

IN MEMORIAM P. D.

Nice, January 30, 1914

If any in an island cradle curled
Of comfort, may make offering to you,
Who in the day of all denial blew
A bugle through the blackness of the world,

---

[1] Written for *Margaret Douglas: A Selection from her Writings*, (Ditchling: St. Dominic's Press, 1931).

An English hand would touch your shroud, in trust
That truth again be told in English speech,
And we too yet may practice what we preach,
Though it were practising the bayonet thrust,

Cutting that giant neck from sand to sand,
From sea to sea; it was a little thing
Beside your sudden shout and sabre swing
That cut the throat of thieves in every land.

Heed not if half-wits mock your broken blade;
Mammon our master doeth all things ill.
You are the Fool that charged a windmill. Still,
The Miller is a knave; and was afraid.

Lay down your sword. Ruin will know her own.
Let each small statesman sow his weak wild oat,
Or turn his coat to decorate his coat,
Or take the throne and perish by the throne.

Lay down your sword. And let the White Flag fade
To grey; and let the Red Flag fade to pink,
For these that climb and climb; and cannot sink
So deep as death and honour, Déroulède.

(1914)[1]

IN OCTOBER

Where are they gone that did delight in honour
Abrupt and absolute as an epic ends,
What light of the Last Things, like death at morning,
Crowns the true lovers and the tragic friends?

Young priests with eager faces bright as eagles,
Poor scholars of the harp-string, strict and strung,

---

[1] Paul Déroulède (1846–1914) was a French author, politician, soldier and playwright. He composed many patriotic poems.

All the huge thirst of things irrevocable
And all the intolerant innocence that died young.

The dark largesse of the last gesture flinging
The glove in challenge or gold in sacrifice—
Where are they gone that had delight in honour
That the world grows so greedy and so wise?

Vow and averted head and high refusal
Clean as the chasm where the dawn burns white,
Where shall they go that have delight in honour
When all men honour nothing but delight?

Out of the infinite came Finality,
Freedom that makes unfathomably sure,
For only a wind of all the widest windows
Can close with such a clang that iron door:

The doors that cannot shut shall never open
Nor men make windows when they make not walls,
Though emptiness extend its endless prison
In the white nightmare of its lengthening halls

Shall they not rise and seek beyond the mountains
That which unsays not and is not forsworn?
Where should they wander and in what other Eden
Find the lost happiness of the hope forlorn,

Look in what other face for understanding,
But hers who bore the Child that brought the Sword,
Hang in what other house, trophy and tribute,
The broken heart and the unbroken word?

This month of luminous and golden ruin
Lit long ago the galleys and the guns.
Here is there nothing but such loitering rhyme
As down the blank of barren paper runs,

As I write now, O Lady of Last Assurance,
Light in the laurels, sunrise of the dead,

Wind of the ships and lightning of Lepanto,
In honour of Thee, to whom all honour is fled.
(1918–25)

THE LAST HERO

The wind blew out from Bergen from the dawning to the day,
There was a wreck of trees and fall of towers a score of miles away,
And drifted like a livid leaf I go before its tide,
Spewed out of house and stable, beggared of flag and bride.
The heavens are bowed about my head, shouting like seraph wars,
With rains that might put out the sun and clean the sky of stars,
Rains like the fall of ruined seas from secret worlds above,
The roaring of the rains of God none but the lonely love.
Feast in my hall, O foemen, and eat and drink and drain,
You never loved the sun in heaven as I have loved the rain.

The chance of battle changes—so may all battle be;
I stole my lady bride from them, they stole her back from me.
I rent her from her red-roofed hall, I rode and saw arise,
More lovely than the living flowers the hatred in her eyes.
She never loved me, never bent, never was less divine;
The sunset never loved me; the wind was never mine.
Was it all nothing that she stood imperial in duresse?
Silence itself made softer with the sweeping of her dress.
O you who drain the cup of life, O you who wear the crown,
You never loved a woman's smile as I have loved her frown.

The wind blew out from Bergen from the dawning to the day,
They ride and run with fifty spears to break and bar my way,
I shall not die alone, alone, but kin to all the powers,
As merry as the ancient sun and fighting like the flowers.
How white their steel, how bright their eyes! I love each laughing knave,
Cry high and bid him welcome to the banquet of the brave.

Yea, I will bless them as they bend and love them where they lie,
When on their skulls the sword I swing falls shattering from the sky.
The hour when death is like a light and blood is like a rose, —
You never loved your friends, my friends, as I shall love my foes.

Know you what earth shall lose to-night, what rich uncounted loans,
What heavy gold of tales untold you bury with my bones?
My loves in deep dim meadows, my ships that rode at ease,
Ruffling the purple plumage of strange and secret seas.
To see this fair earth as it is to me alone was given,
The blow that breaks my brow to-night shall break the dome of heaven.
The skies I saw, the trees I saw after no eyes shall see.
To-night I die the death of God: the stars shall die with me:
One sound shall sunder all the spears and break the trumpet's breath:
You never laughed in all your life as I shall laugh in death.

(1901)

LEPANTO

White founts falling in the courts of the sun,
And the Soldan of Byzantium is smiling as they run;

There is laughter like the fountains in that face of all men feared,
It stirs the forest darkness, the darkness of his beard,
It curls the blood-red crescent, the crescent of his lips,
For the inmost sea of all the earth is shaken with his ships.
They have dared the white republics up the capes of Italy,
They have dashed the Adriatic round the Lion of the Sea,
And the Pope has cast his arms abroad for agony and loss,
And called the kings of Christendom for swords about the Cross,
The cold queen of England is looking in the glass;
The shadow of the Valois is yawning at the Mass;
From evening isles fantastical rings faint the Spanish gun,
And the Lord upon the Golden Horn is laughing in the sun.

Dim drums throbbing, in the hills half heard,
Where only on a nameless throne a crownless prince has stirred,
Where, risen from a doubtful seat and half-attainted stall,
The last knight of Europe takes weapons from the wall,
The last and lingering troubadour to whom the bird has sung,
That once went singing southward when all the world was young.
In that enormous silence, tiny and unafraid,
Comes up along a winding road the noise of the Crusade.
Strong gongs groaning as the guns boom far,
Don John of Austria is going to the war,
Stiff flags straining in the night-blasts cold
In the gloom black-purple, in the glint old-gold,
Torchlight crimson on the copper kettle-drums,
Then the tuckets, then the trumpets, then the cannon, and he comes.
Don John laughing in the brave beard curled,
Spurning of his stirrups like the thrones of all the world,
Holding his head up for a flag of all the free.
Love-light of Spain—hurrah!
Death-light of Africa!
Don John of Austria
Is riding to the sea.

Mahound is in his paradise above the evening star,
(*Don John of Austria is going to the war.*)
He moves a mighty turban on the timeless houri's knees,
His turban that is woven of the sunset and the seas.
He shakes the peacock gardens as he rises from his ease,
And he strides among the tree-tops and is taller than the trees,
And his voice through all the garden is a thunder sent to bring
Black Azrael and Ariel and Ammon on the wing.
Giants and the Genii,
Multiplex of wing and eye,
Whose strong obedience broke the sky
When Solomon was king.

They rush in red and purple from the red clouds of the morn,
From temples where the yellow gods shut up their eyes in scorn;

They rise in green robes roaring from the green hells of the sea
Where fallen skies and evil hues and eyeless creatures be;
On them the sea-valves cluster and the grey sea-forests curl,
Splashed with a splendid sickness, the sickness of the pearl;
They swell in sapphire smoke out of the blue cracks of the ground,—
They gather and they wonder and give worship to Mahound.
And he saith, "Break up the mountains where the hermit-folk may hide,
And sift the red and silver sands lest bone of saint abide,
And chase the Giaours flying night and day, not giving rest,
For that which was our trouble comes again out of the west.
We have set the seal of Solomon on all things under sun,
Of knowledge and of sorrow and endurance of things done,
But a noise is in the mountains, in the mountains, and I know
The voice that shook our palaces—four hundred years ago:
It is he that saith not 'Kismet'; it is he that knows not Fate;
It is Richard, it is Raymond, it is Godfrey in the gate!
It is he whose loss is laughter when he counts the wager worth,
Put down your feet upon him, that our peace be on the earth."
For he heard drums groaning and he heard guns jar,
(*Don John of Austria is going to the war.*)
Sudden and still—hurrah!
Bolt from Iberia!
Don John of Austria
Is gone by Alcalar.

St. Michael's on his Mountain in the sea-roads of the north
(*Don John of Austria is girt and going forth.*)
Where the grey seas glitter and the sharp tides shift
And the sea-folk labour and the red sails lift.
He shakes his lance of iron and he claps his wings of stone;
The noise is gone through Normandy; the noise is gone alone;
The North is full of tangled things and texts and aching eyes
And dead is all the innocence of anger and surprise,
And Christian killeth Christian in a narrow dusty room,
And Christian dreadeth Christ that hath a newer face of doom,
And Christian hateth Mary that God kissed in Galilee,
But Don John of Austria is riding to the sea.

Don John calling through the blast and the eclipse
Crying with the trumpet, with the trumpet of his lips,
Trumpet that sayeth ha!
   Domino gloria!
Don John of Austria
Is shouting to the ships.

King Philip's in his closet with the Fleece about his neck
(*Don John of Austria is armed upon the deck.*)
The walls are hung with velvet that is black and soft as sin,
And little dwarfs creep out of it and little dwarfs creep in.
He holds a crystal phial that has colours like the moon,
He touches, and it tingles, and he trembles very soon,
And his face is as a fungus of a leprous white and grey
Like plants in the high houses that are shuttered from the day,
And death is in the phial and the end of noble work,
But Don John of Austria has fired upon the Turk.
Don John's hunting, and his hounds have bayed—
Booms away past Italy the rumour of his raid.
Gun upon gun, ha! ha!
Gun upon gun, hurrah!
Don John of Austria
Has loosed the cannonade.

The Pope was in his chapel before day or battle broke,
(*Don John of Austria is hidden in the smoke.*)
The hidden room in a man's house where God sits all the year,
The secret window whence the world looks small and very dear.
He sees as in a mirror on the monstrous twilight sea
The crescent of his cruel ships whose name is mystery;
They fling great shadows foe-wards, making Cross and Castle dark,
They veil the plumèd lions on the galleys of St. Mark;
And above the ships are palaces of brown, black-bearded chiefs,
And below the ships are prisons, where with multitudinous griefs,
Christian captives sick and sunless, all a labouring race repines
Like a race in sunken cities, like a nation in the mines.

They are lost like slaves that swat, and in the skies of morning hung
The stairways of the tallest gods when tyranny was young.

They are countless, voiceless, hopeless as those fallen or fleeing on
Before the high Kings' horses in the granite of Babylon.
And many a one grows witless in his quiet room in hell
Where a yellow face looks inward through the lattice of his cell,
And he finds his God forgotten, and he seeks no more a sign —
(*But Don John of Austria has burst the battle-line!*)
Don John pounding from the slaughter-painted poop,
Purpling all the ocean like a bloody pirate's sloop,
Scarlet running over on the silvers and the golds,
Breaking of the hatches up and bursting of the holds,
Thronging of the thousands up that labour under sea
White for bliss and blind for sun and stunned for liberty.
Vivat Hispania!
Domino Gloria!
Don John of Austria
Has set his people free!

Cervantes on his galley sets the sword back in the sheath
(*Don John of Austria rides homeward with a wreath.*)
And he sees across a weary land a straggling road in Spain,
Up which a lean and foolish knight forever rides in vain,
And he smiles, but not as Sultans smile, and settles back the blade. . . .
(*But Don John of Austria rides home from the Crusade.*)

                                                    (1911)

"MEDIAEVALISM"

If men should arise and return to the noise and time of the tourney,
The name and fame of the tabard, the tangle of gules and gold,
Would these things stand and suffice for the bourne of a backward
      journey,
A light on our days returning, as it was in the days of old?

Nay, there is none rides back to pick up a glove or a feather,
Though the gauntlet rang with honour or the plume was more than a
    crown:
And hushed is the holy trumpet that called the nations together
And under the Horns of Hattin the hope of the world went down.

Ah, not in remembrance stored, but out of oblivion starting,
Because you have sought new homes and all that you sought is so,
Because you had trodden the fire and barred the door in departing,
Returns in your chosen exile the glory of long ago.

Not then when you barred the door, not then when you trod the
    embers,
But now, at your new road's end, you have seen the face of a fate,
That not as a child looks back, and not as a fool remembers,
All that men took too lightly and all that they love too late.

It is you that have made no rubric for saints, no raiment for lovers
Your caps that cry for a feather, your roofs that sigh for a spire:
Is it a dream from the dead if your own decay discovers
Alive in your rotting graveyard the worm of the world's desire?

Therefore the old trees tower, that the green trees grow and are
    stunted:
Therefore these dead men mock you, that you the living are dead:
Since ever you battered the saints and the tools of your crafts were
    blunted,
Or shattered the glass in its glory and loaded yourselves with the lead.

When the usurer hunts the squire as the squire has hunted the peasant,
As sheep that are eaten of worms where men were eaten of sheep:
Now is the judgment of earth, and the weighing of past and present,
Who scorn to weep over ruins, behold your ruin and weep.

Have ye not known, ye fools, that have made the present a prison,
That thirst can remember water and hunger remember bread?
We went not gathering ghosts; but the shriek of your shame is arisen
Out of your own black Babel too loud; and it woke the dead.

            (1918–21)

THE MODERN MAGIC

Prester John on his lands looked down
He bore in one mystery mitre and crown,
And the scaly webs of the strange attire
Stripped from the dragon that feeds on fire,
And high over luminous rocks and trees
And the purple fish of his secret seas
And the whole sprawled map of the magical place,
A crystal mirror before his face
For ever stood; in whose circle shone
The world and all that is done thereon.

And the Seven Kings by his throne that stand
Cried, "Tell us the news from the Holy Land."

"Richard the King, of the scarlet ships,
Sweeps over Acre, but swerves and slips
From Godfrey's gate and from God's own crown,
And is shot in the ditch of a small French town.
Such is the news of the world," he said;
"But the signs of the world will never be read
In a glass darkly, by anyone;
We must wait for the sunrise," said Prester John.

Nigh on a thousand years were past:
To the strange priest's paradise pierced at last,
The men of the west, with the wondrous things
Of western wizards and western kings,
And high on their staggering engines borne
A marvel of marvels, the mighty Horn
Within whose cave, like a giant's ear,
Might all men speak and might all men hear
The noise of a battle, the noise of a bird,
Even all the sounds of the earth were heard.

And the Seven Kings said "It is ended then,
The demon of distance, rending men,

Deafness of deserts and random deeds,
When everyone knows what everyone needs,
Seeing that words like winds can come,
All will be Bethlehem, all will be Rome,
And all men answer and understand,
Tell us the news from the Holy Land."

"No battle-noise and no battle-news,
But shaking of shekels and laughter of Jews,
And a rattle of golden balls they toss
High o'er the ruin of Crescent and Cross,
And a usurer's voice in cold command,
These are the sounds from the Holy Land.

O, horns may call us from far away,
But men hear only what men can say,
And words may go as the wide wind blows,
But what everyone wants is what nobody knows:
And the Horn will not tell it to anyone,
We must wait for the Trumpet," said Prester John.

(1925)

"THE MYTH OF ARTHUR"

O learned man who never learned to learn,
Save to deduce, by timid steps and small,
From towering smoke that fire can never burn
And from tall tales that men were never tall.
Say, have you thought what manner of man it is
Of whom men can say "He could strike giants down"?
Or what strong memories over time's abyss
Bore up the pomp of Camelot and the crown.
And why one banner all the background fills,
Beyond the pageants of so many spears,
And by what witchery in the western hills

A throne stands empty for a thousand years.
Who hold, unheeding this immense impact,
Immortal story for a mortal sin;
Lest human fable touch historic fact,
Chase myths like moths, and fight them with a pin.
Take comfort; rest—there needs not this ado.
You shall not be a myth, I promise you.

(English Review, Sept. 1923)

AN OLD RIDDLE

"One pear hanging high
Seven Knights riding by."

Seven Knights a shrine about,
Over a wall of shields look out
Each banner a scroll of fame
Each sword as a thunder-flame
Each face as a sun
But a maid's gifts are as God's gifts
And who shall count thereon.

Seven Knights of the Court of Love
Each has her for a star above
Seven smite in a single name
Seven hearts are hearts of flame
Round where she doth sit
But a maid's choice is as God's choice
And who shall challenge it.

Seven Knights of the world's emprise
Seven in vigil and fast made wise
Seven with high helms crowned and cleft
One shall be taken the other left
Seven swords of love
But a maid's heart is as God's heart
And who shall speak thereof.

Seven Knights their brows that rear
Cleansed and christened of sacred fear
Seven warriors strong and sad
Seven Christs in armour clad
Seven kin and kith
But a maid's will is as God's will
And who shalt strive therewith.

Seven titans, huge and starred
Seven giants of God's own guard
These may merit all years' renown,
Fit for these be the robe and crown,
Heaven's fields befit
But a maid's grace is as God's grace
And who shall merit it.

(early, mid 1890s)

A QUOTATION

Hell cried "My name is Legion"; and heaven then
Sent us a legion of Michaels for our men.

(1924)[1]

A RAID

Why do you groan under graven tables
Hewn with the ten hard words of God?
Writ by the huge unhuman finger
In a land of lepers and locusts trod;

[1] Written for *The British Legion Album*, published in aid of Field-Marshal Earl Haig's Appeal for Ex-service Men of All Ranks.

Why do you seal up your ears from hearing
Music of hatred and heart's desire
Missing the madness of dear Aphrodite
The perfect crash of Apollo's lyre.

Because we ride on a raid, a raid,
Horses bridled, and horse obeyed
Spur by spur and feather by feather
All in a rank and all together
Drums a rolling and trumpets curled
Right to the end of the endless world.

                              (ca. 1910?)

THE RED CROSS WARRIOR

Under the Farm of All the Winds
  Where the long lash of liberty
Whirls through the skies of war, and finds
  Men in great travail, being free.

Speeds them as never slaves were sped,
  Drives them as never beasts were driven,
To the white seas that wash the dead —
  High hatred pure enough for heaven.

The tyrants drudge to enwall a slum,
  Heap hell up slowly, as with a hod,
Carve their crimes deep into the dumb
  Red granite of the wrath of God.

And we beneath unriven sky
  Shame if we cannot save and stay
As stubbornly as these can die,
  As patiently as those can slay;

If when the Red Cross Warrior stands,
  Now reeling as his Dragon reeled,

There be not found unwounded hands
To bear him on the Red Cross shield.

(1915)

A SONG OF DEFEAT

The line breaks and the guns go under,
   The lords and the lackeys ride the plain;
I draw deep breaths of the dawn and thunder,
   And the whole of my heart grows young again.
For our chiefs said "Done," and I did not deem it;
   Our seers said "Peace," and it was not peace;
Earth will grow worse till men redeem it,
   And wars more evil, ere all wars cease.
But the old flags reel and the old drums rattle,
   As once in my life they throbbed and reeled;
I have found my youth in the lost battle,
   I have found my heart on the battlefield.
     For we that fight till the world is free,
     We are not easy in victory:
     We have known each other too long, my brother,
     And fought each other, the world and we.

And I dream of the days when work was scrappy,
   And rare in our pockets the mark of the mint,
When we were angry and poor and happy,
   And proud of seeing our names in print.
For so they conquered and so we scattered,
   When the Devil rode and his dogs smelt gold,
And the peace of a harmless folk was shattered;
   When I was twenty and odd years old.
When the mongrel men that the market classes
   Had slimy hands upon England's rod,
And sword in hand upon Afric's passes
   Her last Republic cried to God.

For the men no lords can buy or sell,
They sit not easy when all goes well,
They have said to each other what naught can smother,
They have seen each other, our souls and hell.

It is all as of old; the empty clangour,
    The Nothing scrawled on a five-foot page,
The huckster who, mocking holy anger,
    Painfully paints his face with rage.
And the faith of the poor is faint and partial,
    And the pride of the rich is all for sale,
And the chosen heralds of England's Marshal
    Are the sandwich-men of the *Daily Mail*.
And the niggards that dare not give are glutted,
    And the feeble that dare not fail are strong,
So while the City of Toil is gutted,
    I sit in the saddle and sing my song.
        For we that fight till the world is free,
        We have no comfort in victory;
        We have read each other as Cain his brother,
        We know each other, these slaves and we.

                                            (1907)

TO A TURK

Warrior by warriors smitten,
    Gambler whose luck has turned,
Read not the small words written,
    Who know what love you earned:
You know, and none shall tell you,
    What and how long and how
They did endure in silence
    That smite in silence now.

A Liberal may belabour
  With rods your reckless dead,
As the Tory licked your sabre
  For the blood he dared not shed;
Since from the creedless chapel
  And the cushioned prize-ring came
The men that feared your glory
  And they that praised your shame.

With us too rage against the rood
  Your devils and your swine;
A colder scorn of womanhood,
  A baser fear of wine.
And lust without the harem,
  And Doom without the God.
Go. It is not this rabble
  Sayeth to you 'Ichabod.'

Because our sorrow has sufficed
  And what we know we know;
And because you were great, Lord Antichrist,
  In the name of Christ you go;
But you shall not turn your turban
  For the little dogs that yell,
When a man rides out of a city
  In the name of God; farewell.

(1913)

TO CAPTAIN FRYATT

(Captain Fryatt was captain of "The Great Eastern". He was captured and executed by the Germans during the 1914 – 18 war and buried in Flanders.)

Trampled yet red is the last of the embers,
Red the last cloud of a sun that has set;
What of your sleeping though Flanders remembers,
What of your waking, if England forget?

Why should you share in the hearts that we harden,
In the shame of our nature, who see it and live?
How more than the godly the greedy can pardon,
How well and how quickly the hungry forgive.

Ah, well if the soil of the stranger had wrapped you,
While the lords that you served and the friends that you knew
Hawk in the marts of the tyrants that trapped you,
Tout in the shops of the butchers that slew.

Why should you wake for a realm that is rotten,
Stuffed with their bribes and as dead to their debts?
Sleep and forget us, as we have forgotten;
For Flanders remembers and England forgets.

(1922)

TO THE UNKNOWN WARRIOR

You whom the kings saluted: who refused not
The one great gesture of ignoble days,
Fame without name and glory without gossip,
Whom no biographer befouls with praise.

Who said of you "Defeated"? In the darkness
The dug-out where the limelight never comes,
Nor the big drum of Barnum's Show can shatter
That vibrant stillness after all the drums.

Though the time come when every Yankee circus
　　Can use our soldiers for its sandwich-men,
When those that pay the piper call the tune,
　　You will not dance. You will not move again.

You will not march for Fatty Arbuckle,
　　Though he have yet a favourable press,
Tender as San Francisco to St. Francis,
　　Or all the Angels of Los Angeles.

They shall not storm the last unfallen fortress,
　　The lonely castle where uncowed and free
Dwells the unknown and undefeated warrior
　　That did alone defeat Publicity.

　　　　　　　　　　　　　　(1925)

THE WIFE OF FLANDERS

Low and brown barns thatched and repatched and tattered
　　Where I had seven sons until to-day,
A little hill of hay your spur has scattered. . . .
　　This is not Paris. You have lost the way.

You, staring at your sword to find it brittle,
　　Surprised at the surprise that was your plan,
Who shaking and breaking barriers not a little
　　Find never more the death-door of Sedan.

Must I for more than carnage call you claimant,
　　Paying you a penny for each son you slay?
Man, the whole globe in gold were no repayment
　　For what *you* have lost. And how shall I repay?

What is the price of that red spark that caught me
　　From a kind farm that never had a name?
What is the price of that dead man they brought me?
　　For other dead men do not look the same.

How should I pay for one poor graven steeple
  Whereon you shattered what you shall not know,
How should I pay you, miserable people?
  How should I pay you everything you owe?

Unhappy, can I give you back your honour?
  Though I forgave would any man forget?
While all the great green land has trampled on her
  The treason and terror of the night we met.

Not any more in vengeance or in pardon
  An old wife bargains for a bean that's hers.
You have no word to break: no heart to harden.
  Ride on and prosper. You have lost your spurs.

                         (1914)

INDEX OF TITLES

A.M. indicates that title is by the editor.
(*unc*) indicates that the poem is uncollected: previously not included in collections of Chesterton's verse.
(*unp*) indicates that the poem has not previously been published.

INDEX OF FIRST LINES

The text of this book has been set in Bembo by the Neumann Press of Long Prairie, Minnesota. Printed on Warren's Sebago paper and bound in Kennet cloth by Thomson Shore, Dexter, Michigan. Cover and jacket design by Darlene Lawless O'Rourke.